D0209277

SOMEONE'S DAUGHTER

SOMEONE'S DAUGHTER

In Search of Justice for Jane Doe

SILVIA PETTEM

TAYLOR TRADE PUBLISHING
Lanham • New York • Boulder • Toronto • Plymouth, UK

Published by Taylor Trade Publishing
An imprint of The Rowman & Littlefield Publishing Group, Inc.
4501 Forbes Boulevard, Suite 200, Lanham, Maryland 20706
http://www.rlpgtrade.com

Estover Road, Plymouth PL6 7PY, United Kingdom

Distributed by National Book Network

British Library Cataloguing in Publication Information Available

Library of Congress Cataloging-in-Publication Data
Pettem, Silvia.
  Someone's Daughter : In Search of Justice for Jane Doe / Silvia Pettem.
     p.   cm.
  Includes index.
  ISBN 978-1-58979-420-7 (cloth : alk. paper) — ISBN 978-1-58979-421-4
(electronic)
  1. Murder—Colorado—Boulder—Case studies. 2. Murder—Investigation—
Colorado—Boulder—Case studies. 3. Cold cases (Criminal investigation)—
Colorado—Boulder. I. Title.
  HV6534.B68P48 2009
  364.152'3092—dc22
                                                              2009009250

When you have eliminated the impossible, whatever remains, however improbable, must be the truth.

—Sherlock Holmes (Sir Arthur Conan Doyle)

ILLUSTRATIONS

CHARACTERS

Acton, Hugh "Huck": Witness to the marriage of Jimmie and Katharine
   Dyer
Ainsworth, Steve: Detective, Boulder County Sheriff's Office
Andes, James: One of two college students who found Jane Doe's body
Bausch, Sandy: One of core group of historical/genealogical researchers
Bender, Frank: Forensic artist who sculpted the bust of Jane Doe
Birkby, Dr. Walter: Forensic anthropologist, assisted at Jane Doe's
   exhumation and reassembled her skull
Bornhofen, Frederick: Chairman of the board and case manager for the
   Vidocq Society
Brooks, Pierce: Former lead investigator, Los Angeles Police Department
Cass, Alan: Family friend of author
Conour, Beth: Boulder County medical investigator, assisted at Jane
   Doe's exhumation
Crawley, Pat: Former longtime resident of Flagstaff, Arizona
Donton, Clayton: Former Navy buddy of Jimmie Dyer
Dyer, Jimmie: Late husband of Katharine Farrand Dyer
Dyer, Katharine Farrand: Missing Denver woman in 1954
Eichorn, Cindi: One of core group of historical/genealogical researchers
Embrey, Twylia May: Missing Nebraska woman in 1952
Everson, Art: Former sheriff (1942–1966), Boulder County Sheriff's Office
Fabian, Robert: Detective, Scotland Yard consultant on Marion Joan
   McDowell case
Farrand, Katharine: Maiden name of Katharine Dyer
Fenton, Dr. Todd: Director, Michigan State University Forensic
   Anthropology Laboratory
Foster, Theresa: Murder victim in Boulder, 1948

xi

Frederick, Dave: One of core group of historical/genealogical researchers

Froede, Dr. Richard: Forensic pathologist, assisted at Jane Doe's exhumation

Garner, Mildred "Midge": Sister of Twylia May Embrey

Glatman, Harvey M.: Suspect in Jane Doe's murder

Goldberg, Dr. Robert "Dr. Bob": Forensic pathologist, assisted at Jane Doe's exhumation

Greenwood, Michael: General manager of Crist Mortuary

Hand, Eula Jo "Jody": Assault victim of Harvey Glatman

Hendricks, Roy: Former detective, Boulder Police Department

Hill, Roy: Former detective, Boulder Police Department

Hubbs, Billie Ruth: Former acquaintance of Katharine Farrand Dyer

Hutchins, James W.: Initial suspect in Jane Doe's murder

James, Dr. Freburn L.: Pathologist who performed Jane Doe's original autopsy

Jaquette, Elaura: Murder victim in Boulder, 1966

Kitt, Jennifer: Great-niece of Twylia May Embrey

Lauer, Norene: Assault victim of Harvey Glatman

Lavigne, Micki: First of core group of historical/genealogical researchers

Little Miss Nobody: Unidentified murder victim, Prescott, Arizona

Little Miss X: Unidentified murder victim, Flagstaff, Arizona

Looney, Bob: Boulder *Daily Camera* reporter in 1954

Matthews, Todd: Media director of the Doe Network, identifier of the "Tent Girl"

McDowell, Marion Joan: Missing Toronto woman in 1953

Nicholas, Karen Anne: One of core group of historical/genealogical researchers

Ostrander, Shirley: Former acquaintance of Katharine Farrand Dyer

Parker, Reverend Charles Franklin: Performed marriage of Jimmie and Katharine Dyer

Pelle, Joe: Sheriff (current), Boulder County Sheriff's Office

Raines, Ed: Husband of author

Ramsey, JonBenét: Murder victim in Boulder, 1996

Ridpath, Susan: Cousin of Marion Joan McDowell

Scanlon, Dr. Richard M.: Forensic dentist, examined photos of Jane Doe's teeth

Smith, Woody: Archivist, Colorado Mountain Club

Starr, Emily: Late sister of Jimmie Dyer

Swanson, Wayne: One of two college students who found Jane Doe's body

Taylor, Carol: Librarian, Boulder *Daily Camera*

Teegarden, Dorse "Dock": Former under-sheriff, Boulder County Sheriff's Office

Teegarden, Myron: Former police chief (1949–1967), Boulder Police Department

Umenhofer, John: Sergeant, Springfield Police Department

Vigil, Lorraine: Assault victim of Harvey Glatman

Wedum, Eleanor: One of the portrayers of Jane Doe in "Meet the Spirits"

Weibel, Bruce: Murder victim, killed by James W. Hutchins in 1954

West, Phil: Lieutenant (then commander, now division chief), Boulder County Sheriff's Office

Wineman, Reverend Andy: Chaplain, Boulder County Sheriff's Office

FOREWORD

The number of missing and unidentified dead that haunt our country's morgues and cemeteries has been called the "nation's silent mass disaster." How many victims are there? We don't know. In a society that statistically researches and tracks almost every aspect of life, this is a gray area of knowledge and a black hole whose depths are unknown. Perhaps this is no better exemplified than in the case of "Boulder Jane Doe"—the tragic story of a young victim cast into a remote Colorado creek bed in 1954. Hers is a compelling and haunting tale, one that is demonstrative of the worst of mankind, yet is also exemplary of the best that people can do when motivated to do the right thing. It is the story of one woman's search to restore a victim's dignity by returning her name, and the enlightened efforts of a cold case detective and his law-enforcement agency to bring a killer to justice.

Life begins with a name and a spanking, and in the end, the name is all that remains. For most, life ends peacefully, surrounded by loved ones who reminisce on the many years of happiness the departed brought into their lives. The perils of life, however, are many and often cut short the years. These dangers recognize no age, gender, or race and bring sorrow and sadness into a place where love and happiness once reigned. Accident, disease, and other misfortunes are seldom reported in the headlines of the day, but one manner of death stands out among all others—murder.

By varying degrees of violence, the lives of young and old murder victims are most often snuffed out quickly. Sometimes they know their killers, sometimes they do not. For some, death is lingering and slow and they ultimately pass on in whatever comfort may be available, attended by doctors and family. In either case, law-enforcement agencies respond to identify and apprehend the perpetrator of a crime historically considered *mala en se*, and what passes for justice for victims and their families proceeds according to law.

Some are not so lucky, however. After receiving fatal wounds, they are not surrounded by clean sheets and those who care. These victims lie in isolated surroundings, trembling in fear and horror while the body shuts down. Baked by the sun or shivering in terrible cold, they are unable to move as minutes turn into hours, or even days, and ultimately they die. Alone and afraid, their only companions are the predators drawing near.

If the victims are found and identified within a reasonable time, law enforcement may solve their murders. From historical times to the present, identification of the victim is a primary requisite in solving criminal homicide. Only then can police seek to learn who had the motive, the opportunity, and the means—known in the trade as "MOM."

But not all murders are solved. They never have been and probably never will. While we have seen unprecedented advances in forensics and police practices in the past half century, even the best of these today cannot always help us if we cannot identify the victims. Once living, breathing human beings with families and dreams, the bodies often cannot contribute to solving the cases if we do not know who they are. While law enforcement usually does its best, if a case cannot be solved using means and forensics available at the time, it becomes an unsolved murder—popularly termed a "cold case" homicide.

As the years pass, those with missing loved ones move on, wondering "What happened? Where are they? Will I ever know?" They, also, are victims of the senseless crime. Similarly, those who investigated the events move on in their careers; they are promoted, transferred, and ultimately retire. As the investigation grows more distant, even they pass away. And life goes on.

If the unnamed victims are not cremated, most are buried simply in paupers' graves at public expense and known to the world only as "John Doe" or "Jane Doe." For these departed, justice is an elusive dream and the killer moves on—perhaps to kill again.

For some, however, there is occasionally hope. A hope that arises from unexpected sources. For Boulder Jane Doe, that hope was local historian and researcher Silvia Pettem and the Boulder County, Colorado, Sheriff's Office. Driven by a compelling curiosity and a historian's mission to seek the truth and find justice, Pettem approached her local sheriff with a plan and a vision. *Could they utilize modern forensic and investigative techniques to identify this young woman, even, perhaps, to solve her crime almost fifty years later?* What resulted is perhaps unprecedented in modern law-enforcement investigations.

Silvia Pettem did not fit the profile, if there is such a thing, of a citizen detective. This middle-aged mother had no police training, no desire to solve crimes. She simply wanted to see a wrong made right; in doing so, she demonstrated the power of one person in our society. It did not take long for her to realize that her naive sense of right and wrong would run head-long into the realities of criminal investigation in the homicide arena. Good intentions were tempered with the realities of law and law enforcement as she learned that the cops have restraints; they have policies and procedures which, while often not making sense to the uninformed, are there for a purpose. In this way, she experienced the same frustrations that confront investigators on a daily basis, but of which the public is generally unaware. Her desire to return Boulder Jane Doe to her family was confounded by modern-day confidentiality restraints and the objective, unbiased processes of homicide investigation. She wanted to find the woman's name; they wanted to find her killer.

From her rural mountain home, Pettem made contacts and won al-lies to her cause around the nation. The internet, unfathomable fifty years ago, became an umbilical cord that stretched coast to coast as volunteer researchers augmented the official investigation with bits and pieces of in-formation gained from sources not commonly found in the usual homicide investigation, but of significant importance in a cold case investigation. Cold case investigators often have to "color outside the box" and Pettem and the detectives did just that. Each gave many hours of their lives in a joint effort to give Boulder Jane Doe back her name and her dignity, sacri-ficing time with their families in search of answers. From the Philadelphia-based Vidocq Society, a nationally acclaimed cold case homicide resource, to *America's Most Wanted* and the American Academy of Forensic Sciences, Pettem told Jane Doe's story.

It was an almost unholy alliance. Highly regarded forensic experts from the Vidocq Society came forward and volunteered pro bono to help ex-hume the young woman's remains and to reconstruct not only her skull and face but also her final hours of life. Dedicated sheriff's personnel and others went the extra mile to solve the crime, each succumbing to that obsessive, compulsive desire to learn the truth about events a half century before. In the course of their efforts they opened the pages of a book looking backward in time, gaining insights into the past, into life in a different era and police practices and forensics that seem prehistoric by modern standards.

I have read the same book. I have experienced the same compulsive and obsessive drive to learn the truth behind a crime perpetrated decades in the past. My experiences involved a series of murders and alleged rapes that occurred in the heart of the Prohibition Era amid a criminal justice system marked by gross political corruption. As have Pettem and the detectives, I spent years digging for clues from attics to archives, traveling thousands of miles to interview elderly citizens about events sixty years earlier and experiencing the frustrations that come when one tries to unravel the past—a past that seemingly does not want to be unraveled.

In my case, a young Native American, by now deceased, spent more than forty years in prison and on parole for crimes he did not commit. While the genesis of Pettem's efforts began while reading the inscription on a small headstone in a local cemetery, the first clues in my case came with second-hand statements by one of the alleged rape victims before her death. This was the beginning of my thirteen-year trek to seek justice and win a complete pardon on the grounds of innocence for a young cowboy. I did identify a living killer, but in the end, the pardon was more important. Like Pettem, I had never investigated a murder before, and did it all on my own time and expense. Along the way I learned to be resourceful as I sought to synthesize the old with the new to find the truth, and ultimately the case was officially reactivated. The truth is there, but the dust of the decades must be blown away to reveal it. The dust is deeper in some cases than in others.

Forensics, the application of science to law, is a fascinating subject. Almost daily the media reports the cases of those convicted by science, and occasionally, those exonerated. DNA and other discoveries have revolutionized the field of investigation, but despite these modern marvels, old-fashioned shoe leather is still what solves cases. The saga of Boulder Jane Doe blends the old with the new and exemplifies the teamwork that cold case investigations require.

For these Boulder investigators, law and citizen alike, the issues common to many cold case investigations became apparent very early on. Lack of original written records and photographs necessitated rebuilding the case from scratch, which is to say, by reading newspaper accounts and starting from there. Newspapers are staples of cold case reconstruction, a treasure trove of information, including names, dates, investigation summaries, and photographs. Other frustrations arose, including red herrings, false leads, and emerging hopes and expectations dashed by tenacious investigation: commonalities in the daily course of cold case investigation.

Pettem's story and the efforts of the Boulder County Sheriff's Office offer revealing insight into a potential slayer, a notorious serial killer whose crimes became the driving force behind the establishment of the FBI's Violent Criminal Apprehension Program (ViCAP) at Quantico, Virginia. For more than twenty years now, this unit has tracked serial killers and others and provided significant assistance to law enforcement nationwide. Chillingly, the investigation reveals potential time and space relationships that the victim could not have foreseen, but which may have been preordained by a sociopathic predator.

Investigations such as this are expensive. A decades-old paradigm suggests that if these cases are not solved within the first twenty-four to seventy-two hours, the chances of solving the case rapidly plunge. People get their stories straight, the suspect gets away, and the likelihood of recovering evidence diminishes. Ultimately, when the case is reactivated, those who need to be located and reinterviewed have often scattered to all points in the nation. This adds to the cost of the investigation. These and other issues are considerations to those who administer budgets, and who have opposed reopening decades-old cases. Instead of being viewed as unsolved cases of murder, they are viewed in light of allocation of budgetary resources. Thus begs the question "What is the value of human life?"

This case, however, illustrates enlightened official approaches to such investigations. It demonstrates the commitment of those in modern law enforcement to adapt and to move forward in a responsible manner that balances the need for prudent management of resources with a commitment to ensuring public safety and sending the message that the law does not forget. We can learn many lessons from this experience.

This effort was rewarding by far. Boulder Jane Doe acquired a legacy as well as a new and extended family. After all was said and done, she did not die nor will she rest in obscurity. The more we learn about victims, the more we may, on occasion, begin to take them into our hearts. After all, we are their last hope for whatever passes for justice. Pettem, sheriff's detectives, members of Vidocq, and others all came to take this unknown waif into their hearts as they sought to close the book on this crime. In the end, they ultimately acknowledged the victim's life and brought answers to others they encountered along the way who suffered from their own cases of assault and missing persons. Thus, from bad came good.

It is this ending, perhaps, that marks the success of their efforts and restores the victim's dignity. Even in those homicides that we solve, we do not always learn all the answers. In this case, perhaps we never will. But we learned a lot and have laid the foundation for the future. What will the future hold? Only time will tell . . .

Richard H. Walton
Author, *Cold Case Homicides:*
Practical Investigative Techniques

INTRODUCTION

June 8, 2004. In the early morning light of what promises to be a warm summer day, I slip through a small iron gate on the north side of Columbia Cemetery in Boulder, Colorado. I am one of the first to arrive on this eventful day, and I savor the walk through the long shadows that filter through a canopy of shade trees and light up the soft green grass, still wet from a recent rain. Within a few minutes, law-enforcement officials, forensic specialists, mortuary and city park employees, and a three-man crew from the television program *America's Most Wanted* park their cars along Pleasant Street on the north side of the city's oldest graveyard. A shiny black hearse pulls up nearby. Already parked under a large ash tree is a big yellow John Deere backhoe. As I survey this burst of activity, I feel both hopeful and anxious, not quite sure what to expect. Never before in the history of the Boulder County Sheriff's Office has anyone exhumed a human body from a cemetery.

Lieutenant Phil West, six foot six with graying hair and a mustache, assembles the fifteen of us around the grave of an unidentified young woman found murdered in a mountain canyon west of the city in April 1954. Even dressed in blue jeans and a casual polo shirt, the lieutenant projects a commanding presence. When he bows his head and says: "Let's have a moment of silence for Jane Doe," we follow his lead.

It is hard to believe that we are standing in the exact same spot where, half a century earlier, a compassionate Boulder community buried the same young woman. I glance at a newspaper photograph I recently found in the Boulder *Daily Camera* archives that shows a group of mourners gathered around her casket at her grave, the men dressed in suits and the ladies wearing pillbox hats and crisp white gloves. They called her "the Mystery

Girl" and "Someone's Daughter." Now the crowd assembled today, myself included, has become her extended family.

As I reflect on the events that led up to this day, the quiet is suddenly broken by the deep throttling sound of the backhoe. The operator slowly lowers the bucket, and we all huddle—riveted—around the grave with our cameras. Eight minutes later, after the backhoe has removed about a foot of dirt, a blue-jeans-clad groundsman calls a halt. Any further machine digging, he says, might damage the contents of Jane Doe's grave or the graves on either side. Two other mortuary employees, holding long metal rods, begin prodding the grave to try to locate the top of the coffin. One of the men picks up a shovel and gently lifts some dirt. The backhoe operator digs some more, loading the dirt into a dump truck. After another foot of earth is removed, the hand-diggers climb back into the grave.

Looking away for a moment, I see the young female hearse driver standing in the background. She is ready to take the coffin to a morgue, where the victim's remains are scheduled to be examined by forensic specialists who have flown in from Arizona and Georgia. The driver's presence makes me uneasy, as Lieutenant West had already told me that in order to protect the integrity of a possible future homicide investigation, I, a layperson, cannot be present for the opening of the coffin. I am deeply disappointed, but I console myself with the knowledge that progress is being made. Moreover, I know that if I had not presented Jane Doe's case to the sheriff in the first place, the exhumation would not be occurring at all.

I anxiously wonder how long the hand-digging will take. Shortly after nine o'clock in the morning, nearly an hour after the first scrape of the backhoe, a groundsman lifts a shovelful of dirt containing a few slivers of wood and a tuft of wavy light-brown hair. At first there is a hushed silence, but this is quickly broken by one of the forensic specialists, who asks to see the old newspaper photograph in order to make sure that the men are digging in the right place. Another of these visiting experts, a man in his seventies, takes a brush and a trowel and lowers himself into the now three-foot-deep grave. He sifts through the dirt and finds more wood fragments and hair. Then he uncovers a bone and pieces of a once-zippered black-rubber body bag.

Seeing the perplexed look on my face, the third forensic specialist—a large man in blue scrubs—leans over to me and explains that the wooden coffin had simply disintegrated underground.

I am almost afraid to look into the grave for fear that Lieutenant West will ask me to leave. But before I have a chance to ask if I can stay, a sheriff's cadet pulls out a roll of crime-scene tape and cordons off a large circle around Jane Doe's grave. All of us remain inside the controlled area. Photographers and reporters, tipped off by the *Daily Camera* librarian who happened to pass by the cemetery on her way to work, emerge seemingly from nowhere. They are quickly pushed back, so that no one but our core group can look down into the grave. As the hearse drives away empty, I feel exhilarated and realize that an unexpected twist of fate has allowed me to be included after all. I stare at Jane Doe's skeletal remains embedded in the soft reddish-brown dirt and know I have reached back in time.

1

AN EXTENDED FAMILY

1

Please give me back my name. No one knows who I am or how I came to die—battered, beaten, and naked on the rocky edge of Boulder Creek. I was found in April 1954 by two college students out on a hike. My murderer, whoever he was, was brutal and vicious, but the compassionate people of Boulder gave me a Christian funeral, with graveside services right here where you are standing. A photo of the burial even made Denver's Rocky Mountain News. *The newspaper's headline read, "Will this grave mark an unsolved mystery?" A local monument maker carved "Jane Doe" into my gravestone. The police think I was about twenty years old. I was too young to die. Can someone tell me who I am and return my remains to my family?*

October 5, 1996. The slender young woman who uttered these words was dressed all in brown, from her sweater to her wool skirt to her brown-and-white saddle shoes. A pair of 1950s-style, white-plastic sunglasses framed her rounded face. Eight years prior to the victim's exhumation, I had also stood in Columbia Cemetery. The ten-acre burial ground—home to gravestones of every shape and size—was resplendent in fall colors from the reddish tinge of the silver maples to the vibrant greens and yellows of ashes, lindens, and locusts to the dark green junipers and the distinctive blue-green hue of Colorado's native blue spruce.

The occasion was the city's first "Meet the Spirits" reenactment, hosted jointly by the Boulder Historical Society and the preservation organization Historic Boulder, Inc., and I was participating in the final dress rehearsal before the spectators were due to arrive. A group of about thirty Boulder residents—mostly like-minded history enthusiasts like myself—had come together to tell the stories of some of the more famous, and infamous, permanent residents of the cemetery. We hoped that by dressing up in period costumes and speaking as if we were the characters we portrayed, we could share Boulder's colorful hidden history with the community at large.

I had come to present the story of Mary Rippon, the first woman professor at the University of Colorado, and I was dressed for the part, wearing a high-necked, ivory-colored blouse handmade by a friend, and a long tweed skirt I had sewn myself. Weeks earlier, I had bought the pattern for the Victorian-era skirt and searched through several fabric stores until I found just the right heavy material, a knobby mixture of dark brown and black. Years of sewing in my stay-at-home-mom days had prepared me for the task, but I had never before made a garment with a slight bustle—designed to give a woman a shapely backside whether she needed one or not.

Pinned to my blouse was a green and silver brooch that had been passed down from my mother's mother, and around my shoulders I had draped a chocolate brown beaver fur wrap which I struggled to keep evenly positioned. The costume was topped off with a large Victorian hat I had borrowed from the historical society. Trimmed with real fur, fake lilacs, and a black ostrich plume, the ostentatious head covering concealed my shoulder-length brown hair, pinned tightly on top of my head.

Trying not to trip, I lifted my unwieldy skirt a few inches off the ground and walked as sedately as I could to join my fellow actors and actresses. Some of the faces looked familiar to me, but their vintage clothing identified them as people from various walks of life and time periods. In addition to Jane Doe, there was a well-suited banker, a uniformed constable, a flashy prostitute, and a leather-coated Indian scout. Most famous of all, and drawing in the crowds, was Tom Horn, a frontiersman and hired gunman who had been wrongfully hanged for murder in Wyoming in 1903. Unlike the others, all of whom were Boulder residents, Tom Horn had been brought by his brother—himself a Boulder resident—to the frontier town for a proper burial. Most of the eclectic group stationed themselves near the graves of their characters.

As we prepared to share our characters' stories, a sense of excitement filled the air. Dozens of people were lined up at the gate waiting to get in as the last of the arriving "spirits" rushed to their graves and adjusted their props. On a century-old dirt lane that meandered through the cemetery, a white draft horse pulled an elegantly restored shiny black 1867 hearse wagon, driven by a man in a top hat and tails. Volunteers dressed in black played the part of mourners. Far from morbid or depressing, the cemetery looked like a movie set, bustling with activity.

I had been happy to leave the trappings of modern life and walk into the past. As a forty-nine-year-old writer and historian, I had spent most of my adult life researching and writing about Boulder County history. The land and its people had become not only my livelihood but also my passion. I knew that the cemetery's first burial was in 1870, when the then treeless and barren prairie was a carriage drive from the center of town. A few years earlier, this same land at the base of the Rocky Mountains had been occupied by roaming bands of Arapaho Indians. In October 1858, when scattered settlements of Arapahos were encamped at the base of the Rocky Mountains, a small group of gold-seekers from the Midwest camped near a rocky outcrop they called Red Rocks, at the mouth of Boulder Cañon—the Spanish spelling in use at the time. There, the prospectors panned and sluiced for gold in the glacier-fed waters of Boulder Creek. When the snow melted, the men worked their way upstream and found more gold in the mountains. Before long, Boulder had become a supply center for the miners.

By the time Colorado was granted statehood in 1876, Boulder's population numbered approximately three thousand, and the graveyard held a few dozen burials. Farsighted citizens planted trees, including the cemetery's few spindly saplings. Two decades later, the town had grown enough that part of its residential area almost reached the cemetery that increased, yearly, its number of burials. Today the cemetery is shaded

By the 1880s, the few trees planted in Columbia Cemetery were beginning to grow. Carnegie Branch Library for Local History, Boulder Historical Society collection.

by mature trees that shelter the final resting places of nearly 6,500 men, women, and children.

On that crisp October day of the reenactment, I was a little nervous about portraying the Victorian woman professor. Although I knew my character well—I had researched her life for a biography—we expected more than one hundred people to attend the day's self-guided tour. As I fidgeted with the script I had quickly composed on my computer and then carefully tucked into the pages of a nineteenth-century maroon-colored textbook—a prop I clutched in my gloved hand—I realized that I would rather be doing research in a library than speaking to a crowd. I asked myself why I had even agreed to be part of this event, but then I remembered that it was a fund-raiser, the proceeds of which would go to the preservation of the cemetery. It was all for a good cause and might even be fun.

At ten o'clock in the morning, the public was admitted through the cemetery's main entrance, a modest but slightly ornate wrought-iron gate that stood between two pillars built of irregularly shaped fieldstones. Volunteers handed self-guided-tour brochures to the graveyard visitors, who then set off on their own, spreading out to visit the graves of the people who interested them the most. When the first crowd of the day gathered around me, I took a deep breath, then began: "I'm Mary Rippon. Most people know me as the first woman professor at the University of Colorado, but they don't know that I married one of my students and had a child."

I then explained that "Miss Rippon," a full professor of German language and literature at the university during the Victorian era, fell in love with one of her students and soon found herself pregnant. This put her in an incredibly difficult situation: She could not continue professionally if her love affair—and pregnancy—became public, so she married her lover in secrecy, then traveled overseas to give birth to their child. Forced to give up custody of her daughter for the sake of her career, Mary eventually allowed her ex-husband to raise the child with his second wife. Though Mary acted as the dean of women to her female students, her personal life remained permanently hidden behind a Victorian veil of secrecy. And though she received decades of praise for being a professor, she received none at all for being a mother.

As I finished recounting Mary's story, my thoughts turned to my own daughters, a twenty-three-year-old new bride and recent college graduate, and a nineteen-year-old who had recently left Colorado to continue her college education in Wisconsin. We shared a close bond, perhaps because ten years earlier I had taken my daughters with me when I divorced their father. The girls and I moved from a primitive cabin in the mountains into a cramped one-room apartment in Boulder where a friend helped me start a mail-order business in out-of-print books, and I struggled as a single mother. There were times when I wondered how we would survive, but somehow we did. Three years later I married one of my book customers. My new husband, Ed Raines, joked that he would do anything for a discount.

I was still thinking about my daughters when two Girl Scouts came by with cider and cookies. I eagerly gobbled up their refreshments, but I longed for a lull so I could wander off and listen to the other characters' monologues. Unfortunately, I never had a chance to leave Mary's side.

By the end of the day, I was tired and talked out as I headed toward my car. My feet ached, so I paused for a moment on my way out of the cemetery and sat under a crabapple tree near Jane Doe's modest gravestone. It was the first time I had ever seen it, and I thought back to the young woman's plea during our rehearsal: *Please give me back my name.* Looking at the small gray stone, I noticed that it was rough on the top and sides but polished and smooth on front. Etched into the polished surface were some stylized leaves that framed a flower with five distinct petals, familiar in Colorado as a cinquefoil. In cemeteries, particularly during the Victorian era, the cinquefoil often was used to symbolize "maternal affection" or a "beloved daughter." How poignant!

Under "Jane Doe, April 1954" were the words: "Age About 20 Years." I was struck by the fact that the murder victim's stated age was right between the ages of my own two daughters. How could the young woman who died forty-two years ago not be missed? I had been talking all afternoon about Mary Rippon and her choice of career over motherhood. She accepted responsibility and financial commitment, but she paid a terrible price—her daughter's love. Now I found myself wondering about Jane Doe's mother. Was she alive when her daughter was murdered? What really happened to Jane Doe?

By the time the next year's "Meet the Spirits" reenactment rolled around, in October 1997, the Boulder community was deep into the ongoing investigation of the murder of JonBenét Ramsey, which had broken ten months earlier. As anyone with a television will recall, the six-year-old girl's mother, Patsy, had gone on national television and stated: "There is a killer on the loose. I don't know who it is. I don't know if it's a he or a she. . . . Keep your babies close to you. There's someone out there."

Nearly every news station simultaneously splashed videos of the elaborately made-up and costumed little girl performing beauty pageant routines and singing songs that included "I Want to Be a Cowboy's Sweetheart." In

Jane Doe's gravestone in Columbia Cemetery was donated by a local monument maker in memory of the community's "mystery girl." Photo courtesy of the Daily Camera.

what had first been presented as a kidnapping, the child was found dead in the Ramsey family's Boulder home the day after Christmas.

Boulder's police chief and mayor reassured their citizens that the city's streets were safe and that a killer was *not* on the loose. But as the only murder in Boulder in the entire calendar year, the unsolved JonBenét Ramsey case dominated the news and left a lot of unanswered questions. Some people believed the Ramsey family was involved, while others swore her killer was an intruder. Nearly a year after it was first reported, the little girl's murder remained unsolved. So, too, was Jane Doe's.

At the second year's cemetery reenactment, the visiting public knew firsthand what it was like to have an unsolved murder in their community. The tour-goers had more interest in and compassion for Jane Doe, and her character drew larger crowds. Again I portrayed Mary Rippon, and again I found myself too busy telling her story to listen to Jane Doe and the stories of the other characters. Still, when I got to the part in Mary's story in which I explained that her daughter's death certificate read "mother's name unknown," I thought about the much greater unknown—the missing identity of a young woman stripped naked, beaten, and dumped like a bag of garbage down an embankment next to Boulder Creek.

Over the course of the next few months, as autumn turned to winter, I frequently stopped by Columbia Cemetery and visited Jane Doe's grave. The trees shed their leaves, which crunched under my feet, and I was reminded of the cemetery's nineteenth-century description as "the city of the dead." I enjoyed the quiet and solitude. Many of the names on the gravestones were familiar to me, and I felt as if I were among friends. Although I do not think of myself as religious or even particularly spiritual, I was drawn toward Jane Doe's grave—and I figured that her spirit must have been guiding me. I could not get out of my mind the first few lines of a poem that Mary Rippon's husband, Will Housel, penned more than a century ago:

> But seems there is a legend, or an old philosophy
> That a spirit sometimes lingers in a blossom or a tree.

As a historian, and—more importantly—as a mother, I made the decision to embark on a solitary quest to acknowledge the life of this unknown woman. Little did I know, at the time, that the victim's murder would profoundly affect my life and draw me into a partnership with law-enforcement officials and the forensic community as we jointly sought justice for her death.

2

In 1998, two years after I first learned of Jane Doe, I was hired by the Boulder *Daily Camera* to write a weekly history column. I had written for the newspaper in the late 1970s, then switched to writing books as well as freelance articles for other local newspapers and magazines. Although I continued to work out of my home, my research allowed me to poke around in the newspaper's archives, and my new position gave me yet another excuse to dig into the lives and events in Boulder's past.

The *Daily Camera*'s archives were housed in a room that always smelled the same—like ink or musty old paper or an odd mixture of both. Wedged between the newsroom and the now-antiquated offices and darkroom of the photography department, the cluttered but quiet space was, to me, a haven—an overflowing treasure trove of microfilm, newspaper clippings, and photographs. As a historian, I grew to love this place. It is where I got to do the work of a historical detective, rummaging through files to research Boulder's colorful characters. The more information I found, the more the people of the past became real to me. I especially enjoyed finding photos of the people I featured in my articles, matching faces with names. Far from seeming mundane, the process filled me with anticipation, much like a prospector searching for gold or a gambler hoping to hit the jackpot at any moment.

I usually began with the small envelope files, which bulged with clippings, old photographs, and long-forgotten obituaries. Then, when I had exhausted those resources, I moved on to the bulkier files that were housed in large manila folders and stuffed into metal cabinets that covered the entire west wall of the room. A gray metal ladder, squeaky and on wheels, was the only way to access the drawers near the top. On a slow news day in the fall of 1998, however, I was only concerned with the files at waist level.

That was because I was searching the "Murder" files in the "M" drawer of the cabinet, in hopes of learning something—anything—about Jane Doe.

The drawer contained a dozen or so dusty old folders filed alphabetically under different murder victims' names, and as I flipped through them, I began to despair of finding any information on my nameless victim. After only a few minutes, however, I spotted, in the very back, a battered manila folder that read: "Murder, Unidentified Girl." What a find!

Inside the folder were brittle, yellowed clippings from the *Daily Camera*. The articles had been glued to numbered sheets of white-glue-stained paper, presumably long ago by a conscientious librarian who also clipped stories from the *Rocky Mountain News* and the *Denver Post*. Throughout the years, careless reporters had mixed up the pages, so I spread them out like jigsaw puzzle pieces and sorted them chronologically. After copying, reading, and absorbing the whole file over a period of several months, I put together a rough scenario of what I thought had likely happened:

Somewhere, in a place where there were no known witnesses, the victim's attacker struck her on her head with a "blunt, broad weapon," as Sheriff Art Everson, in office at the time, had speculated. Possibly, it was the handle of a pistol. Very little blood was found with the young woman's body, leading investigators at the time to believe that her assailant beat her in another location, then transported her, perhaps still alive, to the rocky edge of Boulder Creek, three hundred yards below the parking lot at Boulder Falls.

To get to this spot, Jane Doe's murderer either drove up the canyon from Boulder or down the canyon from the former tungsten mining town of Nederland. Parts of the road were dirt in 1954, but the road was—and still is—the main thoroughfare through the narrow mountain canyon immediately west of Boulder. Today's paved road follows the same roadbed and continues to provide access to the Boulder Falls parking lot, one of the few places a driver can pull off the road. During daylight hours in good weather, the lot is traditionally filled with the cars of tourists who continue to visit the waterfall, a long-popular attraction on a tributary of Boulder Creek that flows in from the north.

If the victim's attacker did bring her to this parking lot, he would have realized that the drop-off to the creek was not steep enough for him to easily discard her body. While reading the articles for the first time, I speculated that the attacker drove downhill until he found a spot where the pitch of the embankment between the road and Boulder Creek had increased. In a successful attempt to erase her identity, he then stripped his slender victim of all of her clothing, jewelry, and personal belongings until all she had left were three bobby pins in her wavy light-brown hair. Then, I speculated, he dumped or threw her limp body out of his car or truck, and she slid to her final resting place on the rocks at the edge of Boulder Creek.

Under the cover of darkness, the unknown assailant left his young victim—naked and alone—to die of shock and exposure. Very briefly, between storms in an overcast sky, a tiny sliver of a waning moon (some called it a "toenail") flickered and went out in the western sky. Within a few hours, falling snow blanketed the body and erased the tracks of her killer and his vehicle.

Throughout the first week of April, the victim's battered body lay exposed to the elements. Each day, it froze in the early morning hours, then baked in the direct rays of the sun. As the snow began to melt, mammals— perhaps joined by ravens or crows—plucked out her left eye, gnawed off her right ear, and tore away at the flesh on her face, neck, hands, and feet, while buds formed on scrubby currant bushes in an annual display of new life. A few tufts of green grass poked through the straw-colored sticks of the previous year's undergrowth. The steepness of the embankment was just enough to keep the victim's body out of view of passing cars.

A week or more had passed before April 8, 1954, when two University of Colorado students accidentally found Jane Doe's body lying on the rocks at the edge of Boulder Creek. Wayne Swanson and James Andes were roomers in a half-century-old, two-story frame house at 1719 Marine Street, a short walk downhill from the university campus. The Swedish family who owned the house took in a few male roomers each year to help pay the mortgage. The college freshmen had just finished the last of their midterm exams and were beckoned out of doors by the warm weather—a very pleasant seventy-two degrees in the mid-afternoon—and the early blooms of spring. The bright yellow flowers of forsythia bushes contrasted with the first pink and white blossoms on fruit trees scattered all over town.

Lanky nineteen-year-old Wayne, from Batavia, Illinois, never turned down a chance to hike. He and James, also an Illinois native, did not waste any time heading into the hills. If the young men reflected the tastes of their peers, their car's radio may have vibrated with Bill Haley and his Comets' brand-new release, "Shake, Rattle, and Roll." Competing for airtime with this first rock-and-roll song to sell a million records was the latest hit from the harmonic Spaniels (and made even more popular by the McGuire Sisters), "Goodnight, Sweetheart, Goodnight."

The two college students were not alone in their desire to drive into the mountains. "See the U.S.A. in your Chevrolet," pleaded Dinah Shore to viewers across America who watched the singer on small lacquered black-and-white television sets. Automobile sales had boomed after World War II. With twenty-nine-cents-per-gallon gasoline, motorists took every chance they could to take to the highways. In Boulder Cañon (still with the Spanish spelling in the 1950s), families parked on scenic turnouts where they fished, had "steak fries," and enjoyed the serenity of the clear cold mountain stream.

After a fifteen-minute drive, Wayne and James parked at Boulder Falls. Instead of taking the short walk to the waterfall, they decided to explore Boulder Creek. James took along his camera. Despite the dramatic increase in warm weather, the first week of April was still too early for the annual spring runoff of melting snow from the watershed that hugged the eastern side of the Continental Divide. The water level in the creek was at its seasonal low, allowing the students greater access to the creek bed.

"We walked down the creek, stepping on stones," James told a newspaper reporter the following day. "I picked up a few pieces of driftwood for a fire, and we laid them along the bank, intending to come back for them later." James added that they worked their way down the east side of the creek, sometimes on one bank, sometimes on the other, and sometimes on rocks in the creek. He estimated that they went a quarter mile down the creek, then climbed up on the road and started back.

At that point, the two students were walking along the shoulder of the road and looking toward the creek for more wood. Suddenly, they noticed what looked like a figure lying on the rocks at the edge of the creek. "At first we thought it was a store window dummy," said James. "We didn't think it could possibly be a human body."

Wayne and James scrambled down the bank and then stopped in horror when they realized they were face-to-face with the partially decomposed body of a nude young woman. She lay on her back, her flesh blackened and bruised. "I don't know what we said," Wayne told the same reporter. "We just left in a hurry."

"It was a funny feeling," the student continued. "We weren't exactly scared in the sense that we wanted to run, but I sure wish we hadn't found the body. But I suppose if we had just agreed it was a mannequin and gone on, our consciences would have bothered us, and we would have had to come back and find out anyhow."

After Wayne and James's startling discovery, they jumped in their car and sped back down the canyon. Daylight was quickly fading when they pulled up on Pearl Street in front of Boulder County's art deco–style courthouse, where they found Sheriff Everson working late in his office on the first floor. At the time, the sheriff's office only had six or seven employees, including a secretary. Although skeptical at first, the sheriff and coroner George Howe accompanied the students back to the scene. The coroner had seen many corpses in his nearly twenty years in office and covered the young woman's battered body with a sheet. The men gently placed the victim on a gurney, carried her back up the hill, slid her corpse into a Cadillac hearse, and drove to Boulder's Howe Mortuary on the corner of Spruce and Eleventh streets.

The sheriff's office had no detectives of its own, so Sheriff Everson asked for and received assistance from the Boulder Police Department, only slightly larger. Boulder Police Detective Roy Hendricks immediately called fellow police detective Roy Hill, and together they viewed the body at Howe Mortuary, where coroner George Howe and his brother, Norman Howe—the mortuary's owner—had moved the unidentified victim down a flight of stairs to the basement. There, in a white tile–lined morgue and embalming room, brightly lit with overhead fluorescent lights, the men placed the slender woman's body on her back on a cold white porcelain table. Her disheveled shoulder-length hair held twigs and pine needles, and her right arm lay at her side. Her left arm was folded so that her left hand—with well-manicured fingernails—rested on her abdomen. A towel covered her genital area. The flesh on her neck and face, except for her forehead, was so ravaged by animals that it appeared incongruously attached to her badly bruised but otherwise intact body.

A telephone call to the Boulder Sanitarium summoned pathologist Dr. Freburn L. James to come at once to perform an autopsy. The young medical specialist would discover that in addition to multiple contusions and abrasions, the woman had sustained fractures to her skull, jaw, left arm, left collarbone, and the first to fourth ribs on her left side. The collarbone and rib fractures formed a nearly vertical line, indicating that all were incurred at the same instant. The victim's only significant identifying feature was an appendectomy scar. She had no fillings in her teeth, which precluded the use of dental records in attempting an identification. She was determined to be approximately five foot three inches tall and was thought to have weighed between 100 and 110 pounds.

Before beginning the autopsy, the mortuary owner dialed Hillcrest [HI] 2-1202.

"I need you here immediately," he shouted in the telephone to Laurence Paddock, son of A. A. Paddock, who was the publisher of the *Daily Camera*. "Bring your camera and bring [reporter Bob] Looney. I've got a story for him!"

The following morning, Detectives Hendricks and Hill were joined at the crime scene by the police department's third detective, Willard Spier.

They searched the area, but, reportedly, did not find anything of importance. The students who found the body and reporters from the Boulder and Denver newspapers climbed around on the rocks, too.

After visiting and photographing the crime scene, the newspaper reporters rushed back to their offices, where they cranked out lengthy articles—the same ones I had avidly read in the *Daily Camera* archives. Only the following one-inch Associated Press "wire" story, however, was sent to major newspapers in the rest of the country. A teletype operator in Boulder relayed the text that was then converted into a code and transported over telegraph lines. His, or her, story read:

> The unidentified body of a blonde girl in her late teens lay unnoticed for about a week only 30 feet from a busy road 9 miles west of here, officers said today. Sheriff Art Everson declared, "There is no doubt she was murdered." Two Colorado University students spotted the body as they returned from a mountain stroll here yesterday.

On the day after James Andes, left, and Wayne Swanson, right, found the victim's body, they returned to the scene to point out the exact location to reporters. Reprinted with permission of the Rocky Mountain News.

Officials also posed at the crime scene. From left to right are Police Detective Willard Spier, Deputy District Attorney Joe Dolan, Police Detective Roy Hill, Police Detective Roy Hendricks, Sheriff Art Everson, and coroner George Howe. When the case was revisited in 2004, the only man still alive was Roy Hendricks. Photo courtesy of the Daily Camera.

Teletype machines in other newspaper offices around the country converted the telegraphed code back into words for print in big-city newspapers. Many residents in rural areas—or across the country where I lived at the time—did not get the news at all.

When Jane Doe's body was found, I was seven years old, living with my parents in an ultramodern house in Lancaster, Pennsylvania. The only child of a middle-class suburban housewife and an electrical engineer, I had had a pleasant and relatively uneventful childhood. My mother was a homemaker but disliked housework and spent a lot of her time writing music and playing the piano. My father designed tubes for television cameras, but during most of my childhood—including April 1954—he would not allow a television in our home. I thwarted his efforts to shelter me from outside influences by going to my best friend's house to watch "Buffalo Bob" Smith and the *Howdy Doody Show*, as well as the latest episodes of *I Love Lucy*. When my parents finally did get a television in

1955, we never missed an episode of the then-new family show, *Father Knows Best*.

Some of my earliest recollections are of Sunday drives with my parents. Long before the days of seat belts and car seats, I stood on the floor of the backseat of our 1950 Plymouth so I could get a better view out the window. My parents took me through Amish farmlands where we watched men in plain dark clothing and straw hats plow their tobacco fields with mules. I learned to recognize tobacco barns, with slats on the sides to allow air to circulate and dry the tobacco leaves that hung inside. When my friends and I were old enough to go to school, we would stop on our way home from the bus stop and suck the "honey" from honeysuckle vines that grew along the side of the country road.

My only fear—admittedly a big one—was of nuclear war. My parents and I lived in a one-story house without a basement, and I remember at a very young age during the Cold War era convincing an elderly neighbor to let us set up a fallout shelter in her solid brick home. I also had an above-average curiosity about prisons, no doubt sparked by the looming presence of the Lancaster County Prison, built in 1852 and still in use. With its commanding stone towers and arched gateway, it intrigued me and looked like a medieval fortress. (I later learned that I was not far off, as the prison was a near-replica of Lancaster Castle and former prison in Lancaster, England.) I remember staring at the imposing red sandstone structure on East King Street every time my mother and I drove from the suburbs into the city to shop at the A&P grocery store. I tried to imagine what the prison was like inside, but I had no experience from which to draw. I thought I was rather knowledgeable for a kid, but none of my friends were missing, and I had no firsthand experience with violence or with domestic or sexual abuse. I knew nothing at all about murder.

During my senior year in high school, I wanted to apply to Penn State University because many of my friends were planning on attending. My mother had been a world traveler and suggested I go somewhere more adventurous for college, somewhere in the West. At the time, I was unaware that my parents' twenty-three-year-long marriage had begun to unravel. My mother, who may have enjoyed a vicarious pleasure in influencing my college plans, came up with the University of Colorado. In September 1965, I moved to Boulder. Although I majored in psychology, I took some sociology and criminology classes that even included a field trip inside the Colorado State Penitentiary.

Like nearly every college student, I was caught up in the present. I lived in Sewall Hall because I liked the 1930s style of the dormitory, but I was unaware at the time that it was one of the best examples of architect Charles Klauder's Tuscan-style sandstone buildings that now define the University of Colorado at Boulder. From my window, I had a view of the Indian Peaks of the Continental Divide, including a bit of the Arapaho Glacier. I shared the room with a Colorado girl from a big family who, to my amazement, could actually sleep with the light on. All of us freshmen girls lived in fear of the housemothers who stood with keys in hand to enforce our ten o'clock weekday, and slightly later weekend, curfew. Every Sunday evening was the cook's night off, and several of us from the dormitory would walk downhill to the Gondolier Restaurant, then located on Broadway near Marine Street.

Rarely did my friends and I venture the few more blocks to Pearl Street, the main thoroughfare of downtown Boulder. Nationally, the Vietnam War was heating up, and singer Bob Dylan expressed the mood of the country with his popular song, "The Times They Are A-Changin." My first year in Boulder, however, the "sleepy college town," as it was called by the press, was quiet. In those pre-pedestrian-mall days, downtown motorists had no trouble finding a place to park, and the F. W. Woolworth Company's store, with its large soda fountain, occupied the entire southeast corner of Pearl Street and Broadway.

Years later, at the *Daily Camera*, when I continued to read the microfilmed and clipped articles from the time of Jane Doe's murder, I could easily envision Boulder in the 1950s—only a decade before I arrived. Unlike the spiritual diversity in Boulder today, the majority of the city's 23,200 residents in 1954 were Christian. Indeed, only a day after the victim's unembalmed body was zipped into a black rubber body bag and placed in a refrigerated room in the basement of Howe Mortuary, a 90 by 215 foot string of brilliant white lights configured in the shape of a cross was illuminated on the side of Flagstaff Mountain, overlooking the city of Boulder. This was not a tribute to Jane Doe but rather a Holy Week tradition that had begun in 1948.

According to the *Daily Camera*, the gigantic cross that glowed from six o'clock to eleven o'clock in the evening was meant to be "spiritually comforting," but reporters were quick to point out that the upcoming Christian holiday was the "first Easter of the H-bomb era." Only a few weeks earlier, on March 1, 1954, the United States had set off the world's biggest manmade explosion when its government tested the hydrogen bomb in the Pacific archipelago of Bikini. In Boulder, researchers at the University of Colorado kept a close watch for fallout, however the collection of atmospheric dust on suction filters in the university laboratory had, so far, not varied more than two percent from normal. One writer stated: "Rejoicing that Christ is risen mingles with fear that man has fashioned a weapon that could doom civilization," adding that much of the free world's burden rested on the shoulders of U.S. president Dwight David Eisenhower.

Churches all over town advertised their upcoming events. The First Methodist Church announced that its Palm Sunday service would be the cantata "Seven Last Words." The musical composition's opening line was: "All people who travel upon the highway, hearken to me, and behold me." A Gallup poll reported that ninety-four percent of the U.S. population believed in God. In fact, that very year, during President Eisenhower's administration, the U.S. Congress modified the Pledge of Allegiance from "one nation indivisible" to "one nation, under God, indivisible."

Friday evening was also date night, and university coeds on the eve of their upcoming weeklong Easter holiday brushed out their Veronica Lake–style hairdos and piled into Fords and Chevrolets with their boyfriends. Some of the students drove east on Arapahoe Avenue for the opening night of the sixth season of the Motorena Drive-In Theater. While munching on popcorn, couples watched the movie *The War of the Worlds*, in which scientists and Marines repelled a Martian invasion of Earth. Violence close to home or the murder of a woman their own age was far from their minds.

Meanwhile, the young murder victim's cold corpse lay in the morgue for two long weeks, while newspaper writers in Denver and veteran *Daily Camera* reporter Bob Looney, in Boulder, published almost-daily articles in the hopes that someone would come forward with an identification. No young women were reported missing from Boulder or from the University of Colorado, but the Denver police came up with the names of two women—one considered too heavy and the other, at age twenty-four, said to have been too old.

Detail-oriented Bob Looney tucked a stubby number-two pencil and three or four sheets of horizontally folded copy paper into his suit-coat pocket and tagged along after police and sheriff officials who combed a ten-square-mile area searching for clues and the victim's clothes. They even went as far west as the mining community of Cardinal, where they sifted through ashes in the woodstove of a recently abandoned cabin. When a slender blonde wearing white moccasins was reported missing from Salt Lake City, Utah, and a mountain resident found a white moccasin in a canyon west of Boulder, the shoe was considered a good clue until it was learned that it had been in the same place for months. After a day in the field, reporter Looney returned to the building that had housed the newspaper offices at Pearl and Eleventh streets since 1891. The wooden floors

A few years prior to Jane Doe's murder, Sheriff Art Everson, right, was photographed with Deputy Don Moore in the sheriff's office on the first floor of the Boulder County Courthouse on Pearl Street. Photo courtesy of the Daily Camera.

creaked under his feet as he sat down at his desk in the newsroom. Pecking away with two fingers on a Royal typewriter, he quoted Sheriff Art Everson as saying: "We just haven't a thing here that's any good."

City officials then announced their intention to bury the victim in the southwest corner of Columbia Cemetery, but the plans did not sit well with the local community. "It would be a darn shame when *someone's daughter* is to be buried in a pauper's grave, and we decided we would try to do something about it," wrote a woman who lived in a boardinghouse in Denver. "We are enclosing this check to start a fund for proper burial of this unfortunate girl." Each resident chipped in one dollar. The group mailed its joint check for twelve dollars to the *Daily Camera*. The newspaper also collected the donations of church groups and individuals, including one from a Boulder police officer. Echoing the donors' sentiments was Coroner Howe, who publicly stated: "We don't know who she was or what religion she followed. We can only do what we think is right."

On April 22, the day of the victim's funeral, a Denver woman arrived at Howe Mortuary and asked to view the body. She explained that she thought the deceased was her daughter from a former marriage—a daughter she had not seen in four years. Little did she know at the time that her daughter was alive and well in Ohio. The woman sat with the corpse for an hour, then reluctantly allowed the coroner to re-zip the body bag shortly before the funeral was scheduled to begin.

At two o'clock in the afternoon, thirty people somberly climbed the concrete steps of the mortuary's original front entrance on Spruce Street. Men, in suits and ties, and women, in dresses, hats, and gloves—average citizens who came from a variety of occupations and Christian denominations—seated themselves on the wooden pews in the chapel. One of the men in attendance was seventy-three-year-old Francis Tobin, a white-haired former miner who ran an investment company from his home. His compassion for the victim may have stemmed from his thirty-year search for information on his missing grandfather, who, he finally learned, had been murdered in 1867 while laying track for the Union Pacific Railroad in Dawson County, Nebraska.

Two of the women, Josephine Gibbons and Jessie Nevills, were sisters. Professionally, the middle-aged women were nurses, but they shared an interest in writing jingles, a popular and often lucrative pastime in the 1950s. Both women won cash and free groceries and participated in radio programs that included "The Phrase That Pays." Josephine, however, was

Individuals, as well as florists, sent flowers to Jane Doe's funeral. One of the accompanying cards was simply addressed "To Someone's Daughter." Carnegie Branch Library for Local History, Boulder Historical Society collection.

the big winner when she entered a "Lovely Lux Girl" contest, and the Lux Soap Company's manager rewarded her with a brand new 1951 Ford.

A few of the women wept when organist Margaret Haskell began to play familiar hymns on the mortuary's small pipe organ. Conspicuously empty, on the right side of the room behind a partially open velvet curtain, was a seating area known as the "family room." The closed casket, in the front of the room, was banked with eight floral pieces. One arrangement, along with others of lilies, roses, sweet peas, and pink and white carnations, was a spray of red gladiolus. Accompanying the gladiolus flowers was a card—most likely from one of the twelve Denver boarders—addressed "To Someone's Daughter."

Reverend Paul Fife of Boulder's Sacred Heart of Jesus Church began the funeral with Psalm 130: "From the depths of despair, O Lord, I call for your help. Hear my cry, O Lord, pay attention to my prayer." A *Denver Post* reporter noted that the preacher mixed Catholic and nondenominational rites and there was "a blank, an almost imperceptible pause at each point in the service where the name of the deceased normally was recited." After the formal service, the casket was placed in the hearse for the short drive to

Members of the local community gathered in Columbia Cemetery for graveside services. Mortuary owner Norman Howe is in the foreground on the left, Reverend Paul Fife and Chamber of Commerce secretary Eben G. Fine are on the right. The two ladies with arms folded behind the left side of the casket are the "jingle sisters," and the man with arms folded behind the right side of the casket is Francis Tobin. Reprinted with permission of the Rocky Mountain News.

Columbia Cemetery. Mourners followed in their cars and then assembled around her grave as Reverend Fife gave the victim his final blessing.

Boulder Laundry owner Francis Gilmore, retired electrician Charles Timberlake, and former highway construction worker Charles Walker, along with coroner George Howe and his brother and mortuary owner, Norman Howe, served as pallbearers, and they gently lowered the casket with its fragile remains into the freshly dug grave. Law-enforcement officers kept watch for any sign of recognition among the mourners, in case the killer might have been in attendance, but they did not note any suspicious activity. "The services were simple," wrote the Denver reporter, "restoring in death the dignity her murderer destroyed in the last violent moments of her life."

Maybe the newspaper's headline that had accompanied the graveside burial photo was right—maybe Jane Doe's grave would mark an unsolved mystery. I decided to dig deeper for clues.

3

While pondering the question of the unsolved mystery, I decided to see if I could find some context—some insight into how the brutal murder of an unidentified young woman had fit into the day-to-day lives of the people of this small western city. I continued to hand-crank the *Daily Camera*'s old microfilm reader and found, however, that it had not fit in at all. Actress Donna Reed was featured at the local movie theater, and average Boulder families appeared to lead stereotypical lifestyles as depicted on their favorite television shows—*Ozzie and Harriett* and *Leave It to Beaver*.

Crimes against women were rare, and murders more so, with one exception, and that was the 1948 murder of University of Colorado student Theresa Foster. Joe Sam Walker, her convicted killer, was locked in prison, but he professed his innocence. Unless someone else killed Theresa, her murder could not have had any connection with the murder of Jane Doe. Parents may have hugged their children a little tighter after reading Bob Looney's newspaper accounts of the Boulder Cañon victim, but there was no indication of widespread fear or hiding behind closed doors.

As I continued reading, I was startled to learn that something suspicious—and possibly related—had happened just two days after Jane Doe's body had been discovered. According to an article in the *Daily Camera*, an Oklahoma state patrolman stopped a 1950 Ford that bore Colorado license plates. While the officer was writing the driver a speeding ticket, he noticed that the backseat of the car was soaked with fresh blood. The officer searched the car and found a red hair ribbon with strands of blonde hair. The driver, who was thrown in jail, said he knew nothing of the girl found in the canyon, but he admitted killing someone else. Samples of blood and hair found in the car were sent to the Federal Bureau of Investigation laboratory in Washington, D.C. An urgent teletype message to Sheriff Art Everson asked him to send samples of Jane Doe's blood and hair as well. Eventually I would learn that the sheriff did send a hair sample.

The more I learned about Jane Doe, the more I wanted to know. My possible involvement in the case, however, had become real to me even before I systematically sorted through all of the *Daily Camera*'s files. On April 30, 1998, my husband, Ed, called and said he would be working late, so I settled in on the couch with our two eight-week-old kittens, Maggie Brown and Nellie Bly. As they jumped all over me, I started flipping through the television channels and literally stumbled upon the CBS *48 Hours* program titled "Never Give Up." It featured Todd Matthews, a young man in Livingston, Tennessee, who had identified a homicide victim found wrapped in canvas and previously known only as the "Tent Girl."

The young woman had been murdered in 1968, two years before Matthews was born. On May 17 of that year, a water well driller, waiting for instructions from his boss, was killing time in Scott County, Kentucky, an hour's drive north of Lexington. The man was searching along a wooded stretch of the roadway for old glass insulators but, instead, found a five-foot-long bundle. He tugged at its tarpaulin cover, and out rolled a partially decomposed human body! The driller rushed off to call the sheriff, who returned with the coroner, who took the body to a morgue. All the medical examiner could determine was that the body was that of a white female, thought to have been between sixteen and eighteen years old, with short reddish-blonde hair. She had been dead for an estimated four to six weeks. The local newspaper was the first to call the unidentified victim the "Tent Girl." In the hopes that credible leads would reach police, the magazine *Master Detective* published a full account in a 1969 issue but, even with the national publicity, her case remained unsolved.

The unidentified victim was buried in the county-owned section of a cemetery in Georgetown, the seat of Scott County. Unlike our Jane Doe's simple gravestone with the engraved words, "Jane Doe, April 1954, Age About 20 Years," the Lexington, Kentucky, community put up a stone with a reconstructed sketch of the victim's face, as well as the following:

> Tent Girl. Found May 17, 1968 on U.S. Highway 25 North. Died about April 26–May 3, 1968. Age about 16–19 years. Height 5-feet-1 inch. Weight 110–115 lbs. Reddish-Brown hair, Unidentified.

Twenty years after the young woman's murder, the well driller moved to Livingston, Tennessee, where his daughter became engaged to Todd Matthews.

Todd's future father-in-law had been carrying around a copy of the 1969 *Master Detective* for years. He showed it to Todd, who immediately became fascinated with the story. Although Todd was a high school senior working part-time in a grocery store and—like me—had no background in detective work or tracing missing persons, he was determined to come up with the victim's identification. He even contacted the coroner and asked that the victim's remains be exhumed, but initially he got nowhere. Then, in the mid-1990s, following the advent of the computer age, Todd began searching missing-person websites on the internet. Late one night, ten years after he began his quest, he sat at his computer and came across a query which read:

> My sister Barbara has been missing from our family since the latter part of 1967. She has brown hair, brown eyes, is around five feet two inches tall, and was last seen in the Lexington, Kentucky, area. If you have any information, please contact me at the address posted.

As Todd's story goes, he woke up his wife by shouting: "I've found her!"

In March 1998, Todd again asked local authorities to exhume the "Tent Girl," and this time they agreed. They obtained her DNA from one of her teeth and compared her profile with one taken from a cheek swab of the victim's sister. A month later, the results positively identified the victim as Barbara Ann Hackman-Taylor, a twenty-four-year-old—who actually was several years older than the estimated age of her body. The victim's carnival-worker husband had told her family that she had run off with another man. Was he the murderer? No one would ever know, as he died of cancer in 1987. Barbara Ann was given a new gravestone, with her own name on it at last.

Todd's successful identification of the "Tent Girl" made a lasting impression on me. I was still reflecting on the television program—and my pieced-together scenario of Jane Doe—a year and a half later, in October 1999, when I met archeologist Jack Smith for a beer in Tom's Tavern. The no-frills beer-and-hamburger joint just west of Boulder's upscale Pearl Street Pedestrian Mall had been in business since 1959 and was popular with long-time Boulder residents. Indeed, my friend Jack was an old-timer himself, and the excuse to meet was so that I could borrow a photograph from him for one of my history columns. The tavern was across the street from the *Daily Camera* office, a sprawling brick building that, in 1963, had replaced the former building that had become old and cramped in reporter Bob Looney's time. I had just turned in my latest article, which was titled: "Jane Doe

Mourned But Never Identified." Her story was fresh in my mind as I slid into one of the restaurant's red-vinyl-seated booths.

I found myself telling Jack about the "Tent Girl" program and how the Kentucky victim's DNA was used to determine her identity. What little I knew about DNA I had picked up from actor O. J. Simpson's murder trial four years earlier, as well as the more recent Monica Lewinsky scandal which identified president Bill Clinton's semen on the White House intern's navy blue dress. I soon learned that the first use of DNA to solve a crime had been in England, in 1986, then the following year it was introduced to the United States in a criminal court case in Florida. My friend suggested that perhaps Jane Doe could be exhumed and her DNA profiled, as had been done with the "Tent Girl" in Kentucky. Was this something I could initiate? On television, it looked so easy, but the reality might be altogether different.

Still, bolstered by the realization that modern technology might make it possible to identify Jane Doe, I passionately talked about her to anyone and everyone who would listen. That included Sergeant Dan Barber, a Boulder County sheriff's deputy I met one day in the Carnegie Branch Library for Local History while doing research for my newspaper column. The uniformed officer was working on a history of the sheriff's office, so I naively asked him if I could read the Jane Doe case file. When he got back to me a few days later, he told me that the case files prior to 1970 had mysteriously disappeared after the then-incumbent sheriff was not reelected. Even if the sheriff's office did have the file, he said, I, as a member of the public, would not be allowed to read it. I understood that there is no statue of limitations on murder and all unsolved murder cases remain open, but I was horrified to learn that the file for this case no longer existed. Equally appalling was the realization that all of the files from the whole era were missing!

The sheriff's office referred me to a former deputy who was the under-sheriff at the time of Jane Doe's murder. Dorse "Dock" Teegarden had been interviewed by the *Denver Post* in April 1999, on the forty-fifth anniversary of the murder. He stated that he was out of town, picking up a prisoner, the day her body was found, but he participated in the subsequent search of mountain cabins. "It was a heartbreaker," he told the *Post* reporter. "We followed lead after lead, but nothing ever panned out."

I contacted the retired officer myself, but he had no new information to add. As he had told the reporter, his theory was that she came from someplace else and got a ride with a trucker who "did her in." He added what I already knew—that most of the people connected in some way to the victim were likely dead themselves. Still, I realized the importance of reinterviewing anyone formerly connected with the case.

My next stop was the Boulder County Coroner's Office, in the hopes of finding any additional shred of information. A clerk in the office confirmed that the "unidentified woman" had a death certificate, but it was not public information and she would not let me see it. When I emailed the incumbent coroner a few days later and asked, again, about the death certificate, he wrote back and related that it did, indeed, list the manner of death as "homicide." The coroner permitted his clerk to give me a copy of the one-page "Verdict of Jury," the office's report following the former coroner's inquest. This court proceeding, held in the Boulder County Courthouse, upstairs from the sheriff's office, took place four days after the students had found Jane Doe's body. The jury of six men included three high school teachers, a carpenter, an auto mechanic, and a University of Colorado law student who also worked at Howe Mortuary. The jurors examined the evidence provided by coroner George Howe and determined that "death resulted from shock caused by severe beating by person or persons unknown, with felonious intent."

The only other information stated in the jury's verdict was that the members estimated that the victim's death had occurred from four to ten days prior to April 8, 1954, and that the body was found on Highway 119, about nine miles west of Boulder in Boulder County, Colorado, three hundred yards east of Boulder Falls, and twenty-nine feet below the roadway along the creek.

Since the official court document failed to give me much new information, I turned to a *Daily Camera* article from April 12, 1954, to flesh out the details. Present at the inquest as a witness was Dr. Freburn L. James, the pathologist who had performed the autopsy. Also in the room was Boulder Police Chief Myron Teegarden, who "identified pictures he took at the scene," although no one, not even his son—the former under-sheriff—has any idea what happened to them. The pathologist, Dr. James, described the victim's multiple fractures, bruises, and abrasions, adding that it was difficult to give the specific cause of death with certainty. He stated that his final conclusion—severe shock—was a term meant to embody all of her injuries, and that it was proper to assume that her skull fracture was the proximate cause of death.

When the district attorney asked if all of the facts were consistent with murder, Dr. James testified, "They are." A dentist who had X-rayed the victim's teeth also testified and stated that based on the position of the lower right third molar, he estimated her age at between nineteen and nineteen and one-half years old—in the upper age range of Dr. James's assessment but below the newspaper accounts and the gravestone that would read: "Age About 20 Years." The unidentified young woman had no fillings in her teeth and only one cavity that needed to be filled. The dentist suggested that the excellent condition of her teeth indicated that she may have spent her childhood in a community with a water supply that contained fluorides.

I hoped to contact the jurors but found that all of them were deceased. Then I wrote to the Federal Bureau of Investigation in Washington, D.C., wanting to know what they had on file since newspaper accounts had mentioned the FBI's request for blood, hair, and fingerprints. My one-page letter was returned with a sticky note that read "too vague." Sometime later, Carol Taylor, the librarian at the *Daily Camera*, suggested I file a request under the Freedom of Information Act, the federal law enacted in 1966 that allows any member of the public the right to obtain information from a federal government agency.

Learning not to take "no" for an answer, I filed the request, then was surprised when a woman from the FBI personally telephoned. She told me that on July 1, 1993, in a "routine records destruction," an archivist had deemed that the file on the 1954 Colorado murder was no longer worth keeping. Unlike the pre-1970 files in the Boulder County Sheriff's Office that had mysteriously disappeared, this file had been deliberately purged. It then took ten months to get the caller's comments in writing, complete with the federal statutes (44 U.S.C. § 3302 and 36 C.F.R. § 1228) that defended the file's annihilation by "burning, pulping, shredding, macerating [soaking in liquid], or other suitable means." If only the agency could have held onto the information just a little longer. As I would soon discover, the government agency's purging of the Jane Doe file was just the tip of the iceberg of a decades-long practice of routinely destroying records of unsolved homicides and missing persons.

Wondering why the FBI would have crime-scene evidence in the first place, I did some background reading on the federal agency. I learned that after World War II, the FBI began to devote a significant proportion of its resources to assisting state and local law enforcement. This was due, in part, to advances in forensic science—the application of science to decide questions arising from crime or litigation. Cardboard files in drawer after drawer of the FBI's fingerprint collection contained lists of criminals and noncriminals alike. In addition to anyone who had been arrested, fingerprints were on file for those who had been federally employed, naturalized, or in the military service. The Boulder County sheriff and the Boulder police chief no doubt believed it was possible that Jane Doe's fingerprints could already have been on file, and a match with the victim's fingerprints would provide a positive identification.

The use of fingerprints for identification purposes can be traced back in time to Sir William Herschel, a British officer who, in 1858, worked for the civil service in India. There, he required thumbprints (or whole palm prints, as sources differ) as a substitute for the written signatures of his illiterate laborers. Sir Herschel's practice was refined by Sir Edward Richard Henry, who developed a print classification system using only the tips of fingers. His method of analysis was based on the assumption that no two persons have exactly the same arrangement of raised skin surfaces, or ridges, and that the patterns of these ridges of any one individual remain unchanged throughout life. Sir Henry classified the number of these ridges as well as the loops and whorls of their patterns so they could be filed and compared. Eventually, the Henry System became the standard in Europe and North America, and its inventor became known as the "Father of Fingerprints."

In 1901, Sir Henry was appointed assistant commissioner at London's Scotland Yard. Three years later, an officer from Scotland Yard attended the World's Fair in St. Louis, Missouri, where he was assigned to guard a display of the British Crown Jewels. At the fair, the London police officer passed on his knowledge of fingerprint analysis to police officers in St. Louis. Although the New York Civil Service Commission had initiated the use of fingerprints in the United States for its applicants as early as 1902, the St. Louis Police Department, in 1904, became the first police department in the United States to officially adopt the new identification technique.

Fueling and influencing the public's interest in forensics, British author Sir Arthur Conan Doyle, meanwhile, had created the fictional character Sherlock Holmes. In *A Study in Scarlet*, published in 1887, Doyle displayed an uncanny ability to describe scientific methods of detection years before they were officially discovered and implemented. In Doyle's novel, Sherlock Holmes was able to discern between human and animal bloodstains fourteen years *before* the inception of serology—the science of identification of body fluids in a crime laboratory.

In 1908, president Theodore Roosevelt's administration initiated the Bureau of Investigation—renamed, in 1935, the Federal Bureau of Investigation. Under the jurisdiction of the United States Department of Justice, a force of thirty-four special agents investigated federal crimes, including those in which perpetrators evaded state laws by crossing state lines. Congress had passed the "White Slave Traffic Act" in 1910, making it a crime to transport any individual over state lines for prostitution or any sexual activity for which the person could be charged with a criminal offense. Crossing state lines certainly was in the mind of the Oklahoma state patrol officer who, two days after Jane Doe's body was found, had stopped the speeding driver of the car with Colorado license plates and discovered fresh blood in the backseat.

J. Edgar Hoover ushered in an era of professionalism when president Calvin Coolidge's attorney general appointed the then twenty-nine-year-old law school graduate to head the federal agency in 1924. One of the director's first accomplishments was to establish an Identification Division to track criminals by their fingerprints. He set up a central card repository of rolled ink finger and thumb impressions. Within two years, law-enforcement agencies across the country began to contribute their identification cards as well. It was in this central repository that Boulder officials had hoped to find a match for Jane Doe.

Still considering how the Federal Bureau of Investigation might be able to help me with the Jane Doe case, I looked up the local branch in Boulder and asked the clerk who answered the telephone if his office had retained any files on the unidentified murdered woman. When I told the man who answered my call that the murder had taken place in 1954, he simply stated, "I wasn't born then."

My confidence was shaken by this lack of information, and I began to have real doubts about my ability to further research Jane Doe. I believed that identification was technologically feasible but highly unlikely without any official law-enforcement files. During the year 2000 and into the beginning of 2001, I stopped occasionally at the cemetery and visited the victim's grave, but Jane Doe was relegated to the back burner as I tackled other research and writing projects.

The murder victim, however, would not let me go. I had started on a mission and felt compelled to continue to move forward. Gradually, I came to the realization that there still could be someone in Jane Doe's family waiting for answers, and those answers were not going to come forth on their own. Knowing that no one else was attempting to solve the case, I rededicated myself to the task. At the same time, I came to the conclusion that this project was more than a one-person job. As a new internet user, I timidly posted my first query—like the sister of the "Tent Girl" had done—on the genealogical website Rootsweb.com. I wrote:

> Do you know of a 17–20-year-old WOMAN who was MISSING in 1954? "Jane Doe" was murdered and buried in Boulder, Colorado, in

April 1954 and has never been identified. If she could have been your
sister, mother, cousin, or friend, please contact pettem@earthlink.net.

Unsure of where my request would lead, I hoped I would hear from
someone, and I wondered how long I would have to wait.

The answer turned out to be fourteen months, which was a tumultu-
ous period for me—and for the nation. After the terrorist attacks against the
World Trade Center and the Pentagon in September 2001, the "Meet the
Spirits" cemetery reenactment that had been scheduled for late September
was put off a month. No one felt like doing it. Meanwhile, my husband
and I had moved into the mountains west of Boulder, where we chose
not to hook up our television. Instead, we began to watch a lot of movies,
mostly film noir and—with Jane Doe nagging at me—anything from the
early to mid-1950s.

One film that kept us on the edge of our seats and gave us a great back-
in-time look at midcentury forensics was *Mystery Street*, released in 1950 by
Metro-Goldwyn-Mayer, Inc. The black-and-white whodunit contrasted
Ricardo Montalban, a rookie cop, with Bruce Bennett, a tall, handsome
Harvard Medical School forensic expert and professor. Rereleased on DVD
as "a revealing-for-the-era procedural," the movie epitomized the film noir
genre, known for its dark themes, stark camera angles, and high-contrast
lighting. The film's documentary style incorporated and explained a crime-
scene investigation within the setting of a classic post–World War II crime
drama. Most of the scenes, including those at Harvard Medical School,
were filmed on location. The fictional story involved the murder of a beautiful young woman who was stripped of her clothes and dumped on the
edge of a beach on Cape Cod Bay, near Barnstable, Massachusetts.

Months later, a birdwatcher discovered the victim's skeletal remains
and called police. Lieutenant Peter Morales, portrayed by Montalban, did
not even know if the deceased was a man or a woman, but his enthusiasm to solve the case set him in search of an academic expert. First, the
lieutenant put the victim's bones, hair, and some poison ivy leaves into in
a cardboard box. Then, carrying the box in his late-1940s black Ford, he
drove to the medical school in Boston, where—long before crime-scene
investigation television shows like today's *CSI*—"Dr. McAdoo" dazzled
movie audiences with state-of-the-art forensics of the early 1950s. Viewing
the film was a reminder that many of the forensic practices in use today are
not new after all.

In the bow tie–attired forensic specialist's orderly and spotless laboratory, he magnified a few strands of hair and determined that they were

lighter at one end than the other. His conclusion was that the victim had
been a bleached blonde. Then Lieutenant Morales handed over the poison
ivy leaves and said that they had been found under the skeletal remains. Dr.
McAdoo explained that if the murder victim collapsed on the ivy leaves and
no one had moved the body, the leafiness of the ivy would give an approxi-
mate date of death. The plant was almost in full leaf when it had stopped
growing, so the expert estimated the date of death at the third week of May
of the year that the skeletal remains were found.

Within days, Dr. McAdoo reassembled what he could of the entire
skeleton but noticed that some of the bones were missing. He instructed
Lieutenant Morales to go back to the scene of the crime and sift the beach
sand to a depth of one foot in a search for more bones, just as forensic anthropologists would do today. By this point in the fictional investigation,
the forensic expert had determined that the skeleton belonged to a woman,
as the bones were lighter and smaller than a man's would have been. He
measured her thighbone and estimated her height at five feet five inches.
One look at an enlarged bone in her foot made him speculate that she
might have been a toe-dancing ballerina.

Then the expert told the lieutenant to search through all the photographs that his police department had obtained of missing young women.
In an attempt to find a match, they would project the photographs of
the women, one by one, on top of an image of the victim's skull. According to the fictional Dr. McAdoo, the procedure—now called photo-
superimposition—had been done only once before, in Scotland.

The next scene showed a discouraged Lieutenant Morales at his
cluttered desk, shuffling through file after file of photographs of faces of
missing women. Before long, however, he and the forensic expert—with
his jacket off and his sleeves rolled up—were seated in a projection room.
One slide projector, with two slots, threw two separate, overlapping images onto a screen. One was of the murdered woman's skull and the other
was an individual image of a missing woman's face. Over and over, various
women's faces were projected onto the screen, and one by one they were
discarded when the women's facial features failed to align with the bones
of the skull.

"If the skull does fit, it may not prove it's the right girl," cautioned
Dr. McAdoo, "but if it doesn't fit, it certainly eliminates the wrong one."
All of a sudden, the men found a startling match, right down to the align-
ment of her teeth.

Excited by this likely prospect, Lieutenant Morales narrowed his focus
to his most likely candidate—a three-months-pregnant nightclub enter-

tainer whose suitcase, left behind at her rooming house, just happened to include a pair of toe shoes. The bleached blonde had been having an affair with a respectable family man. When the lieutenant went back to the beach and sifted sand in his search for more of the victim's remains, he found the bones of her unborn child. He also found a missing rib of the victim—a rib that had been pierced by a bullet.

A search crew then dredged a nearby lagoon and found the stolen car that the woman had driven. Two officers reenacted the scenario of the shooting (with the "victim" sitting in the car) and discovered a .45-caliber bullet embedded in the floorboard at exactly the angle they had envisioned. They then traced the bullet to the pistol of the man with whom the blonde had been having an affair. After a fierce chase through a busy Boston railroad yard, Lieutenant Morales arrested the woman's murderer.

Near the end of the film, the lieutenant explained that "professors work with their heads, and cops work with their feet." The main theme of the story, at least to me, however, was that the use of forensic science was—and still is—extremely valuable in solving crimes. Dr. McAdoo reminded me of Edward O. Heinrich, a 1908 University of California, Berkeley graduate, now generally recognized as America's first academically trained forensic scientist. In 1915, he was appointed chief of police in Alameda, California. Interestingly, he also had a Boulder, Colorado, connection.

Boulder had adopted the city-manager form of government in 1917. One hundred candidates, including Edward Heinrich, applied for the first city manager's job, but he was chosen for the position. In an effort to apply his scientific and police-oriented background, Heinrich announced that he would enforce city ordinances, cooperate with law-enforcement agencies, and maintain complete records of arrests and complaints. After sixteen months on the job, however, he turned in his resignation, stating, "One's country may inspire one to die for it, but a municipality is scarcely worth the supreme sacrifice."

Edward Heinrich returned to California to teach at his alma mater and follow in the footsteps of a suddenly deceased San Francisco handwriting expert. Heinrich's own skills in handwriting analysis led to the conviction of a murderer after he determined from the killer's writing style on a ransom note that he "had the hand of a cake decorator." In another case resulting in the capture of three brothers who had gone on a murderous rampage on a mail train, the detective successfully profiled one of the perpetrators from a pair of overalls. A clothing stain—which turned out to be pitch from a fir tree—and fingernail clippings in a worn left-side pocket led Heinrich to deduce that the search was on for a left-handed logger who was meticulous about his appearance. Called "America's Sherlock Holmes" and the "Wizard of Berkeley," Heinrich was credited with having solved two thousand cases during his career.

Even though the illustrious detective remained in California, he also made time to work as a consultant for Boulder authorities in trying, albeit unsuccessfully, to solve some of the city's toughest crimes. One of his first challenges was to attempt to identify the murderer of Boulder Police Officer Elmer Cobb, who was shot in the line of duty in 1923. Heinrich supplied the Boulder district attorney with "truth serum," a drug used to depress the nervous system and remove the ability to reason, leaving the person being interrogated in a twilight zone of consciousness. The fruitless effort was to try to obtain the confession of a suspected "hit man," and the supposed hirer of the hit man was no less than the Boulder police chief himself. Half of the town's residents were convinced of the chief's guilt, while the other half professed his innocence. The case was dismissed for lack of evidence, and the murder of Officer Cobb has never been solved.

The last time Heinrich visited Boulder was in 1949, when the regents of the University of Colorado had asked his assistance following the bludgeoning death of university student Roy Spore. At the time, a recently published text titled *Homicide Investigation* was billed as required reading for all police officers. The book included a forward by the "great pioneer of modern police methods," August Vollmer—Berkeley's first police chief and the nation's leading figure in the field of criminal justice. Even with the advice of his California colleague, Heinrich could not find a clue, but the student's unsolved murder prompted the university president to sponsor a conference on crime.

At the time, all it took to be a cop in Boulder was a gun and a badge. Unlike today, when most officers have college degrees and police academy training followed by in-house departmental training, Boulder's sheriff deputies and police officers in the mid-twentieth century had no formal training at all. To remedy the situation, Boulder Police Chief Myron Teegarden and Boulder County Sheriff Art Everson followed on the heels of the university. Supplementing the frequent *FBI Law Enforcement Bulletins* and any textbooks the men may have been reading in their spare time, the men established what they called the Boulder Crime School in 1949. The weeklong training program was held in Boulder, but was open to all law-enforcement officers in Colorado, Wyoming, and Nebraska. In 1954, the time of Jane Doe's murder, police standards were in a state of change.

In the spring of 2002, I was hired by the Boulder police chief to research his department's 125-year history. Knowing that, in the past, the

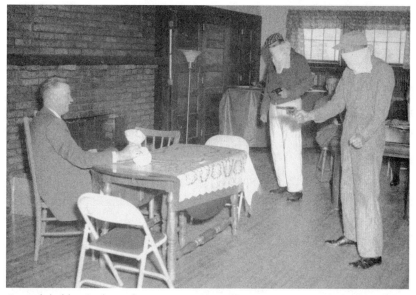

A mock holdup in the early 1950s was part of a training exercise for police officers in the Boulder Crime School. The man at the table is Boulder Police Department Detective Roy Hill. Seated in the background is Boulder County Under-sheriff Dorse "Dock" Teegarden. Photo courtesy of Dock and Dorothy Teegarden.

police department and the sheriff's office had worked together on major crimes, the assignment gave me a perfect opportunity to learn—not in Hollywood terms, but in real life—how these law-enforcement agencies had conducted their criminal investigations at the time of Jane Doe's murder. Although my job was to report on the years 1878 to 2003, I was especially focused on the late 1940s and early 1950s.

I learned that FBI director J. Edgar Hoover personally authorized six highly trained agents to serve in Boulder, as instructors. For the first year's five-day course, the entire class was organized to represent a police department confronted with the actual investigation and solution of a staged kidnapping and murder. The attending officers learned to organize, chart, draw, and photograph a crime scene. Their studies also included the collection of blood and fingerprints, ballistics and gunpowder tests, and the analyses of hair, fiber, handwriting, and typewriting specimens.

The field exercise of the simulated kidnap and murder was staged on the third day of the class. A blonde actress came to the "police department" and said that her "fiancé" had been slugged and was snatched from her side as they sat in the dark in an automobile on a dirt road near the foot of Flagstaff Mountain. The woman could suggest no motive for the attack except that her boyfriend had recently been seen with a large sum of money. She was hysterical and had no idea if he was dead or alive.

After a staged telephone call reported an abandoned automobile on a county road, crime school attendees found the fiancé's "body"—a dummy—in a field southeast of Boulder. To make the crime scene as real-looking as possible, the FBI agents had carefully constructed drag marks and planted a gun as well as spots and pools of blood. The crime-school attendees then conducted a thorough crime-scene investigation, lifting fingerprints from the car and gun and making plaster casts of footprints. They also found key evidence of the "murdered" man's gambling debts on indentations on a tablet of paper that was under a letter that had been written by the "victim." In October 1950, *Life Magazine* gave the Boulder training program national publicity by showing the "capture" of the FBI agent who played the part of a fugitive killer in the second year's simulated case. No mention was made in newspaper reports of seventy-eight-year-old Ed Tangen, identification officer for the Boulder County Sheriff's Office. The noted photographer and fingerprint and ballistics expert died in 1951 and had been a valuable resource in the analysis of handwriting, blood, hair, and fibers.

While conducting my research for the Boulder Police Department, I also needed to learn about the current operations of law enforcement. I told my friends I had turned to a life of crime and enrolled in the department's Citizens' Academy. The classes, which were three hours long and held once a week for twelve weeks, were designed to provide the public with a working knowledge of the modern-day criminal justice system. Topics covered everything, including police procedures in making arrests, laws of search and seizure, drugs, and even a jail tour, but the class on investigations interested me the most. At a later date, and with the chief's permission, I sat in on several sessions of police officer training classes specifically related to crime-scene and death investigations. We learned, in great detail, the procedures and importance of locating, noting, collecting, and preserving evidence that could lead to the identification of an offender.

How thoroughly investigated was the Jane Doe crime scene? No one will ever know since the sheriff's office's case files are gone, and I could not find anyone still alive who was at the scene to talk about it. The police detectives and sheriff's officers may have been fresh out of the Boulder Crime School and eager to do their jobs but, according to the newspaper accounts, there was no crime-scene evidence to analyze. Even Heinrich was unable to help. He died in 1953, one year before the murder of Jane Doe.

Finally, in June 2002, I received a response to my internet query. Virginia resident Micki Lavigne, a preschool teacher who, in her spare time, had volunteered her services as a private investigator for family and friends, sent me a short compassionate email and offered to make the search for Jane Doe her summer project. She created a one-page "Mystery Girl" website and asked me if I had any photographs of Jane Doe.

I knew there were no crime-scene photographs in the *Daily Camera* files, so I asked Alan Cass, a friend who served with me on the board of the Heritage Center Museum at the University of Colorado. Balding and bearded and a few years my senior, Alan had lived in Boulder most of his life. He worked at the university as curator of the American Music Research Center's Glenn Miller Archive, and he had a myriad of eclectic interests, including the research of local murders. If anyone would know about photographs, it would be Alan.

4

Alan revealed to me his interest in homicide victims on my fifty-sixth birthday. On that day, in March 2003, my husband, Ed, and I accompanied Alan and his wife to a parole hearing for the murderer of Elaura Jaquette. In July 1966, during the summer between my freshman and sophomore years at the University of Colorado, the twenty-year-old botany student was brutally beaten, raped, and murdered in an organ practice room in the west tower of the university's Macky Auditorium. At the hearing, in the cafeteria of the Denver County Jail, the ailing and elderly, but still strong-looking convict asked to spend his remaining years with his grandchildren. The parole officer reminded the killer that, unlike him, his victim never had a chance to have grandchildren. Elaura had missed out on so many of life's experiences and, I thought to myself, so had Jane Doe.

Alan had worked as the auditorium's stage manager at the time, but on the specific day of Elaura's murder, he was driving across the Midwest on the way home from a family vacation. The killer, who was the building's part-time custodian—the man we went to see in prison—had changed into a plaid shirt that Alan had left hanging in his office, leaving him feeling personally violated. After the man's arrest, Alan testified at the murderer's trial, where it was learned that the murderer had left a bloody palm print—a key part of the evidence—on a board on top of the victim's body. Our intent in attending the hearing was to glare at him so much that his parole board would make sure that he died in prison—and he did.

When I asked Alan about Jane Doe, I was surprised to hear him say that he was sure that he had seen four to six black-and-white photographs of her corpse years earlier at Howe Mortuary. "I have to warn you," he told me, "they are pretty disturbing due to the condition of her body having been exposed for a period of time along the creek." I immediately felt the clock ticking and a few days later went to the mortuary myself.

As the receptionist listened to my story, she became nearly as interested as I was. She brought out a leather-bound book and opened it up to a one-page funeral record for the "Unidentified Murdered Girl." Most of the information, including when and where her body was found, I already knew. Although the funeral record's stated cause of death used slightly different words—"Shock and exposure and injuries of a beating by persons unknown"—it was essentially the same as that determined during the coroner's inquest. I did learn that the cost of the cemetery plot in Columbia Cemetery, at the time, was sixty dollars, and the opening of the grave was thirty-five dollars, all paid by the *Daily Camera* from private donations. The mortuary had donated a "6/3 Elmo" casket, manufactured by the Iowa Casket Company.

Still on a search for the crime-scene photographs, I followed the receptionist down a narrow dark stairway into a cluttered storage room in the basement. Some of the files were in old metal filing cabinets, and others were in dusty cardboard accordion files stuck behind boxes on the tops of the cabinets. In one of the accordion files, we found an alphabetical index for 1954 and looked under "J" for Jane, "D" for Doe, "M" for murder victim, and finally "U," where we found "Unidentified Girl." There, well-preserved in an old yellowed envelope probably unopened in nearly fifty years, were the sympathy cards that had accompanied the floral arrangements given by members of the community.

We were close, but where were the coveted photographs? They had to be somewhere. My search at the mortuary had failed to produce them, but I remained hopeful about other avenues of investigation. Micki and I placed additional queries on missing-person websites, and by the time another year had passed one researcher had offered to exhume Jane Doe's remains herself. We soon learned, however, that in the state of Colorado, only law enforcement or next-of-kin can authorize and perform an exhumation. In September 2003, I decided it was time to get online and email the newly elected Boulder County sheriff, Joe Pelle.

I should not have been surprised when the sheriff told me that he had never heard of Jane Doe. When I told him about her case, though, he called it "thrilling" and said that he would ask one of his lieutenants, Phil West, to look into the matter. The sheriff added that Lieutenant West would be in contact with me.

On October 2, 2003, my husband and I drove to the Boulder County Justice Center, a two-story complex at Sixth Street and Canyon Boulevard, close to the foothills on the west side of the city. The sheriff's office had moved there from its former location in the Boulder County Courthouse in 1976, after the completion of the Justice Center on the site of the never-finished Park Allen Hotel. Financier and, later, convicted swindler, Allen J. Lefferdink had abandoned this last of his Boulder projects in 1960, leaving hotel foundations which the locals called "the ruins."

By the late 1960s, when Boulder became known as the crossroads in the nation's drug traffic, the dilapidated concrete walls sheltered hippies and transients who needed a place to crash for the night. When the Justice Center opened, it housed—in addition to the Boulder County Sheriff's Office—the Boulder Police Department, the Boulder County District Attorney's Office, the criminal courts of Colorado's Twentieth Judicial District, and the Boulder County Jail with approximately one hundred prisoners. In 1988, the jail inmates—who now number more than five hundred—were moved to a newer, larger jail near the Boulder Municipal Airport. In 1990, the police department relocated to the Public Safety Center building which it shares with the Boulder Fire-Rescue Department, on Thirty-third Street.

As arranged, Ed and I met Alan Cass in the Justice Center lobby before heading to the sheriff's office on the second floor. Because of Alan's knowledge and interest in Boulder murder cases, I had invited him to be present at our meeting. Lieutenant West ushered the three of us into a conference room on the second floor, where we seated ourselves on gray office chairs surrounding a large oval table. Gray cabinets lined one end of the room, a lectern was pushed into a corner, a television was mounted overhead, and a flip chart was perched on an easel. Wall décor included a bulletin board, chalkboard, county map, and calendar.

As we sat down under the glare of fluorescent lights, the tall, soft-spoken lieutenant introduced me to Detective Steve Ainsworth, known in the sheriff's office for his handlebar mustache. Both men were longtime county employees nearing the age of fifty, and although they were wearing street clothes, the pistols on their belts made me a little uncomfortable. Then I began to relay the story of Jane Doe. I had been worried that I would be nervous, but I was so moved by the circumstances of the young woman's death that the words just flowed from my lips.

After patiently allowing me to talk for an hour or so, Lieutenant West and Detective Ainsworth asked a few questions and made copies of Alan's and my photocopied newspaper clippings. They told us they were enthusiastic about revisiting the case. "Your goal—to identify Jane Doe—is an admirable one," said the detective, "but it's only the first step in solving the crime and apprehending her murderer." Lieutenant West nodded in agreement.

I was surprised to hear that these law-enforcement officers were equally, or even more, interested in the perpetrator. At that point in time, my main focus had been only on the victim. When our meeting ended, I said I would continue my research and keep them posted on everything I found. Though I did not say so explicitly, I naively expected the same in return. In the years ahead, I would learn a lot about the rules and procedures that law-enforcement officials are required to follow—protocol that prevented them from giving me information, even if they wanted to.

On the way out of the building, Alan asked Ed and me if we had recognized Detective Ainsworth. "He was the detective lent from the sheriff's office to the Boulder Police Department to work on the JonBenét Ramsey case," he said. We commented that we had remembered him addressing the Ramsey case on the *Today Show*.

Two weeks after I made my presentation, Lieutenant West drove Detective Ainsworth and me to Denver, where we spent all day at the Denver Public Library, Colorado Historical Society, and Colorado State Archives. We did not turn up much that was new, but we did find some records of Boulder County arrests from the same time period and learned that the state archives is the repository for Colorado State Penitentiary records—with mug shots, biographical information, and notations on the crimes, sentences, and paroles or pardons of particular inmates. I was pleased that my companions were taking the time to look into the case with me. I felt relaxed in their presence and, over the course of our outing, I almost forgot they were cops. The detective, in particular, impressed me with his compassion as he showed me photographs of his adopted and foster children.

Detective Ainsworth also brought along a printout from the website of the Doe Network—a volunteer organization devoted to assisting law enforcement in solving cold cases and concerned with unexplained disappearances and unidentified victims from North America, Australia, and Europe. Their mission coincided with ours—to give the nameless back their names and return the missing to their families. In fact, one of the group's administrative team members was Todd Matthews, the young man whose determination led to the identification of the "Tent Girl." We submitted Jane Doe—as Case File 433UFCO—to the Doe Network's extensive database, which included a few cases older than the Boulder victim. In 1928, a young couple, Bessie and Glenn Hyde, disappeared on a rafting trip in the Grand Canyon. Their craft was found upright and fully stocked with supplies, but no sign of either of its occupants has ever been found. In another case, socially prominent Dorothy Arnold, known as the "vanishing heiress," disappeared from New York City in 1910. No trace of her has been found, either, even though a convict, said to have been hired to dig her grave in a cellar of a house near West Point, New York, claimed that she had died after a botched abortion.

The photograph and accompanying text that Detective Ainsworth had in his hand showed Marion Joan McDowell—Case File 758DFON—an attractive young woman who had been abducted near Toronto, Ontario, in December 1953, four months before Jane Doe's body was found. In spite of the distant geography and the time lapse, we wondered if she could have been our murder victim. We were still discussing the missing young woman when we returned to Boulder, where I took the officers to the cemetery to see Jane Doe's gravestone.

A week or two later, I attended my first meeting of Families of Homicide Victims and Missing Persons, or FOHVAMP for short. Knowing of my interest in Jane Doe, a *Daily Camera* crime reporter had told me about this nonprofit organization that offers surviving family members support, guidance, and education to keep unresolved homicides in the public eye. Founded in 2001 by Colorado residents Howard Morton and Mark Reichert, the group helps families turn their grief into action, with the goal of finding justice for their loved ones. Howard's son was murdered in 1975 in Arizona, and Mark's brother's murder occurred in Denver in October 2000. Both cases remain unsolved.

My drive to the meeting took me south of Denver to the B & B Café in the small town of Castle Rock, named for a prominent butte just off the interstate highway. The restaurant was owned by one of the member, who opened especially for us, so we could exchange stories and heap our plates with potluck items that each family had brought to share. I went to represent Jane Doe, but—at this point in my quest—I was not as emotionally involved as were the others in the room. Howard pointed out that there are more than twelve hundred unsolved murders with a Colorado connection, adding: "FOHVAMP is a club we would not choose to be part of."

Broadcast reporters represented all of the local television networks, and several of their anchors went from table to table and booth to booth to film each of the family members and record their stories. When they got to me, I explained that I was unrelated to "my" murder victim, but that I was representing her family. I was, in fact, my victim's advocate, and I summarized what I knew of Jane Doe. Afterward, I talked with a University of Colorado sociology professor who, with some of his students, were researching cold cases. I felt that I was among friends.

From listening to the sometimes tearful firsthand accounts of the families, I began to learn just how strongly the odds are stacked against anyone trying to solve a cold case. Todd Matthews, now the media director of the Doe Network, defines a cold case as one in which "all leads have been exhausted—and/or the law-enforcement agency is no longer following leads or looking for new ones with any luck." The statistics, I learned, are discouraging: According to the National Crime Information Center (NCIC)—a computerized database of criminal history maintained by the Criminal Justice Information Services (CJIS), which is itself a branch of the FBI—there are currently 106,062 reported missing persons and 6,862 unidentified remains throughout the United States and Canada. But the data can only be accessed and entered by law-enforcement personnel, and because law enforcement is under no obligation to enter such information into the system, the number of missing and unidentified persons may be much higher than these figures indicate. Since 1999, out of the almost seven thousand open cases involving unidentified remains, Doe Network volunteers have brought resolution to the families of only forty-seven victims. Still, for those families, it was worthwhile.

Of course, the more recent cases—especially those involving witnesses and crime-scene evidence—receive the most attention from beleaguered police departments. Because there is no statute of limitations on murder and all unsolved murder cases legally remain open, well-funded law-enforcement agencies address the backlog of their older cases with cold case squads. But the efforts of these dedicated detectives are often hampered by a lack of files, especially when the cases are older than ten or twenty years. As I had quickly learned from the Boulder County Sheriff's Office, it, like many others, lacked the staff and finances for even one dedicated cold case detective. Lieutenant West had assigned Detective Ainsworth to the Jane Doe case, but everything else the detective investigated had a higher priority.

Many of the people at the FOHVAMP meeting said that they felt their cases were shoved into the background—almost as if their presence was a reminder to law-enforcement officers that they had failed in apprehending the killers of their loved ones. When I left the B & B Café that day, the consensus that I perceived among the family members who were present was that the police either were not doing enough or were not able to do enough, which is why it sometimes falls to laypeople like myself to investigate these unsolved crimes.

On November 6, 2003, Lieutenant West invited me to a meeting with Boulder Sheriff Joe Pelle, along with the Boulder County coroner and two of his colleagues. I had mentioned the idea of exhuming Jane Doe's remains in my very first contact with Sheriff Pelle, and Lieutenant West and Detective Ainsworth had agreed that it would be a good idea. Still, up until this time, no formal decision from higher up had been made.

After we were seated around a different conference table—in a room adjoining Sheriff Pelle's office—Lieutenant West explained why he wanted to reopen the Jane Doe case. He started by presenting the history and background of her murder and the subsequent investigation as we knew it from the newspaper articles, adding that the sheriff's office no longer retained its original case file. "This is our window of opportunity," added Detective Ainsworth. "With new technology, including DNA, facial reconstruction, and the internet, we may at least be able to identify the victim, and her siblings, if any, may still be alive." We discussed the need for a facial reconstruction, and Detective Ainsworth gave me an assignment—to go through high school and college yearbooks and find typical hairstyles from 1954.

I spoke in favor of the lieutenant's and detective's opinions, but those on the coroner's side of the table argued that reopening the case would not be the best use of the sheriff's time and money. After considerable discussion, Sheriff Pelle said that he would like to pursue the case, but he was unable to justify using thousands of dollars of taxpayers' money when there were more recent homicides to be solved. He agreed, however, to go ahead with the exhumation if I was able to raise the money myself.

Alan Cass wanted a full report, so we met the next day over coffee at Starbucks, within walking distance of his office on the University of Colorado campus. We brainstormed a list of names of people to ask who might know something about the long-ago murder. I agreed to search the University of Colorado alumni directory for contact information on the students who found Jane Doe's body. We made a list of local contacts who we knew were still alive—including the former under-sheriff and two former sheriffs, the elderly police detective who was at the scene the day after the murder, the son of the coroner in office in the 1950s, and a retired district attorney. Any or all of these people, we figured, could have some small clue or clues that might prove helpful down the road.

The task of fund-raising was more daunting. While pondering various options, I decided to go in search of the missing case files. The sheriff officials stated again that they had nothing at all prior to 1970, so I posed my question to a records clerk at the Boulder Police Department since newspaper accounts stated that both agencies had worked together on the case in 1954. When the clerk came back empty-handed, I pleaded for permission to look in the police files myself. These files were, and are, public record, but the room where they are stored is not publicly accessible. To my advantage, I had completed my book on the history of the police department and was on a first-name basis with many of the employees. When I eventually was given permission to search in the records room—to my absolute surprise and delight—I found a misfiled microfilm with some Jane Doe–related correspondence! This was not the missing sheriff's office file, but it was a whole lot better than nothing. The box was labeled "1954 Homicide, Unidentified Female," and it was on a cartridge reel that read "Detective Case Files."

The bulk of the file consisted of letters about missing persons, mostly from distraught relatives all over the country. A woman from Tuttle, Oklahoma, wrote that her daughter had been missing for two months. The daughter had a tattoo on her left hand between her thumb and forefinger which the mother said connected her with a "dope ring." A Springfield, Missouri, mother stated that her daughter had been missing since March 21, and she enclosed a high school photograph showing a smiling young woman with shoulder-length blonde hair. Another Missouri mother, this one from Excelsior Springs, wrote that her daughter had been missing for six weeks and asked if the victim was wearing a class ring. Two people reported missing nieces—a woman from Chicago, Illinois, and a man from a small town in eastern Colorado. A Crooksville, Ohio, woman who wrote that she had not seen her sister in some time gave a description and wanted to know if her sister could have been the murdered woman.

Several police departments in various parts of the country also responded to the one-paragraph newspaper report. A detective in Nassau County, New York, forwarded a photograph and description of a missing young woman in his jurisdiction. The Springfield, Illinois, police department wrote to say a sixteen-year-old bleached-blonde waitress of his city had run off with a soldier returning to Camp Carson, Colorado. A young woman with a scarred wrist was missing from Pittsburgh, Pennsylvania.

Unlike the instant communication we rely on today, the tracing of missing persons—even in this homicide case—was done by regular or air mail. A Dallas, Texas, man whose wife was traveling to California, most likely by bus, wrote that he had not heard from her since she had left a few days earlier, and neither had she reached her destination. He said that he went to the Dallas Police Department to give her description but they had no additional information on the "unidentified woman found near Boulder." The Dallas police then told the husband to write directly to the Boulder police chief. In addition to giving his wife's description, he enclosed a domestic airmail stamp and urged the chief to reply as quickly as possible as to whether the victim could be his missing spouse.

Carbon copies of the police chief's responses to each inquiry were also recorded on the microfilm. Although each letter was individually addressed, the letters themselves were very much the same. The chief explained to each writer that he did not believe their daughter, niece, sister, wife, or—to the police departments—missing person was the unidentified murder victim. And he always reiterated the woman's physical description, adding that she was "about twenty years old" and "blonde."

As I read through the rest of the material, I also found copies of letters to and from Federal Bureau of Investigation director J. Edgar Hoover. Since the director had helped the Boulder police chief and the sheriff set up the Boulder Crime School, I thought perhaps he had taken a special interest in Boulder cases. More likely, though, he was just doing his job of lending federal resources to law-enforcement agencies across the country. On a now-microfilmed file card dated the day after the students found Jane Doe's body, Detective Roy Hill of the Boulder Police Department wrote: "After lunch, the Sheriff and I went to the mortuary, and I tried unsuccessfully to get a fingerprint from the left thumb of the victim which was the only finger with any skin left."

The same reel of microfilm also included a copy of a photograph of the victim's thumbprint. It looked like a black blob with just a few ridge impressions around the edges. I suddenly realized that the newspaper accounts that had mentioned a fingerprint on file had been completely misleading. The FBI had, indeed, filed away a print of Jane Doe's thumb, but since most of her skin was missing, it was not of any use as a method of identification, at all.

Four days after Detective Hill tried to get the thumbprint, he assisted the under-sheriff in taking "close-up photos of the victim's teeth." The detective also noted that he removed some of the victim's hair and sent it to the FBI lab for examination, but his report neglected to specify if he clipped a lock off of the end, or if he removed it next to the scalp as "Dr. McAdoo" had done in the film *Mystery Street*. The newspaper article about the Oklahoma speeder who was arrested with blood in his backseat mentioned that the FBI had also requested a blood sample from the Boulder victim, but there was no mention of her blood type in the correspondence. There may not have been any blood to sample.

In May 1954, the FBI issued its laboratory report with the results of the microscopic analysis of Jane Doe's hair. The official verdict was that her hair had come from the head of a Caucasian, and the color was "light brown." After the police chief received the report, he conscientiously wrote "light brown," instead of "blonde," in all of his future correspondence.

Elated with my find, I paid for a printout of the sixty-three pages, then went to Kinko's and made a copy for the sheriff's office. Detective Steve Ainsworth was out of the office when I dropped off the packet, but he emailed me the next day: "I got a chill down my back when I saw this on my desk this morning."

5

Other new developments kept my research equally exciting. Online, I Googled the name of the original pathologist who, according to the newspaper articles, had performed the autopsy on Jane Doe's body. Much to my surprise, I found him in the Pacific Northwest almost immediately. In November 2003, I wrote to the man, saying that I hoped that my letter reached him, as it concerned historical research of a very unusual nature. I asked him if he was the pathologist named Dr. Freburn L. James who had owned the James Clinical Laboratory in Boulder, Colorado, in 1954. Then I gave him some background on the Jane Doe case, explaining that I had approached the sheriff about exhuming the victim's remains.

Dr. James's return letter reached me two weeks later. "I have long been concerned that no one reported a missing daughter, girl friend or wife, and that no positive identification of 'Jane Doe' was ever made," he wrote, in part. He told me that he had submitted an autopsy report to the Boulder County coroner and called it an "interesting but tragic case." The next time I visited the sheriff's office, I left a copy of Dr. James's letter for Lieutenant West and Detective Ainsworth. The detective checked with the coroner, whose office did not have a copy of the autopsy on file, and then called Dr. James, who said that he still had his personal copy in a filing cabinet in his living room! The elderly pathologist sent a copy to the detective, who then made another copy for me. We both were thrilled to get it.

The official four-page document identified Dr. James as the autopsy surgeon, George Howe as coroner, and the date, time, and location as "April 8, 1954, 9:45 p.m., Howe Mortuary, Boulder, Colorado." Under a place for the victim's name was written, "Unidentified White Female about age 17–20." The pathologist's external examination—citing her skull fracture and a series of fractures on her left side—had been accurately described in the newspaper accounts. Internally, Dr. James examined her skull, heart, lungs, stomach, pancreas, liver, and spleen, as well as her endocrine, urinary, and genital systems. Her last meal had contained carrots, meat, and potatoes. The postmortem examination did not reveal sexual abuse, but the pathologist stated that too much time had elapsed since her murder, and any evidence would be inconclusive. He also noted: "There is no evidence of past pregnancy, and there are no signs which would prove a past pregnancy," indicating that Jane Doe most likely had not been a mother.

I was already aware of her stated height and weight, but the newspaper accounts failed to take into consideration that the corpse had lost fluids between the time she was murdered and the time she was found. When alive, she would have weighed more than the estimated 100 to 110 pounds, but how much more I did not know. As to her hair, the pathologist described it as "light brown, almost blonde," with no evidence of bleaching or dying, adding that it appeared to have a "faint-reddish cast." No wonder there were so many discrepancies in the newspaper accounts. I got the feeling that no one had a really accurate description of the victim at all.

In Dr. James's letter to me he also wrote: "The case became of interest, at the time, to one of the detective-story-type magazines and was published a few months later under the title 'The Battered Blonde of Boulder Bend.'" He added that he did not have a copy, but he urged me to look for one. Then I reread some of the old newspaper articles, including the *Rocky Mountain News* story from April 9, 1954, the day after Jane Doe's body was found. The reporter began: "The battered blonde of Boulder Creek died slowly among the creek bed's jagged rocks, a pathologist said Friday—after she was hurled in." The title of the article was "Mystery Girl Still Alive When Hurled into Creek."

Just as the newspaper accounts had misled the public about Jane Doe's thumbprint, the reporters continued to promote her as a blonde. Perhaps the writers just liked alliteration, or they thought it would make the victim more alluring and sell more newspapers and magazines. The inaccurate publicity, however, did not bring forward any families of missing girls with light brown hair.

I started an internet search for the detective magazine in the hopes that it would provide more details on the case. A flood of new titles had followed the pulp magazines and digest-size mystery fiction publications made popular, beginning in 1941, with *Ellery Queen's Mystery Magazine.* At first, when I looked for any title replicating the newspaper reporter's alliteration and Dr. James's memory, all I found were references to a 1949 movie titled *Beautiful Blonde from Bashful Bend.* The movie starred Betty

Grable, with Cesar Romero and Rudy Vallee. According to its write-up, it followed the antics of a saloon-bar singer who had "the biggest 6-shooters in the West."

By December 2003, I was feeling optimistic about Jane Doe. I had started to reconstruct a case file—beginning with old newspaper articles. The events came to life when newspaper archives revealed the photographs of the students who found her body, the detectives at the crime scene, and the people gathered around her grave. Funeral records led to the flower cards, and the coroner's "Verdict of Jury" gave me the location of the crime scene. Reading the police department correspondence was almost like going back in time. Rounding out the newly gathered material was Dr. James's report from the original autopsy.

Lieutenant Phil West, Detective Steve Ainsworth, and I had convinced a somewhat reluctant sheriff to consider revisiting this very cold case. Meanwhile, Alan and I had a list of people to contact, although I discovered that some, like Detective Roy Hill, were deceased. I looked forward to regular meetings with the lieutenant and detective and hoped we would share information and resources.

In one of Lieutenant West's emails he wrote: "Certainly, IF (after all these years) we identified a suspect, we would have to handle that confidentially, but I see no reason to exclude you from most anything else." All that was missing was money for the exhumation. I had no idea where I would get it, but I knew that I could not let the opportunity slip away.

Talking up the need for money, I found several people willing to contribute. At first no one was sure how to handle the funds until a board member of the Boulder History Museum suggested that the nonprofit museum could be the repository for tax-deductible funds earmarked for Jane Doe's exhumation. I wrote up a formal proposal and waited for the board members to vote. The idea was unanimously accepted, and the Jane Doe Fund was established. Equally exciting was the news that Sheriff Pelle had scheduled a press conference—specifically to address the Jane Doe case—for early February 2004. We were on our way!

I followed Alan Cass's suggestion, too, to look up contact information on the students who discovered Jane Doe's body. I located and found both of them, and I was delighted to learn that one of the men, Wayne Swanson—then nearly seventy years old—lived in an assisted-living home in Steamboat Springs, Colorado. I reached him through his brother Denny, who invited me to visit. He even told me to bring an overnight bag.

On January 27, 2004, I jumped in my car for the four-hour drive on snowpacked mountain roads. The wind was strong but the sun was bright as I headed south on the Peak to Peak Highway, through Nederland and Black Hawk, and then west through Clear Creek Canyon to Interstate 70. Once past Idaho Springs, I climbed steadily, skirted the historic silver-mining town of Georgetown, and then drove through the Eisenhower Tunnel at an elevation of 11,112 feet. Nearly two miles later, when I emerged on the other side of the Continental Divide, snow was falling heavily.

At Silverthorne I turned right toward Kremmling and the last leg of my journey—over Rabbit Ears Pass, named for a rock formation that, obviously, looked like the ears of a rabbit. The snow had been plowed into huge piles on either side of the road, there was very little traffic, and the sun was brilliant. I was struck by the beauty of immense evergreen trees, heavily laden with snow. After the summit, the Yampa Valley opened up in front of me, and I drove downhill again before pulling into the town of Steamboat Springs. There, as planned ahead of time, I called Wayne's brother Denny, who had agreed to take me to see the former student. I knew from the University of Colorado's online alumni directory that Wayne had been a social studies major and had graduated in 1959.

Denny said to meet him at his place of business, the True Value Hardware store. We then drove to the Doak Walker Care Center, where Wayne had lived since having a stroke two years earlier. The modern and well-maintained skilled nursing facility was named in memory of a football legend and longtime Steamboat Springs resident. I recognized Wayne as soon as I first glimpsed him in the hallway. Although he was struggling with a walker, he bore a strong resemblance to the lanky lad whose photograph I had seen in the newspaper clippings from 1954. Wayne was five years older and a little shorter than Denny. He had never married and had no family other than his brother.

Wayne, Denny, and I sat down in a lounge where I got out my stack of photocopies of the old newspaper clippings. I was pleased that the former student could confirm all of the information in the articles. I showed Wayne the photograph of him and James Andes, the student who was with him when they found Jane Doe's body. Wayne said they each had separate rooms in the rooming house on Marine Street, between the University of Colorado and downtown Boulder. Wayne liked to hike and admitted, "When I should have been home studying, I was hiking in the mountains."

The brothers' parents had often brought their young sons from their midwestern home to vacation in Colorado, just as my husband's parents had brought Ed on fishing and rock-hunting trips from Texas, instilling in him an appreciation for the state's geology and mining history. I was reminded, too, of family trips with my young daughters, who continue to call Colorado home. Denny added that his family's love for the mountains was the reason that Wayne had gone to the university and why both of the brothers had chosen to live in the state.

Wayne and his college friend James were both were from Illinois. Wayne told me that on the day they found Jane Doe's body, they "just wanted something to do for the afternoon." James, a business major who earned his spending money with a part-time job at Joyce's Market, had a car. With a few hours on their hands, the students drove into the mountains. According to Wayne, they had parked at the Boulder Falls turnout and were walking on the roadway when they spotted what looked like a store mannequin on the rocks at the edge of the stream at the bottom of an embankment.

"We were scared," Wayne said, as he turned toward me—the situation as fresh in his mind as if it had just happened. Wayne then told me that he turned to James and asked, "What should we do?"

Denny had warned me that in addition to the effects of his recent stroke, Wayne also suffered from Parkinson's disease. Often, because of the disease, he was unemotional, but the former student became animated when he spoke of Jane Doe. Even though I had read the story in the newspaper clippings, Wayne wanted to tell it to me all over again.

"After we found the body," Wayne said, "it was late in the afternoon and starting to get dark. We got in James's car and drove immediately to the sheriff's office, then came back up with the sheriff. I'll never forget seeing the girl being lifted up and placed on a stretcher."

Wayne then told me that he, James, and some newspaper reporters even went into the morgue. "I had recently had a biology class and had dissected animals," Wayne told me. "Seeing the girl's body didn't bother me, but one of the local newspaper reporters, also in the room, started to get sick." This breach of protocol would have been unheard of today.

According to Wayne, the two students were never interviewed by the sheriff or the detectives from the Boulder Police Department. They were, however, thrust into the limelight by the press, who asked them to tell and retell their story. Wayne remembers that he and James hung around the morgue until midnight.

"We were just kids," Wayne recalled. "No one asked us to leave."

The next day Wayne and James went to their parents' homes for Easter vacation. Wayne thought James had left his car in Boulder and, most likely, they both boarded the same eastbound train. I asked him if he had heard any more about the victim after their weeklong vacation. He said he saw an article or two in the newspaper, but then everyone forgot about her. Jane Doe may have remained forgotten for a long time, but I was touched when Wayne told me, "In later years, I wondered about her every time I turned on my television and heard news of Boulder."

When Denny and I were getting ready to leave the assisted-living home, Denny told me that he still maintained Wayne's former residence at the Bear Claw Condominiums, and he offered me the comfortable two-bedroom condo for the night. When I let myself in, I felt as if I were invading Wayne's privacy, or at least continuing my visit with him. All around me were his personal photographs, including a framed black-and-white print of the former student on his twenty-first birthday. He was sitting on a railing in front of the screen door of his parents' home and looked just as he had in the old newspaper articles.

The condo was in the highest building on the slopes of the Steamboat Springs Ski Area, and a gondola passed on one side while a chairlift went by on the other. The air was clear and cold, and the local newspaper announced the resort's fifty-five inches of packed powder. Wayne's outdated ski passes hung from a spice rack in the kitchen. The rooms were tastefully furnished with western and Native American art, along with books on health, cooking, and travel. Compact discs of George Gershwin and Frank Sinatra lined the shelves. Wayne even had a pillow embroidered with the phrase "Screw the golden years." I liked the man and was glad for the opportunity to put his name with his face.

I wished that I could have had that same opportunity to meet and get to know the other student, James. I looked him up the *Boulder City Directories* and determined that he left Boulder during his sophomore year, but he later returned and obtained a bachelor's degree in business from the University of Colorado. After graduation, he joined the trust department of the First National Bank, in Boulder. During the intervening years, he had joined the Army, taken some courses at Northwestern University, and worked in a couple of banks in Chicago. I found him in an out-of-state location and wrote to him. He called me, but he got my husband instead. He shouted into the telephone to Ed that I was to "never" contact him again.

Within an hour after I got home the day after my visit with Wayne, a reporter called me from the *Rocky Mountain News*. He wanted some information on Sheriff Joe Pelle's upcoming press conference in which he would announce the reactivation of the Jane Doe case. I did not tell the reporter about my visit with Wayne, but I filled him in with a few answers to his questions on Jane Doe. At the end of the conversation—in which I thought I was simply giving information—I was shocked to hear him say, "The story will be in tomorrow's paper."

The crime reporter of the *Daily Camera*, the publisher of my history columns, had formally interviewed me, too, but she was holding her story for the day of the press conference. When I next entered the *Camera's* newsroom, my editor made it very clear to me that "leaking information" to another newspaper was unacceptable. That was not my intention, I explained, and I quickly learned about competition and the importance of a scoop. I was completely unaware that Jane Doe had become front-page news.

A few days later, on the morning of February 4, 2004, Sheriff Pelle faced a bank of television cameras and a dozen print and broadcast journalists. In the training room near his office, he announced his commitment to the Jane Doe murder investigation, assuming, of course, that I could raise the funds for her exhumation and DNA comparisons. Wearing a gray jacket, light blue shirt, and a dark tie, he told the media that I, a local historian, had convinced him of the importance of the case by mounting a "firm but polite campaign."

The sheriff said that he believed the case was still worth pursuing "if only to reassure ourselves that everything that is humanly possible has been

The author spoke about the case with the media in January 2004. Jane Doe's small gravestone is on the right. Photo courtesy of the Daily Camera.

done to identify her." He reiterated what Lieutenant West and Detective Ainsworth had stressed in our recent meeting—that even with the advances in forensic technologies like DNA comparisons, this was the last, best opportunity to resolve the case. He added that Jane Doe's parents most likely were dead, and that any siblings who could assist in the investigation were probably in their sixties or seventies. Detective Ainsworth, also in a coat and tie, then spoke solemnly and said, "If it were my sister, I'd want people to do what we're doing."

Then the president of the board of the Boulder History Museum stepped up to the plate and announced the museum's agreement to accept individual tax-deductible donations earmarked for the investigation. On camera, I formally kicked off the "Jane Doe Fund" with a check for one hundred dollars and felt excited and optimistic.

Lieutenant West had asked me to address the historic aspects of the case, so I pulled out my prepared notes, giving a brief background on what I knew of the murder as well as the outpouring of compassion from the community. I announced, too, that a volunteer webmaster had created a Jane Doe website, complete with almost all of the published articles on the case since 1954. The only part of my remarks that the media picked up, however, was about life in the 1950s.

I explained that in 1954, the year of Jane Doe's death, Dwight David Eisenhower was president, and Senator Joe McCarthy was on a witch hunt for Communists. A postage stamp was three cents, and an average house sold for twenty-two thousand dollars. At the time, Perry Como, Frank Sinatra, and Patti Page were popular singers. Elvis Presley had just recorded his first record, "Careless Love." A favorite television show was *I Love Lucy*, women's hairstyles were soft and curly, and poodle skirts were the latest fad.

Immediately after the press conference, Lieutenant West led the journalists and their camera crews on a tour of the cemetery. Their press kits included the "Unidentified Woman's" death certificate, which the coroner's office had previously told me I was not allowed to see. Since I, too, was a member of the press, I picked up a packet for myself.

Even though the weather was cold and overcast, I watched, elated, as stylishly dressed television anchors took turns standing in the snow next to Jane Doe's grave and filming segments for the evening news. The search for Jane Doe's identity had gone public. I had been invited, that day, to address the Boulder Luncheon Optimist Club with a talk on Boulder history, but when I arrived, I was so full of my recent news that I spontaneously spoke, instead, on the reopening of the Jane Doe case.

The media attention was aimed at Boulder and Denver residents, but the internet spread our case far and wide. The very next day, I began posting the latest news articles on the brand-new Jane Doe website, which included a message board, contact information, and an icon to click to make donations. The Boulder History Museum started receiving checks, and I was mailed and emailed notes of encouragement from people across the country. One donor, Carl Wright, even sent poetry, including a few lines of Alexander Pope's "Elegy to an Unfortunate Lady"—so appropriate for Jane Doe. The poem began:

> By foreign hands your dying eyes were closed.
> By foreign hands your comely limbs composed.
> By foreign hands your humble grave adorned.
> By strangers honored and by strangers mourned.

In a continued quest for funds, I searched the internet for additional sources. When I came across the website for the United States Department of Justice and emailed for referrals, the person who responded to my request suggested that I call the Philadelphia-based Vidocq Society. Founded in 1990 by professional forensic experts, the society's stated mission was, and still is "to act as a catalyst and provide guidance to law-enforcement agencies to assist them in solving crimes." Founding member William Fleisher had proposed naming the organization for Eugène François Vidocq, generally recognized today as the "father of modern criminal investigation."

Monsieur Vidocq, born in France in 1775, was a fugitive from justice who offered his services as a police spy and informer. The crook-turned-cop became so successful at catching criminals that he was named the first chief of La Sûreté Nationale when it was the criminal investigative bureau of the police department in Paris. Beginning in 1811, he directed a force of twenty-eight detectives, all of whom were also former criminals. Among Monsieur Vidocq's various accomplishments, he developed a card index system for record-keeping and introduced the science of ballistics in police work. He also was the first to make plaster-of-Paris casts of foot and shoe impressions, as the officers in the Boulder Crime School had done during their mock investigation.

Part of the Vidocq Society's expertise, I learned, was assisting with exhumations. When I sent chairman of the board and case manager Frederick Bornhofen the details on our case, he replied that his organization would be glad to help, free of charge. By the spring of 2004, our team was on a roll.

6

My fellow researcher, Micki Lavigne, and I—connected by the internet—continued to search missing person websites. We corresponded with the Doe Network's Todd Matthews, with Alan Cass, and with each other. Sometimes we briefly mentioned our personal lives—I learned that Micki was married and had a son and two stepdaughters in high school—but mostly we discussed all possible Jane Doe candidates that we culled from the old newspaper articles that had been transcribed by the volunteer webmaster and then posted on the Jane Doe website for the whole world to see.

In April 2004, Vidocq Society board chairman Frederick Bornhofen communicated directly with Lieutenant West, who informed me that the exhumation was planned for early June. He also said that three Vidocq Society experts would be flying in from Arizona and Georgia. I asked for, and received, as an in-kind donation, free accommodations for our guests from the Hotel Boulderado. It felt great to have the backing of the local community as well as the community at large. Now I had become the catalyst—bringing together the forensic specialists and the sheriff's officials. Jane Doe's exhumation was really going to happen.

Before it could begin, however, the sheriff's office had to obtain a search warrant to satisfy Boulder Revised Code 4-26-4(c), which read: "The [city] manager shall not issue any disinterment permit unless the applicant presents a valid order of a court of competent jurisdiction approving the disinterment." Detective Ainsworth filed the necessary legal affidavit, outlining the background of the case and including my initial interest in making use of modern technology to attempt to identify the victim's remains. He stated that he believed there was probable cause—in the form of the newspaper accounts, the coroner's "Verdict of Jury," the funeral record, and the unidentified woman's death certificate—to show that Jane Doe had been murdered.

From researching cemetery records, the detective also said that he believed there was specific evidence "which could be of great assistance in identifying the victim and furthering the criminal investigation of her murder." Specifically, this was Jane Doe's remains, buried in "Section B, Lot 015, Grave 3NE" in Boulder's Columbia Cemetery. The request of the court was approved.

In just a few months, in addition to promised pro bono assistance from the Vidocq Society, we had more than three thousand dollars in the bank. Michael Greenwood, general manager of Crist Mortuary, offered his grave-opening services for free, saving us an additional three to four thousand dollars. We did not need any more money for the exhumation, but we began to build up a fund for Jane Doe's DNA profile and hoped-for future DNA comparisons with potential family members. For my birthday that year, I asked my husband and daughters for contributions to the Jane Doe Fund. I met fairly regularly with Detective Ainsworth and Lieutenant West—who also made a donation—and I kept them apprised of our growing bank balance. Alan Cass was a donor, as well.

Along with all of these generous donations and offers to help, however, came controversy. In the newsletter of the preservation organization Historic Boulder, Inc.—one of the sponsors of the "Meet the Spirits" event—a Boulder resident wrote a long editorial titled "Resurrecting Another Easter Spirit?" He referred to Jane Doe as "a long-fallen leaf off a family tree" and asked that she not be exhumed. The writer called her the "patron saint" of those who "crave solitude, anonymity, unlisted numbers, silent cell phones, pagers that never ring, bill collectors with amnesia, impenetrable spam-filters, and a place to hide in the soothing shadows of total, complete, heavenly peace and quiet."

As had been my experience, the writer first learned of Jane Doe during one of the cemetery tours. But, unlike me, he stated that he preferred to continue to think of her as a "faceless, unknown, nameless waif" and the subject of "affectionate and poignant" legend. "She is somebody only as long as she is nobody," he wrote. "Her memory lives only as long as her anonymity survives. As soon as we find her, we lose her. She truly dies, forever, the moment we bring her to life."

Although the writer failed to give any of his own personal, religious, or moral beliefs, he made it clear that he wanted Jane Doe to rest in peace. Even in 1954, however, coroner George Howe anticipated disinterment when he told a reporter: "The body will be placed in an airtight rubber bag to prevent further decomposition. That way, we'll be able to exhume the body for possible identification any time within two years." I thought past my hopes of finding the victim's immediate family and reflected on the community at large. I became convinced that we—as members of society—had an obligation at least to try to find out who killed her. As Lieutenant West and Detective Ainsworth had told me, the way to start was to search for her identity.

My husband defended our quest by posting his comments on the Jane Doe website's message board. Titled "Why This Is Important," Ed started out by stating: "Mankind has built a civilization through our principles. First and foremost, our individual worth is based upon a mutual recognition that each of us counts." He explained that no matter what beliefs we hold concerning our origins, purpose, or ultimate end, we have agreed to recognize our fellow man's individual identity, even when circumstance has seemingly stolen that identity.

Ed also wrote that the ultimate denial of respect—murder—is recognized as our civilization's worst crime, and those who commit it will be hunted down to the end of their days. In conclusion, he stated: "What is proposed in the Jane Doe case is nothing more than what we have all pledged to each other. We acknowledged that pledge in the rules of our civilization. If we fail to act on our agreement, we will have negated the value of civilization itself."

I began to think of Jane Doe as a friend and continued to visit her grave. And I noticed that someone—maybe even the controversial letter writer—continually left fresh flowers.

With her exhumation just weeks away, Lieutenant West and I discussed publicity. In order to keep the donations coming in, I gave interviews on several Denver-area radio shows, including *Colorado Matters*, an affiliate of National Public Radio. At the same time, a reporter from a local television network expressed interest in covering the event, but the lieutenant, hoping to garner more significant media attention, said he preferred to grant exclusive coverage to just one national show. When I suggested *America's Most Wanted*, he agreed immediately and invited the film crew to the exhumation. This long-running television program focuses on the apprehension of fugitives wanted for various crimes. When the producer of the show said yes, we were confident that—within a few months—our case would be on the air, and there would be more leads than we could handle.

In preparation for a big publicity hit, and with hopes that it might shed light on Jane Doe's identity, I reread the correspondence that I had found in the Boulder Police Department's records room. From the microfilmed correspondence, I made a spreadsheet of the twelve missing young women documented in the police files. Information on most of them was very skimpy, but the one who seemed most promising—because of a Colorado connection—was Josephine Proctor. I found typed notations that reported a visit by her uncle to the Boulder police station on April 26, 1955, more than a year after Jane Doe's body was found.

The police report was unsigned, but it stated that a man from Akron, Colorado, in the eastern part of the state, came into the Boulder police station "inquiring about the girl whose body was found in Boulder Cañon on April 8, 1954." The man thought the victim might have been his niece. Josephine had been missing for a little more than a year, and her grandmother, living in Denver, refused to talk about her disappearance.

Josephine's husband also lived in or near Denver. As stated in the police report, the uncle suspected "some kind of foul play due to the reticence on the part of the grandmother to tell him anything about the girl." The missing woman was described as five foot three inches in height, of slender build, with perfect teeth, and—like Jane Doe—as having had an appendectomy, but she was twenty-six years old and had borne two children. Nothing was mentioned about the color of her hair. What I found particularly interesting was that Josephine was not automatically ruled out, even though she had given birth and was older than the estimated age of the Boulder victim. Perhaps because the case had remained unsolved for a year, the officers took this new lead seriously.

There was also another letter in Josephine's case file, given to the police as evidence by her uncle. Written by the uncooperative grandmother to another family member, it stated that Josephine's husband had left her for another woman. "He went back drunk and was a-going to cut her [Josephine's] throat with a butcher knife," wrote the grandmother.

According to the letter, Josephine then left her two children in Iowa with her mother-in-law and moved—around the time Jane Doe was murdered—to Denver. When Josephine's uncle told his story to a detective at the Boulder Police Department, no one had seen or heard from the missing woman in a year. Josephine's husband, however, had custody of the couple's two children. "He was as mean as the dickens," Josephine's grandmother wrote. "If they [the children] ever mention their mother and he hears them, he takes off his belt and whips them." There was nothing more that I could find about this missing woman in the police files. She sounded vulnerable to me, and that very vulnerability made her more likely, in my opinion, to have become a murder victim.

I decided to take the information that I had and research it some more. At the Denver Public Library, I found the uncle's obituary, which listed his survivors. One was Firman McBeth, an elderly Iowa farmer. He also was Josephine's uncle, although he was approximately her same age. When the man's wife answered the telephone, I explained that I was tracing a missing person who was murdered and who might have been a member of her husband's family. He was out having coffee, but she told me, "Be sure and call back, honey."

When I did reach Firman a couple of hours later, he was eager to talk and described Josephine as "thin, blonde, with a reddish complexion, and a face like an Indian." He said she had stayed with him for a while, without her children. Then, in May 1962, the man's brother, Andrew McBeth, and his family were all murdered. "Josephine came a-running and thought she would get some money," said Firman, who added that she went away empty-handed. "I put her on the bus in Ottumwa [Iowa]," he said. "She didn't say where she was going."

I learned that all five members of the Andrew McBeth family were murdered on their farm near Martinsburg, Iowa. At the time that Firman and I talked on the telephone, the murderer, who was a nephew and is since deceased, had been serving five consecutive life sentences in the Iowa State Penitentiary for first-degree murder. I was immediately reminded of author Truman Capote's book *In Cold Blood*—the story of the 1959 murder of the Herbert Clutter family on a farm near Holcomb, Kansas. The setting, the era, and the circumstances were very much the same.

Then I was jolted back to the present and asked Firman if he was sure the murders had taken place in 1962. He said "yes," then turned the conversation back to Josephine. "I worried about her for so long," he said, sadly. "I never saw her again." Since she returned in 1962, I told him, she could not have been the murder victim from 1954. Trying to leave the conversation on a positive note, I said: "Maybe she'll come back again."

I had ruled out my first potential Jane Doe candidate, but at least I gave the elderly man the hope that Josephine was still alive. I also was concerned that my telephone call about missing and murdered family members might have been difficult for this elderly stranger on the other end of the line to comprehend. On the contrary, he seemed to enjoy talking with me. "I'm tickled to hear from you," he said.

My inquiries about Josephine Proctor were in mid-April 2004, exactly fifty years after Jane Doe's body lay in the morgue awaiting burial in Columbia Cemetery. All over Boulder, the fruit trees, again, had come into bloom. As April turned into May, spring made its way uphill, into the higher elevations of the mountains and into Boulder Canyon. The pines and firs were green year-round, but the scrubby bushes along the creek had just leafed out, and their pale new greenery again obliterated the brown harshness of winter. I treated myself, at the time, to my first semi-professional digital camera. When I thought about where I wanted to go to try it out, my car practically drove itself up Boulder Canyon. Specifically, I set out on a mission that, most likely, no one had undertaken for half a century. I wanted to see if I could find the exact location where Wayne Swanson and James Andes had found Jane Doe's body.

First, however, I knew I had to do my homework. I went to Boulder's Carnegie Branch Library for Local History to learn all I could about the construction of the road. From research I had done in the past, I was aware that its first segment—from Boulder to the Magnolia Road turnoff—was part of a road built in 1865 between Boulder and the "Gregory diggings," the name given to the gold-mining and milling area of Central City and Black Hawk. Then, in 1871, after prospectors discovered silver ore at Caribou, at ten thousand feet near Boulder County's western border on the Continental Divide, a toll road company extended the one-lane dirt wagon-road fifteen or so miles due west—up the steep, narrow, and previously untraveled canyon.

From 1914 to 1917, when horse-drawn vehicles mingled with Stanley Steamer Mountain Wagons and yet another mineral—tungsten—was mined in upper Boulder Canyon, the Colorado State Penitentiary set up a work camp in the mountainous terrain. The convicts worked in chain gangs to widen the dirt road from one lane to two.

In the decades to come, private contractors with steam shovels and trucks regraded and continued to improve the road. The new road workers eliminated sharp curves, established new rights-of-way, bypassed many of the old bridges, and built three new ones. By 1953, after yet another construction crew blasted rock cuts, bored a 340-foot tunnel, raised the roadbed, and paved most of it, the *Daily Camera* called the "Boulder Cañon" road a "highway" and "one of the finest in all the Rockies."

Newspaper photographs of the "new" road, in 1953, looked familiar to me. What was modern then—if the road still followed the same roadbed—was a typical, two-lane, safe, but winding, mountain road still in use today. The only way to know if major changes had been made in the years since Jane Doe's murder, in 1954, was to hike along the streambed, as the students had done, and look at the road and creek close-up.

In the newspaper photograph of the students at the crime scene, there were several large and distinctive rocks. If they had not been disturbed

In 1953, the tunnel and the rest of the highway improvements through Boulder Canyon were complete. Carnegie Branch Library for Local History, Boulder Historical Society collection.

throughout the years, maybe I could still find them. I also had found a second photograph, taken from the road and looking down to Boulder Creek. My only other source of information was from the inquest at which the coroner had stated that Jane Doe's body was found "300 yards east of Boulder Falls, 29 feet below the roadway along the creek." I took my new camera and photocopies of the old photographs and parked at the Boulder Falls turnout. Then I walked along the roadway and looked for a fir tree that showed up between the road and the creek in the second photograph. The only tree in the general vicinity was too small to have been there fifty years ago, and it also appeared to be too far away. Then, digging around in the underbrush, I found a stump where a tree had obviously rotted away. I was getting closer.

Not very good at estimating distances, I was not optimistic that I had walked the three hundred yards, but that must have been my lucky day. Near the rotten tree stump, I climbed down the steep twenty-nine-foot embankment to Boulder Creek. On the way down, I wound the camera strap around my neck, since I needed my hands free to grab on to the bushes in order to keep from sliding straight downhill and into the cold rushing water. When I got to the edge of the creek and was able to stand on a foot or two of level ground, I pulled the photocopies of the old photographs out of my pocket and studied them again. Sure enough, I was below the tree stump that could have been the fir tree in the newspaper photograph.

When I looked again at the photograph of the students at the scene, I noticed that to the right of Wayne Swanson was a large boulder, larger than him, and on the rock face was a dark-gray discoloration. I had made a quilt or two when my daughters were young, and I remembered piecing together a pattern called a "bear's paw." The dark shape on the rock reminded me of one of those quilt pieces, as it had a similar stylized jagged outline. Suddenly, I recognized the identical rock! There was no mistaking that large boulder with the dark "inclusion," as my geologist-husband later informed me. I felt completely exhilarated. The discovery was a bona fide breakthrough in the case, and it made me feel even more invested in the quest.

In front of the students was a rock about two or three feet long with a visible white quartz vein running along its top and side. That rock was there, too, and it had not moved in fifty years. What this meant was that the roadbed had no major changes since 1953. I had found the exact location where Jane Doe's body lay for a week or more.

Excitedly, I quickly pulled off the lens cap, screwed on the sunshade, and took both horizontal and vertical shots and zoomed in for close-ups.

A fir tree, now nothing more than a rotten stump, loomed over two Boulder police detectives when this photograph of the crime scene was taken, the day after Jane Doe's body was found. Photo courtesy of the Daily Camera.

The rock with a "bear-paw" inclusion that the author found in 2004 perfectly matched the rock shown in the photograph, taken in 1954, of the students pointing to the place where they found Jane Doe's body (see photo on page 16).

Then I backed up, at creek level, to take in the scene from a slight distance. That's when I saw the third distinctive rock, a medium-sized horizontal boulder with a depression on the top. In the old photograph, that notch-like shape was directly behind Wayne Swanson's head.

As soon as I got home, I downloaded the photographs onto my computer and printed them out. I called Lieutenant West and told him that I had found the crime scene. It may not have been where Jane Doe initially was beaten, but it was where she had been left to die after her murderer dumped, rolled, or knocked her down the embankment. I made arrangements to take the lieutenant and two other men from the sheriff's office to show them the site.

A few days later, the investigators and I rode up the canyon together. They were excited, too, and we discussed and looked forward to the exhumation. I knew it was two weeks away, but the lieutenant asked me not to reveal the date to anyone, as he wanted to avoid what he called a "media circus." It felt good to have put together a case file, convinced the sheriff to reopen the investigation, and received the support of donors, friends (including Micki), and family, as well as to be participating in a working relationship with relevant law-enforcement personnel and receiving the promise of forensic assistance—all topped off with the discovery of the crime scene.

The questions I had about Jane Doe were no longer mine alone to solve.

One day not long thereafter, as I drove from Boulder to my home in the mountains, I listened to an "oldies" station on my car radio. A popular 1950s trio called the Fleetwoods sang a ballad titled "Tragedy." I had never heard the song before, but the words reminded me so much of Jane Doe that I immediately bought the compact disc and played it over and over at home. The refrain that continued to haunt me was:

> Blown by the wind,
> Kissed by the snow;
> All that's left is the dark below.

2

TWISTS AND TURNS

7

I first met Dr. Walter Birkby, Dr. Richard Froede, and Dr. Robert Goldberg—from the Vidocq Society—at their hotel, the Hotel Boulderado. The five-story brick landmark was Boulder's first large downtown hotel, opening on New Year's Day 1909. Sid Anderson, the general manager, provided rooms for the visiting forensic experts, and the hotel's upscale dining room proved to be the perfect setting for the sheriff to host an elegant pre-exhumation-day dinner for the Vidocq guests, a few members of the sheriff's office, and myself.

Dr. Froede, a forensic pathologist, and Dr. Birkby, a forensic anthropologist, both came from Tucson and were described by Vidocq Society board chairman Frederick Bornhofen as "the cream of the crop." White-haired Dr. Froede was in his mid-seventies. He had served as a military pathologist in the United States Air Force for twenty-one years, retiring from the Air Force in 1976 with the rank of colonel. At that time, he also was chairman of the Department of Forensic Sciences in the Armed Forces Institute of Pathology.

Then, from 1976 to 1987, Dr. Froede was professor of pathology and chief of forensic sciences at the University of Arizona, in Tucson. He also served as chief medical examiner in Pima County, Arizona, and was medical examiner for eight other Arizona counties, as well. In 1987, he returned to the Armed Forces Institute of Pathology as a Distinguished Scientist in Forensic Sciences and was appointed the first Armed Forces medical examiner in 1988. A past president of the American Academy of Forensic Sciences, he also served in many other prestigious positions and continues to act as a consultant in forensic cases.

His colleague, Dr. Birkby, with graying hair and a crew cut, was two years younger. With a background in both physical and forensic anthropology, he specialized in human osteology (the branch of anatomy concerned with the study of the structure and functions of bones) and the recovery and identification of human remains. He had begun his professional career as a graduate teaching assistant at the University of Kansas in 1961. Then he moved to Tucson, where he earned his doctoral degree in anthropology at the University of Arizona and climbed the ladder to become adjunct research professor of anthropology. He also served as curator of physical anthropology at the Arizona State Museum.

Dr. Birkby's additional work as a consultant in forensic anthropology drew him into criminal and civil cases all over the country, with clients that included everyone from private law firms to city, county, and state governments; the Bureau of Alcohol, Tobacco, and Firearms; and the Federal Bureau of Investigation. As Vidocq Society members, both Drs. Froede and Birkby frequently traveled, at their own expense, from their homes in Arizona to meetings in Philadelphia to apply their collective forensic skills and experience to cold case homicides and unsolved deaths.

Conversations at the adjoining dinner tables ranged widely from graduations to weddings to travel plans, but we discussed only one topic—the murder of Jane Doe. Even though the subject that drew us together was somber, the evening was not. To the contrary, Lieutenant Phil West, Detective Steve Ainsworth, and I were practically bursting with excitement as we prepared for the big day.

Over a two-hour meal, Lieutenant West explained the plan for the next day. Groundsmen from Crist Mortuary's maintenance department would remove the coffin and place it in a hearse, then the Vidocq Society experts would accompany Jane Doe's skeletal remains to the neighboring Jefferson County morgue—better equipped than Boulder County's for the anticipated autopsy. The lieutenant reminded me that I could not be present at the morgue when the coffin was opened because—if the murderer were ever brought to trial—my presence at the autopsy could compromise the investigation. I knew that he would want to keep private any information that only the murderer would know, but I found the reasoning, in a situation with only skeletal remains, a little hard to understand. I agreed, however, as I certainly did not want to do anything that would jeopardize the case.

At eight o'clock in the morning on the following day, I went to the cemetery ready to witness the drama unfold. Although I had supplied the historical research, the exhumation was a team effort, and each of us would contribute in our own areas of expertise. I watched, mesmerized, as the mortuary's backhoe driver removed more than twelve inches of dirt, and four groundsmen hand-shoveled and probed two or three feet of earth—all in an attempt to locate the top of the coffin. I was so focused on the deepening hole that I was unable to move. And when, instead of a coffin, I saw wavy light-brown hair, a bone, and pieces of a black vinyl body bag emerge from the ground, I was shocked—there was no coffin at all! Since the coffin had disintegrated underground, its opening had become moot. No one told me to go away.

Of the three Vidocq Society men, Dr. Froede was in charge. Dr. Robert Goldberg (or "Dr. Bob," as he asked me to call him), also a forensic pathologist, was the large, bearded man at my side who kept up a running commentary. He had flown in from his home in Atlanta, Georgia. After receiving a law degree from North Carolina Central University, he graduated cum laude from the World University Dominicana Medical School in the Dominican Republic. His professional career included working as a consultant to the United States Department of Justice for twenty-two years, and he had frequently been interviewed by the media on various murder cases, including those of Washington, D.C., intern Chandra Levy and California resident Laci Peterson.

The lack of a coffin prompted an abrupt and dramatic change in plans. Beth Conour, a thirty-three-year-old local forensic anthropologist, had taken a couple of days of vacation time from her job as a Boulder County medical investigator to be part of the team. With a master's degree in biological anthropology, she had agreed ahead of time to help in any way but had no idea that morning of the important and unique role she soon would play. Luckily, Beth kept an archeological kit—complete with a trowel, toothbrushes, and paintbrushes—in her car. She retrieved the tools and handed them to Dr. Birkby, who climbed into the grave and began to brush off pieces of the victim's skull. Meanwhile, then-Detective Mike Wagner dashed off to a hardware store to buy additional brushes and trowels.

Before long, Beth and Dr. Birkby were both inside the grave, standing on soil that still covered the victim's lower body. A six-rung aluminum ladder was brought in so they could easily climb in and out of the deepening grave, but the ladder soon assumed a new use—laid horizontally as scaffolding. Whenever Dr. Birkby was not in the grave using the hand tools to meticulously uncover and remove the fragile remains, Beth lay flat—with her head pressed against one of the rungs of the ladder and her arms extended—to continue carefully uncovering, brushing off, and removing the remains. Mixed in with the bones and the wood fragments of the coffin were clumps of down feathers from a pillow that had once been placed by a caring person under the victim's head. Beth called the removal of the contents of the grave "grueling and satisfying," comparing it to an archeological dig which continued, on the first day, for six straight hours.

As portions of the young woman's skeletal remains became exposed, her teeth seemed to grin at us from the grave. I reached down and touched her hair, surprised to find myself needing that physical connection. I stayed by her side while Dr. Birkby and Beth passed bone after bone to a technician who bagged the remains and then marked the bags. Late in the afternoon, an eerie mist rolled in and blanketed the "city of the dead." Crist Mortuary general manager Michael Greenwood and his employees set up a green canvas tent over the open grave. Sheriff cadets shored up the grave's earthen sides with plywood in preparation for an expected storm that, eventually, produced a considerable amount of rain.

At home that evening, I turned on my computer and found multiple emails that echoed the past. The correspondence was from a woman named Debbie, whose mother was—for a short time—thought to have been Jane Doe. As it turned out, the first and only arrest in the Jane Doe case had nothing to do with Jane Doe or Debbie's mother. The arrest was for a man who had, in fact, murdered Debbie's father. Debbie's life and Jane Doe's death had been and still were intertwined. The timing of her emails was surreal.

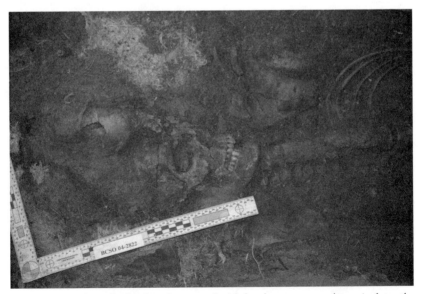

Jane Doe's teeth, embedded in the ground with her bones, seemed to grin from the grave.

During the exhumation, Boulder County Sheriff Joe Pelle, left, talked with forensic anthropologists Dr. Walter Birkby and Beth Conour—both inside the grave. In the background, also looking down, are Dr. Richard Froede and Captain Dennis Hopper.

Members of the Boulder County Sheriff's Office, city parks employees, and the general manager of Crist Mortuary joined Vidocq Society members as they watched Beth Conour (inside the grave) remove Jane Doe's remains. Lieutenant Phil West is on the far left. Detective Steve Ainsworth, in the print shirt, is seated in the foreground.

Months earlier, when I had reconstructed Jane Doe's case file, I had read the old newspaper articles on James W. Hutchins, the man who had been pulled over for speeding in Oklahoma. After a high-speed chase, an Oklahoma highway patrolman had stopped Hutchins in the Cookson Hills area of Sequoyah County, once the hangout of bank-robber "Pretty Boy Floyd." Before the officer had even finished writing the man a speeding ticket, he saw that much of the backseat of the car was soaked with blood. Portions of the upholstery had been removed, and splotches of dried blood clung to the interior of the car, which bore Colorado license plates. Only two days earlier, the students had found Jane Doe's body.

Fresh in the officer's mind was an all-points bulletin from Sheriff Art Everson of Boulder County, Colorado, to law-enforcement agencies in the bordering states of Nebraska, Kansas, Oklahoma, New Mexico, Arizona, Utah, and Wyoming. The report of the murder of an unidentified young woman and an accompanying plea to watch for any suspicious activity had been entered into a teletype machine in the Boulder office, then printed out in police stations in various parts of the country. The Oklahoma patrolman who questioned Hutchins had just been briefed about the "blonde in Boulder Cañon" at the beginning of his shift.

Hutchins claimed not to know anything about the "dead girl," but the patrolman arrested him anyway and locked him in the Sallisaw, Oklahoma, jail. Oklahoma officials took blood and hair samples from the car and immediately sent them to the Federal Bureau of Investigation laboratory in Washington, D.C. Meanwhile, the Oklahoma officials contacted Boulder authorities, who sent samples of Jane Doe's hair to the FBI as well. On the day after Jane Doe's murder hit the newspapers, the *Rocky Mountain News* headline read, "GI Suspect Nabbed in Girl's Murder."

The reporters had not waited, however, to get the whole story. Hutchins continued to deny having killed Jane Doe, but he eventually confessed to another murder—that of thirty-two-year-old Bruce Weibel. Weibel's daughter Debbie—the writer of the emails that were flooding my computer—had read of our victim's upcoming exhumation and reached out to me on that very same night.

"I'm trying to think of what you are doing today and what feelings you must be going through," Debbie wrote. "I think Jane is very pleased to know how much everyone there still cares and loves her. What a very special group of people I have come in contact with because of sweet Jane."

Debbie had been working on her family history and had searched for her father's name on the internet. On June 2, 2004, six days before Jane Doe's exhumation, she had found his name in one of the articles from

1954 that the webmaster had posted on the Jane Doe website. In response to the article that explained the details of her father's murder, she wrote on the website's message board: "I am Bruce Weibel's daughter. The little red ribbon, in the backseat of the car, was mine."

I asked her to email me directly, rather than through the website. She wrote and wrote, sometimes several times per day. I also reread the newspaper articles from the Denver and Boulder newspapers and pieced together the connection between James W. Hutchins—who had murdered Bruce Weibel—and Jane Doe.

In going over the original accounts, I learned that Weibel had driven from his home in Texas to visit his sister in California. On his way back to Texas, he had called his sister from Flagstaff, Arizona, where he asked her to wire him fifteen dollars that he planned to pick up in Albuquerque, New Mexico. He never made it. Somewhere, in a lonely stretch of desert on United States Highway 66, between the two southwestern cities, Weibel saw a man hitchhiking and stopped to give him a ride. The man was Hutchins, who then murdered Weibel and stuffed his body under a bridge thirteen miles east of Gallup, New Mexico. In Weibel's 1950 Ford sedan, Hutchins continued due east on his way home to North Carolina—through the rest of New Mexico, the Texas panhandle, into Oklahoma, and then into the arms of the law.

Even after the Oklahoma police determined that Hutchins had killed Weibel, their discovery of the red ribbon with blonde hair made them concerned that a blonde-haired woman—perhaps Jane Doe, perhaps Weibel's wife (Debbie's mother), Geraldine—had been murdered as well. Hutchins's arrest had been made prior to the official FBI laboratory results indicating that the victim found in Boulder Cañon actually had "light brown" hair. Fired up by the media reports, the police were still looking for evidence in the murder of a blonde. Debbie (who actually was the blonde in the family) wrote that she was twenty months old at the time, and that her redheaded mother later told her that they had not accompanied Weibel because she, Debbie, was sick.

As I continued to read the old articles, I learned that although Debbie's family had lived in Dallas, Texas, at the time of her father's murder, they had formerly lived in Derby, Colorado, northeast of Denver in Adams County. That was why Weibel's 1950 Ford still had Colorado license plates. The first of several headlines on the story read: "Fear for man, wife, baby." Again there was speculation as to whether Jane Doe had given birth. In one of several newspaper accounts, a reporter indicated that a Denver physician confirmed that Geraldine Weibel had given birth, to Debbie, in

1952. The writer also noted that the pathologist who had performed Jane Doe's autopsy had stated that it was unlikely that the murder victim had borne any children. A dentist who was interviewed indicated that, unlike Jane Doe, Geraldine Weibel had fillings in her teeth. In Boulder, Sheriff Everson quickly ruled out Weibel's wife as the Boulder murder victim and located her, and the toddler Debbie, safe in Dallas.

After rereading the newspapers of fifty years ago, I reoriented myself to the present. The initial part of Jane Doe's exhumation had taken nearly all day, and Drs. Froede, Birkby, and Goldberg were unanimous in their opinion that the next day would be as long or longer. I knew I needed to sleep, but that night I was awakened by heavy rain, huge claps of thunder, and bright flashes of lightning. I thought of the victim's remains, some removed and some still in her plywood-covered grave. Although I was not superstitious, I almost wondered if her spirit was angry with us for disturbing her half-century of peace.

The next day I again stood at Jane Doe's side. As the depth of her grave increased, someone brought in a bright light, powered by a generator in the sheriff's command vehicle, parked nearby. This motor home–like vehicle also contained a small table where coffee, donuts, and sandwiches mysteriously appeared and were well-appreciated. I stayed until late in the day, when Beth Conour and Dr. Walter Birkby jubilantly removed the victim's last bones—tiny phalanges from her toes. I watched, too, as the mortuary's groundsmen came back and refilled the grave with dirt. Then they replaced a metal stake with a sign that explained that Jane Doe's gravestone had been removed, for safekeeping, by the Boulder Parks and Recreation Department. Before Crist Mortuary General Manager Greenwood left the cemetery, he stated his commitment to re-inter the remains at the appropriate time in the future. His generous offer included reburial either in Jane Doe's former grave or wherever we, in our investigation, determined that she belonged.

Before the Vidocq Society consultants flew back to their respective homes, Dr. Birkby, Dr. Froede, "Dr. Bob," and I talked about the exhumation. We met over breakfast, again at the Hotel Boulderado, and the men told me that the sheriff's office had treated them with "professionalism, kindness, and care." I could not have been happier, but I was emotionally drained as well.

The previous few days had also been emotionally draining on Debbie. She had learned, through her recent research on her father's family, that she had a stepbrother. She also learned, for the first time, of a mutual relative who knew how to reach him. She called and gave her contact information to that relative, assuming that her long-lost sibling would pick up the telephone and call her at any minute. Instead, Debbie set herself up for disappointment when the telephone did not ring. She told me about it in one email. In another, she contrasted her life with Jane's, asking if it was meant to be for the city and people of Boulder to find Jane's identity in the hopes of finding the victim's family.

"Maybe whatever is left of her family would rather not know about Jane," wrote Debbie. She then added: "I'm finding out even for a real live person that mysteriously appears out of nowhere, I don't think it makes any difference. My relatives might very well wish that I had not found them, and that breaks my heart. Once again, I open my heart up and out to you, as I feel like Jane's own-personal-very-big family in Boulder cares more about her, than my family cares about me."

In the days to come, I began to search for the transcripts of Hutchins's murder trial. After the accused killer had stuffed Weibel's body under the bridge, an American Indian woman on horseback found the victim, with his stocking feet resting on the third strand of a barbed wire fence. I contacted the McKinley County District Court in New Mexico and learned that the transcript was, indeed, on file. I purchased a postal money order to cover the thirty-five-cents-per-page photocopying costs and waited for the 103-page packet to arrive in the mail.

When Hutchins was caught in Oklahoma, he had been driving Weibel's Ford and had the car-owner's identification. Hutchins told police that he had met Weibel in Oklahoma City, and that the man had asked him to drive the car to Fort Smith, Arkansas. The more likely scenario was that Weibel, weary and driving alone, picked up Hutchins in New Mexico. Wiebel probably let Hutchins take the wheel while he climbed into the backseat to get some sleep. The Oklahoma police became suspicious of Hutchins's alibi when they were unable to find Weibel to confirm the story.

"He didn't like our questions, and we didn't like his answers," a police spokesman told the press. "He's hiding something, and we aim to find out what." The information the Oklahoma police learned was that Hutchins, an airman, had been absent without leave from Nellis Air Force Base in Las Vegas, Nevada, and he was in a hurry to get to his home in Forest City, North Carolina. An autopsy of Weibel showed that he had been shot three times, just above the eyes, with a .22-caliber pistol that police found, with three missing bullets, in the car.

I read all through the transcripts of the January 1955 trial of James W. Hutchins. While awaiting trial, he had been given, and had passed, a psychiatric examination. At his arraignment in December 1954, he had been charged with "murder in the first degree" of Bruce Weibel. First-degree murder was defined as "the unlawful killing of a human being, with malice aforethought, either express or implied." Hutchins had pled "not guilty," claiming self-defense.

"It was either him or me," he said of the crime of which there were no witnesses. The transcripts showed a flurry of paperwork as to whether, or where, Hutchins had made his initial confession. Entered into evidence was the murder weapon—the .22-caliber revolver belonging to Hutchins. Police had also confiscated another pistol, a .38-caliber, two cowhide-leather "Ruff'n'Ready" holsters, a leather billfold with identification, photographs, and receipts, and various items of clothing. Hutchins's attorneys asked the court to produce an FBI report on "the criminal record of Bruce Roy Weibel," which the district attorney refused to do.

For four days, the jurors heard testimony, from the Oklahoma trooper who stopped Hutchins for speeding to the woman who discovered Weibel's body. The jury deliberated for just a few hours and then rejected both first- and second-degree murder charges. They settled, instead, on "voluntary manslaughter," defined in New Mexico's statute as "the unlawful killing of a human being without malice, i.e. upon a sudden quarrel or in the heat of passion." Further definition of the "heat of passion" required that "there must have existed in the mind of the slayer such emotions as either anger, rage, sudden resentment or terror as may be sufficient to obscure the reason of an ordinary man, and to prevent deliberation and premeditation, and of such character as to render him incapable of cool reflection upon the character and result of his acts, and to exclude malice."

On February 7, 1955, the district court judge sentenced Hutchins to the New Mexico Penitentiary at Santa Fe for a period of not less than five years and not more than ten years. In the microfilmed files that I had uncovered at the Boulder Police Department several months earlier, I found a copy of a telegram from the district court in New Mexico addressed to the Boulder officials at the time.

"Was case of murdered girl spring '54 solved?" questioned the New Mexico district attorney. What had come up in the trial that made them want to know about Jane Doe? I, too, had many questions, but I had no one to turn to for answers. I thought I could contact the former New Mexico district attorney, but a search of online Social Security death records indicated that he had died in 1998.

In one of Debbie's emails, she had explained the circumstances surrounding her mother's identification of her father's body. As Debbie related, Sheriff Bill Decker of Dallas County had knocked on her mother's door and told her that police officials believed they had found her husband's body. Debbie's mother was asked to identify him, necessitating travel from Dallas, Texas, to Gallup, New Mexico.

"My mother told him she had no car, no money," wrote Debbie. "I think Sheriff Decker must have been one of the nicest men in the world. He looked at my mother (she was so very pretty at that age) and said 'okay.' He got on the radio, told his officers the situation and to set up highway patrolmen at the state line. They transferred her, one to the other, until they got to [Gallup] New Mexico."

Debbie then added that, along the way, the officer went into a drugstore and left Weibel's widow outside waiting for him. She pulled a newspaper off of a newspaper rack and was stunned to see a photograph of her late husband's corpse, wrapped in barbed wire, on the front page. She broke down right then and told the officer she did not need to go look at his body, she knew it from the newspaper. "But," added Debbie, "they took her anyway."

Debbie had no idea what had become of her father's murderer. I was unaware, too, until a few years later when a reader of the Jane Doe website submitted some startling information on the website's message board. After Hutchins was released from the New Mexico prison for the murder of Bruce Weibel, he returned to his home in North Carolina, where he killed again—and this time he murdered three sheriff's deputies. After Hutchins's case went all the way to the United States Supreme Court on a last-minute plea of insanity, the former airman was executed by lethal injection in North Carolina in 1984—the first person to die in North Carolina's death chamber in twenty-two years. The story is told in the film *Rutherford County Line*.

A few weeks after Jane Doe's exhumation, I got a telephone call from Dr. Bob of the Vidocq Society. All three men had agreed to stay on the case as consultants. I was a bit in awe of these learned experts and almost felt, when I answered the call, as if Sherlock Holmes himself was on the other end of the line. Dr. Bob had witnessed numerous exhumations. Jane Doe's had been my only one, but just by being there with him and with the others, I believed that we shared a bond. "It's clear to me that Jane has somehow touched your soul," he said. "Listen to your heart and do your best."

Dr. Bob was outgoing and talkative and called often. Every time I picked up the telephone and heard his deep voice, I felt as if I had my own personal advisor and mentor. He told me that we were doing God's work—speaking for those who could not speak for themselves. He also kept me laughing, telling me that—in his opinion—the members of the Vidocq Society were as diverse as the part-human space creatures assembled at the bar in the 1977 epic fantasy film *Star Wars*. Sometimes, for me, his long telephone conversations came too late in the evening, but he also seemed equally content to talk with my husband. If Ed happened to answer the telephone, they would discuss topics as diverse as firearms training and their favorite songs of the doo-wop era.

One of the first times Dr. Bob called, he gave me an assignment. At Jane Doe's exhumation, he had pointed out a kneecap fracture, consistent with being hit by a car. The fractured patella had not been mentioned in the original autopsy report by Dr. Freburn James, but it was assumed that the pathologist had simply missed it when he examined her body.

"Go find cars that would have been on the road in 1954 and measure the height of their bumpers," Dr. Bob said to me. "Jane Doe probably was a couple of inches shorter than you, but see if you can determine if the bumpers would have been at her knee level." My job, at first, seemed an impossible task, but I knew someone who knew someone else who was a serious collector of antique automobiles. Luckily for me, the collector owned 222 shiny restored cars and trucks, and he had ten that fit the time frame. With a tape measure in hand, I wandered the large warehouse and measured the bumpers of vehicles from a 1935 Ford pickup to a 1954 Pontiac sedan.

The following day, I emailed my results to Dr. Bob and explained that the only horizontal bumper that definitely was at my knee level—about nineteen inches—was a 1949 Mercury. The 1950 Ford, like the one Hutchins was driving, was too low. But some, like the 1952 Hudson Hornet, had so much chrome, both horizontally and vertically, that they could have hit me in the knee, as well. The horizontal bumpers of the later models seemed too low, but I concluded that if Jane Doe were struck by one of the nine- to eleven-inch vertical bumpers, it also could have hit her—or me—on the knee.

Two months later, in August 2004, I was still thinking about Jane Doe when an unexpected lead suddenly hit me as I strolled the aisles of the Rocky Mountain Antiquarian Book Fair in Denver. A rare book and ephemera dealer who had read of my involvement in the case approached me to discuss a magazine called *Dood*. He said the self-described "off-campus humor magazine" had only been published once, in 1956, and its centerfold contained a postmortem photograph of Jane Doe's face!

The book dealer told me, too, that a smaller copy of the photograph was part of a collage on the front cover. The rest of the publication, he said, featured photographs of nude and semi-nude women. Between the images were 1950s-era risqué jokes and rhymes such as: "I was young, she was willen, now I'm using penicillin."

"The magazine is in such bad taste that I hesitated to even mention it," the man told me, adding that he assumed the sheriff's office already had the photograph but, if not, he would be glad to lend it to us. The publication itself was not for sale. He had bought it at a used bookstore in 1994 after that store's owner acquired it as part of a larger collection at a garage sale. Explaining that we had no photograph of Jane Doe at all, I practically begged him to let me see it, but he did not have the magazine with him at the book fair. Our conversation was on a Saturday, so I arranged to borrow *Dood* on Monday, in Boulder. For me, it was a long weekend.

As we had agreed, the book dealer left the publication in the patron box of the Carnegie Branch Library for Local History. My hands trembled as I took the thirty-six-page booklet out of its envelope—I thought I was about to see the facial features of the woman I had been trying to identify for so many years. Needless to say, I was not mentally prepared for the black-and-white image that confronted me. As I had read, and as Alan Cass had told me, most of the flesh on Jane Doe's face had been eaten away. However, her teeth were still in place, and I could see the long wavy hair I had recently touched at her grave.

Underneath the photograph was the caption: "This is an actual photo of the corpse found in Boulder Canyon by University students Wayne Swanson and Jim Andes." After a short news article was the question: "Who Dood it?"

Did the magazine's publishers know something that we did not?

A few days later, I took the magazine to the sheriff's office. Lieutenant West was on vacation, so I put it in the hands of Detective Ainsworth, who was ecstatic. He traced down Bob Latham, *Dood*'s elderly former editor, who lived in Florida. After the detective had a chance to speak with him on the telephone, he gave me permission to give him a call. The former editor told me that a student who had worked in the morgue had taken Jane Doe's photograph, immediately causing me to wonder if the unnamed student was the same man, a law student at the time, who had worked in the mortuary and was also a member of the jury at the coroner's inquest. I attempted to contact the former law student but found that he—like so many others in this search—was deceased.

Bob also told me that following *Dood*'s publication, Sheriff Art Everson had met with him, demanding to know the photographer's name, but the former editor told me that he "played the hard-core journalist" and refused to reveal his source. A half century later, Bob said he had forgotten the photographer's name. I asked him why he published the photograph, and he told me that he thought it would be a "shocker." He then told me that he had obtained one of the nude photographs in the magazine from a contemporary of his, Hugh Hefner, whom he had recently visited in Chicago. His friend had edited *Shaft*, a humor magazine at the University of Illinois, and was just starting out with *Playboy Magazine*, composing the layout of text and photographs on his kitchen table in a cramped apartment. The two men, said the former editor, had a lot in common.

Dood magazine also included photographs of the scantily clad and redheaded stripper "Tempest Storm." At the time of the magazine's publication, she performed at a nightclub in Denver called the Tropics, where her stage act was accompanied by simulated thunder and rain. Bob bragged about the day he escorted Tempest Storm to the University of Colorado campus, in Boulder. A reporter and photographer from the *Daily Camera* covered the event. The stripper parked her red Cadillac convertible near the Old Main building, then she and the former editor started walking toward the student union building. "Men came out like ants," he said. "It was like being in a river." The extremely well-endowed showgirl never even took off her mink coat, but she was mobbed and nearly started a riot among hundreds of sex-starved college men.

Also baring almost all was another stripper—"Gilda"—a former child film star. As Shirley Jean Rickert, Gilda had been the little blonde girl in the *Our Gang* comedy series of the early 1930s. On the day of *Dood*'s release, Bob drove the shapely blonde from Denver to Boulder to autograph copies. Even the copy I held in my hands contained a hand-written note: "Love'n'stuff, Gilda." The former editor and two of his college friends had printed two thousand magazines and sold them all on the same day for twenty-five cents apiece. University of Colorado officials would not allow the financial transactions on campus, so the editor and the stripper, in a wool coat, set up shop across the street in front of the Sink, a 3.2 percent beer establishment. Gilda, perched on the back of an open convertible, was only at her post for twenty minutes, however, when Boulder police came to break up the crowd which they claimed was blocking traffic on Thirteenth Street. Students let some of the air out of the tires on the police car, but the officers still managed to get Gilda to drive away.

Stripper "Tempest Storm" was featured in Dood, *an "off-campus humor magazine," which published a centerfold photograph of the face of Jane Doe's corpse. Photo courtesy of the* Daily Camera.

Gilda, the Our Gang *comedy-star-turned-stripper, also posed for* Dood *and autographed copies for college men eager to buy the publication. Photo courtesy of the* Daily Camera.

The former editor's comments to me were salacious, but they did not help in identifying Jane Doe. She was not even mentioned in a newspaper account, a few weeks later, that told of a resolution drafted by the Boulder Council of Churches to crack down on the distribution of "lewd, suggestive, and immoral publications." According to the *Daily Camera*, the action, headed for the Boulder City Council, had been prompted by *Dood*, stating that its publication, sale, and distribution were offensive to Christian ideals.

By the time of my conversation with *Dood*'s former editor, word about the only known photograph of Jane Doe had reached Dr. Walter Birkby and Dr. Richard Froede, the forensic anthropologist and the forensic pathologist I had met at the exhumation. When Dr. Bob called me again he said, "Birkby is climbing the walls dancing, and Froede says this case is taking on three lives of its own."

The magazine did not get me any closer to solving the case, but it did provide a window into a sleazy underworld in the prefeminist era. That Jane Doe's face had appeared in such a magazine struck me as immensely degrading. I was even more committed to finding justice for Jane Doe. Now that the exhumation was behind us, I put my hopes in her bones.

8

Jane Doe's remains took weeks to dry out. Lieutenant Phil West told me that because they were now part of an official homicide investigation, I would not be allowed to see them, even though I had been present when they were recovered. I had to rely, instead, on information from the forensic specialists, who told me that the bones were extremely fragile. Indeed, the experts were worried that they might crumble and turn to ash before Jane Doe's DNA could be extracted. What if we had come this far for nothing?

In September 2004, the Boulder County Sheriff's Office express-mailed Jane Doe's bones—along with her teeth and hair—to Dr. Walter Birkby in Tucson, Arizona. The forensic anthropologist who had personally removed many of her remains from her grave then laid them out and inventoried them in a workroom in the back of his home. He rearticulated some of her long bones but concentrated mostly on her skull, which had broken underground into more than one hundred pieces. Putting her skull back together, he modestly told me, was like doing a jigsaw puzzle. Actually, it was quite a bit more complicated.

First, Dr. Birkby had to clean the dirt off the bones and stabilize the individual pieces with polyvinyl acetate resin. The water-resistant film kept the bones from fragmenting even more. For up to an hour, he let them dry. Only then was he comfortable handling them, beginning to get a feel for how the pieces would fit together. Complicating the process was the fact that a half century of pressure from wet soil had caused the bones to warp.

Starting with the largest fragment, Dr. Birkby searched until he found an adjoining piece, then he bonded the pieces together with Duco Cement. When that was good and dry, he glued on another piece. If he found that he had glued on the wrong piece, he could dissolve the cement with acetone and start over. Dr. Birkby volunteered all of his time and spent six weeks reassembling Jane Doe's skull. Between prehistoric remains and police cases like Jane Doe's, the former University of Arizona anthropology professor had reassembled thousands of skulls during his career. Of Jane Doe's, he called it "satisfying but time-consuming."

Dr. Birkby, along with Dr. Richard Froede, also compared the fractures that he saw in his laboratory to those in the original autopsy report obtained from the private files of Dr. Freburn L. James, the original pathologist on the case in 1954. The men noted the injuries that Dr. James had recorded, most noticeably the fracture on the lower right side of her skull. She also had numerous broken bones on the left side of her body. These fractures were identified as follows: left humerus (upper arm), left maxilla (part of her upper jawbone), left mandible (part of her lower jawbone), and left clavicle (collarbone), as well as her left first, second, third, and fourth ribs. Of the clavicle and ribs, Dr. James wrote, "These fractures form a nearly vertical line which suggests that all were incurred at the same instant."

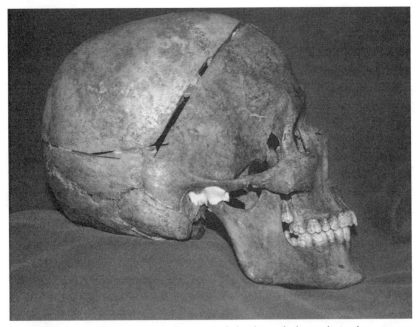

The straight cuts on Jane Doe's skull were made by the pathologist during her autopsy, and the jagged lines show the skull fracture that extended through her frontal, temporal, and parietal bones. Photo by Detective Steve Ainsworth, courtesy of the Boulder County Sheriff's Office.

In their examination of the skeletal remains, Drs. Birkby and Froede also examined her pubic bones in an attempt to confirm what Dr. James had written in his autopsy report—"there are no signs that would prove a past pregnancy." During childbirth, the ligaments that connect the two halves of the pelvis at the pubic symphysis—where the bones are joined at the front—are stretched, often leaving pits and striations. If the pubic bones show these marks, they indicate that the decedent gave birth, but their absence leaves open the question. Jane Doe's pubic bones were smooth, confirming Dr. James's initial determination that she probably had not been a mother.

Doctors Birkby and Froede also confirmed the previously unreported right kneecap fracture that had led to the speculation that Jane Doe might have been hit by the bumper of a car. In that scenario, her right leg would have been on the ground, and the impact of the car would have caused her knee to pivot. The left-side injuries then may have been caused as she was thrown against the side or hood of the car, and the skull fracture could have come as she fell back down on the ground.

Meanwhile, Lieutenant West invited me to a "dummy toss," held during the third week of September 2004, when Dr. Bob again visited Boulder. The lieutenant explained that the purpose of the exercise was to use a mannequin to simulate the initial scenario—the possible dumping or throwing of Jane Doe's body. He wanted to know if it was likely that one man had disposed of her body, or had it required two?

On the appointed day, a cool one for early fall, Dr. Bob met me at the Justice Center, where we were joined by Lieutenant West, Patrol Deputy John Appelmann, and Detectives Steve Ainsworth, John Zamora, and Steve Kellison. Patrol Deputy Appelmann was in uniform, but the rest of the law-enforcement officers were casually dressed in blue jeans. We climbed into two cars—an unmarked green SUV and a sheriff's white four-wheel-drive vehicle—then drove to the crime scene in Boulder Canyon, where we parked on the side of the road. Two of the men unloaded the plastic mannequin, or dummy, which looked like a large doll. Since it weighed more than the slender murder victim, one of the men took off one arm below the elbow, as well as one leg below the knee, in order to get its weight down to approximately 110 pounds.

As I had done a few months earlier, I pointed out the distinctive rocks and the exact location where the students had found Jane Doe's body. One of the men climbed down the forty-five-degree embankment to creek level. Detective Ainsworth followed and set up a video camera. Another detective, standing where we believed the killer may have stood half a century earlier, threw the mannequin down the steep slope. Then, Lieutenant West threw a rope down the embankment, and the man at the creek's edge tied it around the mannequin's waist. When it was secure, the men at the top pulled the "body" uphill so it could be thrown down again. No matter how it was thrown, by one man or two, it landed in the exact spot to which the students had pointed in the newspaper photograph from April 9, 1954.

The uniformed deputy, meanwhile, used a light detection and ranging device (commonly called LIDAR) to measure the distance from the edge of the road—where the "body" was thrown—to the edge of the creek where it had landed. Using pulsed laser light to determine distance, the LIDAR "gun" looked very similar to the more familiar radar gun feared for decades by speeding motorists. While Lieutenant West and the others were tugging on the rope, the uniformed officer—perhaps wanting something else to do—turned his LIDAR on motorists driving by. "You can always tell if they're speeding if the passenger suddenly jolts forward," Detective Ainsworth commented to me. "The driver knows he's speeding when he sees the radar gun and slams on his brakes, but the passenger often is unaware."

We got some very strange looks from the passersby, whether speeding or not, and the drivers of the speeding cars must have felt relieved when they were not pulled over. Instead, what the drivers and their passengers saw was a small group of men cheerfully pulling from the creek what appeared to be a deformed and naked body, as well as a middle-aged woman running around with a camera. The situation was so absurd that I could not help but laugh. How insensitive we all appeared to have been!

The conclusion to the dummy toss strongly suggested that it would have been physically possible for one man to have thrown Jane Doe's body down the embankment. Even so, it initially was speculated that two men could have been involved since the original autopsy did not reveal a lot of "road rash," indicating that two men might have thrown the victim higher into the air, clearing the brush and rocks on the bank.

While we were standing at the crime scene, Lieutenant West and I also discussed the possibility that if the perpetrator or perpetrators had looked for a place to dispose of the victim's body, he or they must not have been very familiar with the surrounding mountainous area. At the time, it was full of open mine shafts, left over from previous gold, silver, and tungsten mining operations. Most local newspaper readers of the era were aware that, in 1950, just four years before Jane Doe's murder, a man had killed his wife and thrown her body down the seventy-feet-deep

In the "dummy-toss," no matter how the mannequin was thrown, it always landed on the rocks at the edge of Boulder Creek in the same place pointed out by the students who had found Jane Doe's body.

Dew Drop mine south of the town of Ward. After the victim's husband confessed two months later, sheriff's officials had managed to recover the woman's body from the abandoned gold mine's murky depths. There are plenty of rumors of other mine shafts still holding bodies, but their numbers will never be known.

Still speculating along the side of the road, we also discussed the "bumper theory"—that perhaps Jane Doe may have been hit by her killer's car after escaping from a sexual assault. In that case, the car would have been the murder weapon, and it could have propelled her down the embankment, but that was one simulation that the Sheriff officials did not try to replicate. Lieutenant West and one of the deputies then dragged the battered mannequin along the highway's narrow shoulder and lifted it back into the green vehicle. The traffic in the canyon was busy that day, and the people driving by continued to have very puzzled looks on their faces.

After the dummy toss, Dr. Bob, Lieutenant West, Detective Ainsworth, and I had lunch at a Mexican restaurant on the east side of Boulder. We talked about Jane Doe, of course, and I asked Detective Ainsworth if he was going to compare her DNA, when it was profiled, with the already profiled DNA of the now elderly brother of Marion Joan McDowell. Although the detective had talked about the case of the missing Toronto-area teenager nearly a year earlier, this was the first time that Dr. Bob had heard about her. We filled him in on what we had learned, from the Doe Network, about the young woman's December 1953 disappearance. "An abduction with no trace of her ever being found," Dr. Bob said, with a look of amazement on his face. "It could well be her."

With a renewed interest in Marion, and a lot of email support from my fellow researcher, Micki, I decided to read all the firsthand accounts I could find on the seventeen-year-old's abrupt disappearance. Not many newspapers offered digitized full-page images of issues from the 1950s, so I felt lucky when I found some of what I was looking for on the website of the *Toronto Star*. I started with a December 7, 1953, article that described the previous night's assault on the teenager from Scarborough Township, Ontario. As the petite, blue-eyed blonde sat with her boyfriend in the front seat of his parked car in a lovers' lane in a Toronto suburb, the door on the boyfriend's side of the car was wrenched open, and a male voice ordered him out. The boyfriend was hit on the head with what later was believed to have been the butt of a gun, then shoved into the backseat of his own car.

The boyfriend's next memory was of Marion lying unconscious on top of him and of being driven to an abandoned farm. There, the driver—whom the boyfriend described as slim, short, and hooded—got out and lifted Marion's limp body from the car. The boyfriend believed that the attacker then stuffed her into the trunk of another car. He had no idea if she was dead or alive. She was never heard from again, and her body has never been found.

The online newspaper articles certainly held my interest, but they cost money. After I downloaded all I could for a lump payment on my credit card, I decided to order free microfilmed copies through inter-library loan at the Boulder Public Library. All the librarian said was available was Toronto's other major newspaper, the *Toronto Telegram*. Two weeks later, my local library notified me that the microfilms had arrived. I checked them out and took them to the *Daily Camera* library, where I had full access to the newspaper's microfilm reader and printer. Alone, on a Saturday afternoon when no one would interrupt me in my familiar surroundings, I reread the details of Marion's assault and abduction, then continued with the day-by-day story as it had unfolded to the reading public.

I soon learned that after the attack, Marion's dazed and injured boyfriend had managed to drive his car to his family's home. His parents then took him to the Scarborough police station, where he was questioned and released. At some point he was given a lie detector test that he "passed with flying colors." In the days to follow, the police dragged ponds and flew over surrounding forests and farmlands. Investigators interrogated men recently released from jails and mental hospitals. The police also requested attendants to check the trunks of all cars that stopped at service stations for gasoline.

Marion's mother was reported as "near unconscious with grief." In large-type newspaper headlines, she begged readers: "I don't want anybody punished. Bring her back. Let us know where she is, please. . . ." Marion's aunt pleaded with the young woman's girlfriends to talk with her in confidence, in the hopes that someone would be able to provide information on the attacker. Marion's grandmother stated that Marion never would have run away. Ross McDowell, the abductee's father, a low-paid factory-worker, put up a hefty reward for information, but he quickly gave up hope of finding her alive. Instead, he aggressively led a group of relatives and searchers to look for her body.

Of major concern to family members was their desire for Marion, if she was dead, to have a Christian burial. I thought back to the Boulder community that had raised funds for Jane Doe's burial in Columbia Cemetery and to the coroner who said, "We don't know who she was or what religion she followed. We can only do what we think is right." If Marion was Jane, I reasoned, at least she did get the Christian burial that her mother and father had wished for their daughter.

School officials directed all children in the rural areas near Toronto to have their families check farm buildings, ditches, and forests. Missing-persons reports on Marion were sent all across Canada. What seemed odd to me, though, was that there was no mention of these reports going to the United States, even though the Toronto area was close to the border between the United States and Canada. The four-month gap between Marion's December disappearance in Toronto and the finding of Jane Doe's body in April made it unlikely that Marion was Jane, but it still could have been possible.

Each day's Toronto newspaper gave more information on Marion's family. The stories continued to follow the family members in their grief as they became emotionally devastated by crank calls and letters. One note demanded a fifty-thousand-dollar ransom, but when Marion's father replied, he got no response. Readers learned that the young woman had worked as a typist at a "Mutual Street photo-engraving firm," earned thirty-eight dollars per week, lived with her parents, and paid them room and board. Like Jane Doe, she used bobby pins in her hair.

An editorial writer recalled the case of theater tycoon Ambrose Small. In 1919, he had received a check for one million dollars and then disappeared on the streets of Toronto after his money had been safely deposited in a bank. Even the fictional Sherlock Holmes's creator, author Sir Arthur Conan Doyle, had been consulted, but the case remained unsolved. Doyle died in 1930 at the age of seventy-one.

In a similar attempt to solve Marion's case, the *Toronto Telegram* hired private investigator Robert Fabian. The former chief of London's Scotland Yard murder squad was flown from London to Toronto in August 1954, eight months after Marion's abduction. He planned to combine his trip to Toronto with an address to the upcoming International Association of Chiefs of Police convention in New Orleans, Louisiana, topped off with a visit to Hollywood, California, where he would offer his advice on a movie based on his book, *Fabian of the Yard*.

The whole front page of the August 11, 1954 issue of the *Telegram* featured a photograph of the dapper but stern-faced officer, with bowler hat and overcoat, looking every bit the "world's greatest detective," as the newspaper's headline proclaimed. Then age fifty-three, Fabian—who used only his last name, without a title—had joined the famed London force in 1921, solving cases in England that included the "Black Butterfly" and the "Witch of Meon Hill." He was considered "a devil to work for" and his motto, related the newspaper reporter, was "Keep your eyes and ears open and use your brain."

The Ontario Provincial Police, however, saw Fabian as an interference and predicted that he would be unable to find any clues. His reported search, however, did sell many more newspapers for the *Telegram* in its constant attempt to outshine the *Toronto Star*. In fact, many years later, one of the newspaper reporters—after he retired—confessed to having made up the copy material attributed to Fabian, calling the detective's concocted investigation "facts from a Scotch bottle." That got me to wondering who was doing the drinking when the *Telegram* wrote of the detective's prior street beat in London: "Although a water-drinker, he [Fabian] haunted the dives of Soho night after night, off duty and on, until he knew by sight and name almost the whole fraternity of crooks." Credit was given to these former contacts for helping him solve many of his later cases.

"If anyone can do it, Fabian can," announced the headline in a subsequent issue of the August 1954 newspaper, heralding the detective as the "champion of champions." His slightly more modest comment was: "Perhaps I'll be lucky." Reportedly, Fabian visited and reconstructed the crime scene, then concluded that no stranger to the area could have been responsible for Marion's attack and abduction and questioned why there were no fingerprints on the boyfriend's car. He pondered about the attacker's motive but finally concluded that the perpetrator must have been a "sex-fiend."

The *Telegram* announced that, from twelve o'clock noon to one o'clock in the afternoon and from seven to eight o'clock in the evening, Fabian himself would answer a special telephone line—Empire 3-4516. "Somebody knows a lot about this case," he stated, "and I'm ready to listen to anonymous phone calls or any other kind." He arrived at his makeshift office in a big sedan surrounded by youthful admirers and signed their autograph books. Photographed with his pipe in hand, the London detective was portrayed as the modern-day Sherlock Holmes, checking on every detail and definitely on track to crack the case.

Meanwhile, the police were flooded with "sightings" of Marion, although none proved to be her. The competing city newspaper, the *Toronto Star*, released the Ontario State Police's belief that Marion had been murdered at the scene, as a large quantity of blood had been found in the boyfriend's car. The Canadian officials had previously withheld this information, they stated, out of compassion for Marion's parents. Fabian, however, upped the *Telegram*'s circulation by theorizing that Marion was still alive.

None of this competition and sensationalism helped the grieving McDowell family. On September 4, 1954, less than a month after Fabian arrived, the *Star* announced that the famed detective had quit and flown away. By then, Marion's father had moved in with his mother-in-law, and Marion's mother was hospitalized and in seclusion following a nervous breakdown. The victim's brother, Ross McDowell, Jr., however, joined the East York Police Department in what would, for him, become a lifelong career and a lifelong and fruitless search for his sister.

Articles decades after Marion's murder reinforced the fact that the likelihood of its resolution had quickly faded into the past. A 1986 obituary of Sergeant Norman Brickell, the officer on duty the night Marion was abducted, stated that her case was the one case of his career that haunted him most of all. Police Inspector Harold Adamson, who had organized what then was the largest manhunt in Toronto's history, died in 2001. With his passing, the Toronto newspapers again reflected on the lack of any clues whatsoever in the nearly half-century-old mystery.

By mid-October 2004, Dr. Walter Birkby had finished reassembling the more than one hundred pieces of Jane Doe's skull. Detective Steve Ainsworth flew to Tucson, where he photographed the skull from various angles. Then the detective sent his photographs, along with a photograph of Marion, to Dr. Todd Fenton, a former student of Dr. Birkby's and the director of the Michigan State University Forensic Anthropology Laboratory in East Lansing, Michigan. There, like the fictional Dr. McAdoo had done in the 1950 film *Mystery Street*, Dr. Fenton would place a photograph of Jane Doe's skull over a photograph of Marion—the process known as superimposition—to determine if their bone structures were similar, and if it was possible that Marion could have been Jane Doe.

We were eager to learn the results, but when Dr. Bob called me the next time, he said: "Cold cases are like menopause. Sometimes they're hot and sometimes they're cold. The case won't be solved overnight. It has to internalize." Dr. Bob was careful to give any real news directly to Lieutenant West. In early November, the lieutenant told me that the superimposition of Marion's photograph on the photographs of Jane Doe's skull was under way, adding, "Hopefully, we will have results by the end of the week. That in turn will dictate whether or not they [Michigan State University] will pursue the DNA comparison."

A few weeks later, Lieutenant West emailed to tell me that he had recently received another telephone call from Dr. Bob stating that since the photographs were taken from slightly different angles, Dr. Fenton was having problems obtaining an accurate superimposition. To remedy the situation, Dr. Bob asked for authorization to have Dr. Birkby ship the skull from Tucson, Arizona, to the Michigan State University laboratory to allow Dr. Fenton to rotate the skull and make the most accurate comparison possible. In the lieutenant's correspondence with me, he added that he was initially reluctant to have the reassembled skull put in the mail, but he had been assured that it could be done safely. "We acquiesced," he said, "and presumably Jane is on her way to Michigan."

"As a bonus," Lieutenant West added, "the University [of Michigan] agreed to do a nuclear DNA extraction for us, so Dr. Birkby sent a long bone along with the skull for sampling. We'll see where that goes."

One day, at home, I got a telephone call from Pauline Arrillaga, a Phoenix-based Associated Press reporter intrigued with the Jane Doe case. The thirty-three-year-old woman had read the media coverage on the exhumation and volunteered to fly to Colorado to give us national coverage. Lieutenant West was in favor, but he specifically instructed me not to mention Marion McDowell, as we were awaiting the results of her photo-superimposition. Understanding my boundaries, I jumped at the chance to get the word out about Jane Doe.

"You will get so many leads," Pauline enthusiastically promised me when we walked into the sheriff's office so she could interview Lieutenant West. Then I showed both of them, on my laptop, the first of many versions of a PowerPoint program I had put together on the case.

Our next stop was Columbia Cemetery. Even though Jane Doe's remains had been removed during the exhumation, Pauline and I visited her gravesite. The Boulder Parks and Recreation Department had moved her stone to an off-site storage building, so we went there to see it. Afterward, Alan Cass rode with us to the turnout near Boulder Falls in Boulder Canyon. We parked and got out and walked along the shoulder of the highway to the site where the college students had found Jane Doe's body. Colorado was blessed with a few days of what I had grown up calling "Indian summer," and the warm fall day probably was similar to the warm spring day when Wayne Swanson and James Andes had taken their hike. Pauline was impressed with the beauty of the canyon—the solid bank of Douglas firs on the north-facing canyon slope, and the Ponderosa pines on the sunny side.

When we got back to town, Pauline and I went to the *Daily Camera* building, where I took her into the archives and showed her the file of old, yellowed newspaper clippings that had hooked me on the case. We walked past Howe Mortuary, where, in the basement, Dr. Freburn L. James had performed the autopsy. Upstairs, in the same building, strangers had gathered two weeks later for the funeral of their "mystery girl." The funeral records and the flower cards I had looked at there had recently been moved to the Carnegie Branch Library for Local History. The library was right around the corner, and we went there, too, so I could show the records and cards to Pauline. I especially wanted her to see the one addressed "To Someone's Daughter."

Eagerly I awaited the publication of the Associated Press story, which Pauline assured me would be reprinted in hundreds of newspapers across the country. Not all of the papers released the article on the same day, but nationwide readers first read the story on December 11, 2004, the same day it was picked up by *USA Today.* Pauline emailed, "I just hope it helps in some small way." A few days later, Lieutenant West emailed me that he had received two "leads." He added that one was probably a crank—an anonymous letter identifying the "killer," but the other was from a woman who thought Jane Doe might have been her long-lost cousin.

I was itching to hear her story so I could discuss it with Micki. My researcher friend and I had swapped hundreds of emails and continued to search missing-person websites, but we needed a name to plug into the genealogy databases. When I asked Lieutenant West, however, he told me he would forward the cousin's name the following week, adding, "I want to let the lady who has been providing this information know who you are first and that it's okay to share the information with you."

Lieutenant West's next email filled me in on the details of the missing woman named Christa. The lieutenant also copied me on an email in which he formally introduced me to the woman who had contacted him. I was pleased when he told her that he was supportive of my efforts. "Ms. Pettem has spear-headed the resurrection of the 'Jane Doe' case," he wrote. "She is very interested in promoting the investigation and has been kept abreast of developments in the case, including the information that you have provided." When he concluded, "Ms. Pettem has our confidence and our endorsement," I really did feel part of the team.

The background information on Christa reached my desk a few days later, and I read that, in 1954, at the age of eighteen, she was thought to have run off with an older man from Port Washington, New York. Her parents were German immigrants who kept a low profile in the years following World War II. They never filed a missing persons report as they assumed she would one day return, but she never did. I contacted her hometown library and asked if it held any high school records, but no one with Christa's name was found. A few days later, the woman who originally contacted Lieutenant West emailed me to say that a family friend remembered that she still lived in New York state in 1955. It was after that that she had disappeared, so Christa could not have been Jane Doe.

Before long, complete strangers also contacted me directly to share their thoughts and stories. Another newspaper reader forwarded the obituary of an Oklahoma woman, explaining that the woman's daughter had been missing since 1952. I contacted a family member who offered to do whatever he could to help, but his description of the missing daughter—she was five feet seven inches with almost black hair and had given birth to at least one child—was too far from the slender, light-brown-haired victim to be plausible.

A woman in western New York State said that a thirteen- to nineteen-year-old girl—too young to have been Christa—was found in a cornfield in the town of Caledonia in 1979. That victim also was buried as a "Jane Doe" and has never been identified. "I think of her very often," wrote the New York State woman. "You never know, she could be the girl next door that just kinda disappeared."

An Arkansas reader told me about her brother Tony, who disappeared at the age of sixteen, in 1978. The woman poured out her feelings about her local law-enforcement agency, which she said refused to take his disappearance seriously and simply labeled him a "runaway." I got a glimpse into what having a missing family member is like for the remaining family. "The years went by and life goes on," she wrote, "but forgetting was never an option—no matter how hard I tried."

Todd Matthews, who had inspired me with his identification of the "Tent Girl," also wrote and said: "Others probably don't know the time and love you have put in this, but I do." An eighty-one-year-old woman in Maine, without access to the internet, called to say that she prays every night for Jane Doe. A California woman wrote: "Because of you, a difference is going to be made. It is your heart that will speak for this young woman, and it is her spirit that is helping you." Even a sympathetic journalist in Chicago took the time to say, "I understand the difficulty and frustration of trying to dig into the past to find the truth, right a wrong, or just understand how people lived."

Just when I thought that the Associated Press story had run its course, I got an email from a woman in Nebraska named Jennifer Kitt. She had read the story—published on the day after Christmas—in her local newspaper, the *North Platte Telegraph*. "I have been reading about Jane Doe and have a story for you," wrote the young woman. "My grandma had a sister run away in 1952 at age eighteen, never to be heard of again."

Jennifer added that the young woman—her great-aunt Twylia May Embrey—matched the description of Jane Doe. The family had searched for many years but always came up empty-handed. A few of Twylia's siblings were still alive and healthy, and the family had high school photographs, information on her date of birth, and even her original Social Security card. Added Jennifer, "I'm not sure if you're interested, but these two people—Jane and Twylia—sure sound similar."

Not interested? How could I not be interested? We talked on the telephone the next day. "I had to think about it for awhile," said Jennifer, "but then my aunt called my grandma and they seemed so certain. We want to know if Twylia is Jane Doe."

9

"My grandma talks about Twylia all the time," Jennifer Kitt told me on the telephone. Even though I had never before spoken with the Nebraska woman, I had a feeling that she had told the story I was about to hear over and over. Jennifer explained that her grandmother, Mildred Garner—called Midge by everyone who knew her—was the oldest of eight siblings. Twylia, born in 1934, was thirteen years younger than Midge and was the second-youngest in the family. Midge often sat by her telephone in the hopes that Twylia would call, but no one had heard from her kid sister in more than fifty years. Eagerly, I asked Jennifer to fill me in on everything she knew about her great-aunt Twylia May.

As Jennifer related, the spunky Nebraska farm girl had left home in 1952, on the day she graduated from high school. Like the family of Christa, in New York, Twylia's family assumed she would return, so they never filed a missing person's report. Jennifer sent me several photographs, including one of the young woman with just the hint of a smile, her curly light brown hair swept back from her face. The more I saw and heard about Twylia, the more captivated I became with her story. A few days later, I took the photographs to Lieutenant Phil West, who seemed almost as excited about this new lead as I was.

At the time, neither Dr. Bob nor Lieutenant West had received a final report from Dr. Todd Fenton at Michigan State University. Since the Boulder County Sheriff's Office was waiting for the results of the forensic anthropologist's comparison of Marion McDowell's photographs with Jane Doe's skull, Lieutenant West asked Detective Steve Ainsworth to forward Twylia's photographs, as well.

Near the end of January 2005, Dr. Fenton emailed his results. Of Marion McDowell, the young woman abducted from Toronto, Dr. Fenton

Twylia May Embrey was last seen in North Platte, Nebraska, in 1952. Her family wanted to know if she was Jane Doe. Photo courtesy of Mildred Garner.

explained that he had performed two different analyses—first a photo-photo analysis comparing Marion's round-faced photographs with photographs of Jane Doe's skull. Then he did a skull-photo superimposition, in which he overlaid Marion's photograph onto a digital image of the actual reassembled skull sent by Dr. Walter Birkby. Dr. Fenton described both of these procedures as "not promising," adding that "they indicate that the skull and photo do not match."

The shipment of Jane Doe's skull to Michigan State University had included a leg bone for nuclear DNA extraction in the university's biology laboratory. We knew that a profile of the victim's DNA would not, in itself, give us any specific information, but the profile was required for future comparisons with possible family members who we hoped would come forward.

When Dr. Fenton was done comparing Marion's photograph, he did a skull-photo superimposition with Twylia's photograph and indicated that there was no match with her, either. Although I was aware that Dr. Fenton's skull-photo comparison was more sophisticated than the photo-photo superimposition I had seen in the film *Mystery Street*, I still knew little about this procedure, and I was skeptical. Lieutenant West consulted with Dr. Bob, however, and told me that in his opinion—since the photographic comparisons were not close—a comparison of Jane Doe's DNA profile with DNA profiles of family members of Marion and Twylia was not warranted at the time. I accepted the fact that Marion's abduction from Toronto made it unlikely that she would turn up in Colorado, but I still thought there was a slim possibility that Twylia could be Jane Doe. A few months later, I would find out that I was not alone.

Sadly, Jane Doe's remains were now spread among three places—her skull was in Dr. Fenton's forensic anthropology laboratory, her leg bone was in the biology laboratory, and the rest of her bones and her hair were neatly packed in labeled cardboard boxes stored at Dr. Birkby's home in Tucson, Arizona.

In order to move the case along, Lieutenant West and I discussed publicity, which led to the need for a sculpted facial reconstruction. The lieutenant predicted that when the *America's Most Wanted* camera crew completed its televised segment on Jane Doe, the producer would want to elicit a reaction from the public with a visual image they could relate to, rather than only showing her reassembled skull. The concept made me think back to what I had read in newspaper accounts from 1954, when Sheriff Art Everson had made similar comments on Jane Doe.

In one of the early *Denver Post* articles, written the day after the students discovered Jane Doe's body, a reporter recapped the murder of another unidentified woman—found in 1952 near Black Hawk, in neighboring Gilpin County, Colorado. Like Jane Doe, the female Black Hawk victim was dumped along the side of the highway, but her body had also been set on fire. According to the newspaper report, a Denver police artist, identified in the story, had reconstructed the victim's head from strands of black hair, bits of bone, and a few teeth. At the time, only one in three American households had a television but, even so, the head was shown to a national television audience.

The Black Hawk case has never been solved, but the newspaper writer reported that Sheriff Art Everson had planned to contact the same artist, adding that the sheriff believed a reconstruction of the Boulder Cañon victim's head would help in her identification. Even though I did not see any more mention of a reconstruction in the newspapers, I wondered if the Boulder authorities ever did contact him. An internet search revealed the man's name and address, still in Colorado. In response to a letter, his daughter told me that her recently deceased father had been proud of his work and had kept a photograph of the Black Hawk victim's reconstruction for many years. The daughter, however, had never heard of Jane Doe.

The concept of a sculpted facial reconstruction in the identification of unknown human remains was not new, even in 1952. That year's edition of the textbook *Modern Criminal Investigation* related the case of an unidentified male skeleton found in a house in Brooklyn, New York, in 1916. Using a medium called "plastelina," an artist sculpted a head that was based on the shape of the victim's skull. Dark brown hair had been found with the man's remains, so the sculptor obtained hair of the same color from a barber and attached it to the head. Going on the assumption that the victim was an Italian, he inserted brown glass eyes. When the head was shown to the sister of a missing person, she quickly cried, "This is Domenico La Rosa." If only it could be so easy for us.

In February 2005, in response to Lieutenant West's request for a facial reconstruction, Vidocq Society board chairman Frederick Bornhofen jumped in and arranged for Jane Doe's skull to travel again. This time, Dr. Todd Fenton mailed it from East Lansing, Michigan, to Philadelphia, Pennsylvania—to Frank Bender, the forensic artist and Vidocq Society co-founder known as the "recomposer of the decomposed." Lieutenant West emailed me, "I think that's the best resolution that we could hope for."

As I would see firsthand, Frank worked out of an old converted one-story butcher shop on South Street. The building had snug living quarters in the rear and was set inconspicuously into an eclectic mixture of mostly brick commercial buildings dating from the nineteenth century. Frank had quickly gained fame for his artistic skills in 1989 after an age-enhanced bust that he created of fugitive John List resulted in List's arrest for multiple murders just eleven days after the head-and-shoulders sculpture was televised to twenty-two million viewers on *America's Most Wanted*.

Frank blended art and science to bring Jane Doe's face to life, as well. First he consulted a standard chart that showed the average amount of flesh at various reference points on the face of a Caucasian woman. Then he began the process of putting a clay face over the actual skull by gluing on twenty-one tissue-depth markers that he cut from white eraser sticks. Using his hands, he pressed non-hardening clay between and flush with the markers, working quickly for several hours. Afterward, in one step removed from the victim's bones, he used sculpting tools to intuitively refine and detail the whole face, including her ears, nose, and mouth. Later he would remove the clay from her skull, but first he had to make what he called the "mother mold."

To prepare the clay surface, Frank sprayed it with a special silicone mold release, then used a brush to apply synthetic rubber until the molasses-like coating was a quarter of an inch thick. As the rubber began to dry, he mixed a batch of fiberglass-reinforced plaster which would become the mother mold and spread it on top of the rubber coating, inserting shims made of strips of aluminum printing plates. When the mother mold was dry, he pried it apart at the shims and removed it, also prying apart and removing the synthetic rubber imprint. He replaced this cured rubber back into the two portions of the mother mold, bound them tightly together with a bungee cord, turned them upside down, and applied plaster, again reinforced with fiberglass, on the inside to make the final head-and-shoulder sculpture. When the plaster was dry, Frank pulled off the mother mold, then sanded, refined, and painted Jane Doe's bust with oil paints. Finally, the permanent three-dimensional figure was ready for the world to see.

During this same time, the nuclear DNA extraction from Jane Doe's femur had been completed. Finally, the sheriff's office had its long-awaited genetic profile. All of us optimistically looked ahead to the unveiling of the facial reconstruction and its quick, we hoped, exposure on national television to bring in the leads that we expected and needed.

I continued to keep Micki informed of our progress. Even though my fellow researcher was in faraway Virginia and committed to working on the Jane Doe case, she also was intensely curious about Twylia's mysterious disappearance. Keeping an open mind—and wanting to satisfy my own curiosity about Twylia—my husband Ed and I set out on a six-hour drive across the eastern plains of Colorado and into the farmlands of western Nebraska. I wanted to see where Twylia had come from and to meet with Jennifer and Midge, Twylia's now elderly sister.

At North Platte, Ed and I turned off Interstate 80, crossed the South Platte River, passed the usual fast-food restaurants, big box stores, and gas

Forensic artist Frank Bender posed in his Philadelphia studio in the spring of 2005 with his recently completed bust of Jane Doe. Photo courtesy of Frank Bender.

stations, and then turned onto North Elm Street and into a tidy neighborhood with both 1920s-era bungalows and post–World War II homes. Jennifer, a thin blonde in her late twenties, explained that Midge's home was about a half-hour's drive away. She would take us there, and she had also invited a *North Platte Telegraph* reporter who was following Jane Doe's and Twylia's stories. After Jennifer made arrangements for the care of her children, Ed, the newspaper reporter, and I climbed into Jennifer's white van. We headed south on Highway 83 to the tiny town of Wellfleet, Nebraska—out in the "boondocks," as described by the locals.

As we left the flat Platte River Valley for open and hilly prairie land, the reporter asked me a lot of questions about my search for Jane Doe's identity and why I was interested in Twylia. I explained that the experts had already ruled her out as Jane Doe, but I believed that whoever Jane Doe was, she could have come from a similar rural midwestern background. I theorized that in 1954 it was possible for a runaway teenager to have been murdered far from home without the news filtering back to her family.

I also was aware, and a little apprehensive, that I was about to meet Midge, a real flesh-and-blood sibling of a long-lost family member. I wanted to know, firsthand, what Twylia's sister had experienced in the past fifty-two years. I figured that by meeting her, I would gain insight into what the situation might be like for siblings, if any, in Jane Doe's family. As for Twylia, I was just too intrigued to give up. Even if Twylia was not Jane Doe, I had resigned myself to trying to solve two mysteries—who was Jane Doe and what happened to Twylia?

When we reached Midge's green-and-white half-century-old frame house on a dusty street on the edge of a town with no paved streets at all, I felt as if we had gone back half a century in time. She greeted us warmly and invited us into her modest home. At the age of eighty-three, she had short reddish-brown hair and was still full of energy, but a pleasant tough-ness in her manner convinced me of a lifetime of hard work. I knew at once that she was a genuine part of America's heartland. We settled into soft, comfortable chairs and passed around scrapbooks of her family's pho-tographs. Twylia, I learned, was free-spirited and rambunctious, loved to draw, and loved horses. When I asked Midge if she knew why Twylia might have left home, she said that her sister had a fight with their father, a Nebraska-born farmer just scraping by with a few crops and a few cows.

The truth, I suspected, was more than a typical parent-teenager squab-ble. Before leaving home, I had found a genealogical website that listed all seven students—Twylia was the only girl—in her tiny graduating class at Maywood High School. I managed to locate a former male classmate who told me he used to dance with her to the lively Roy Rogers cowboy tune, "Don't Fence Me In." The classmate also gave me the name of Twylia's closest female friend, who was a year younger. I found a telephone number for that friend, now living in Iowa, and I gave her a call. She told me that Twylia had confided in her that she had been raped by her father. That, I felt certain, was the real reason she vowed never to see him again.

After visiting in Midge's home for an hour or so, we all climbed into Jennifer's van for the nine-mile drive south to Maywood. With a popu-lation of 278, the town was the epitome, to me, of the rural Midwest. Commercial Street, the main street in town, had a post office, a small food market, and a grain elevator. It also had a few other businesses, including an insurance company, where we found another of Twylia's sisters. We discovered that the old school building had been replaced with a newer one, but we went inside, where alumni photographs hung in the hallway. Jennifer pointed out Twylia's portrait, along with the senior yearbook photographs of her six classmates.

I reflected again on Jane Doe when Jennifer, Midge, Ed, the reporter, and I drove up a short hill and walked around in the Maywood Cemetery. When we found the unembellished graves of Twylia's parents and one of her brothers, I realized that if Twylia was Jane Doe, or if Jane Doe was someone like Twylia, this is where I would envision a reburial of her remains. Midge and her surviving siblings may have wanted her back, but she had fled her abusive father, and his remains were right under my feet! Maybe, I speculated to myself, returning Twylia's remains to Maywood might not be the right thing to do after all.

Two months earlier, after Jennifer first read of Jane Doe in the *North Platte Telegraph*, I had urged the editor of that newspaper to follow up with a local story of her own. The reporter who accompanied Ed and me to Midge's home and to Maywood had written that local story, relating Jennifer and Midge's longtime search for Twylia and the new possibility that she might have been Jane Doe. An elderly man in North Platte just happened to read the newspaper that day and called Jennifer to tell her that he was one of Tywlia's former boyfriends. When we got back to North Platte, Jennifer, Ed, and I met with the man at a coffee shop. He explained that for a few months after Twylia had graduated from high school, she worked as a waitress in a café located on Front Street, across from the North Platte railroad depot. The former boyfriend told us that he had reluctantly watched as Twylia willingly got into a large yellow Cadillac convertible, with Nevada license plates and bull horns mounted on the hood. A man was at the wheel. The North Platte resident said he assumed Twylia was headed west, adding, "She sure was pretty."

There were other stories, too, about Twylia's westward disappearance, including rumors that may or may not have been true. One related a possible affair with Twylia's brother-in-law, Virgil Valentine. For part of the summer between Twylia's junior and senior high school years, she had stayed with Virgil, his wife (another of Twylia's sisters), and their children on their farm in eastern Colorado. Jennifer suggested that Ed and I stop and visit with Virgil on our way home. We found him very open and friendly. He used to "roughhouse," he said, with Twylia, but their relationship was never more than that. A year or so after Twylia left home, however, Virgil received a letter from her that she asked him to read and then burn. He was the last family member to have heard from her. He did not tell us what was in the letter, but he thought it had been postmarked in Colorado.

Another story was provoked by the sudden appearance of a truck driver who contacted Twylia's family in 1981, claiming that he had dated her, too, and that she had gone to California. This renewed interest in Twylia's whereabouts prompted Midge to write a letter which she sent in care of the Social Security Administration, asking that it be forwarded to her. "We want desperately to see you," Midge pleaded, adding that their father had died and their mother was nearly blind and in a nursing home. All Midge got in return, however was a form letter from Social Security officials stating that they, too, had no address for the missing sister. Before my husband and I left Nebraska, Jennifer loaded us down with copies of her family's history, including dates and places of birth of Twylia's and Midge's siblings and parents. When I got home, I shared the information with Micki.

All of my gut reactions told me that even if Jane Doe was not Twylia, she might easily have suffered from similar tangled and/or abusive family relationships. Genealogical research, or what I prefer to call historical detective work, however, cannot be based on instincts; it has to rely on facts. I had learned this the hard way, by simply plunging into this type of research in the early 1980s. At that time, my first husband, two daughters, and I were living very simply in a primitive mountain cabin. We had no health or dental insurance and limited funds, so when our eleven-year-old daughter needed braces on her teeth, I shopped around for an orthodontist who was willing to exchange his professional services for detailed research on his family's history. It was a slightly offbeat arrangement, and I had to convince an experienced genealogist to teach me the tools of the trade, but it worked for us.

Of course, the world has changed in twenty-five years, and the internet has altered the landscape of genealogical research. Old information, such as pre-1900 marriage records, as well as many recent public records that include property transactions, can be found quickly online. But the time period from World War II to the 1970s is a researcher's "black hole." Many of the records overlapping Jane Doe's era are only available by the "gumshoe" method—by letter, by telephone, or by visits to courthouses and archives in person.

Another source of information is people who were at the scene, but there were no eyewitnesses, that we know of, to Jane Doe's murder. Only one man who visited the crime scene at the time was still alive—retired Boulder Police Detective Roy Hendricks. Alan Cass had mentioned him in our brainstorming session shortly after Sheriff Joe Pelle said he would consider reopening the case. The detective, called "Hoot" by his fellow officers, was in his nineties and still lived in his rural Boulder County home. Except for one lady friend and occasional visits to the American Legion Hall, he was reclusive and kept to himself. I tried calling and knocking on his door to no avail. In my wildest dreams, I thought that maybe he would show me long-tucked-away field notes or photographs.

Eventually, the elderly detective's friend returned my telephone calls and told me he did not want to talk to anyone. Detective Steve Ainsworth had tried, too, but even he was not allowed in the door. This, I learned, is not unheard of when younger investigators attempt to contact their retired predecessors.

Thinking I could, instead, meet Roy Hendricks in public, I recruited the help of retired Boulder Police Officer Larry Kinion. He and I had become reacquainted at the recent funeral of yet another retired officer, and we lamented that Roy's funeral could be next. For several hours on an April afternoon, Larry sipped beer while I had a couple of glasses of iced tea in a smoky dining room at the American Legion Hall north of Boulder. The bartender had tipped us off that Roy was expected for the three o'clock airing of *Millionaire* on television. We talked with several people we knew, but the man we came to see never arrived. Eventually, former Boulder County district attorney Stan Johnson and I did have an enjoyable visit with Roy in his home—arranged through his son, Ron Hendricks, who was visiting from out of state—but the former detective, unfortunately, had no new information to add.

Meanwhile, in a constant search for new leads, Micki emailed to tell me that she had been corresponding with a woman whose aunt Georgetta had disappeared from Oklahoma in 1948. The information was sketchy but, according to Georgetta's niece, the family had been dysfunctional, and Georgetta had been sexually abused by her father. The young woman had left home on her eighteenth birthday and was never heard from again—the very same scenario we had heard from Twylia's family. Perhaps the family dynamics of abusive fathers and runaway daughters was more common than I had previously thought. Georgetta's niece sent me a photograph of her aunt, which I forwarded to the sheriff's office. I explained to the niece that within a few months we would have the sculpted reconstruction of Jane Doe's face and if she thought Georgetta looked like Jane Doe, she should contact the authorities directly. At a later date, I followed up with the niece, who wrote to me: "I cannot believe that you could not even assist me with getting the DNA done at my cost just to put my family's mind at ease. Thanks for nothing." I tried, to no avail, to explain that as a layperson, my hands were tied. The case belonged to the sheriff's office, not to me.

As I continued to search for Jane Doe's identity, I also kept looking for Twylia, starting with the assumption that she was alive, had married, and thus had a different last name. I subscribed to a private investigator website and printed out page after page of women named "Twylia" with birth dates the same as, or close to, Twylia's—October 15, 1934. From my master list, I picked the most likely ones and emailed their names and telephone numbers to Jennifer and Micki, who started telephoning them one by one. Before long, we had ruled out ninety women. Comments on the Jane Doe message board's website reflected both the search for Twylia as well as progress on Jane Doe. One person following our quest wrote: "It is as though this young woman has reached out from the grave to seek justice and recognition. I, along with thousands of others, will follow this case. There is just something special about it."

I thought so, too, and my interest in Jane Doe expanded to include other cold cases. Ever since I had attended my first meeting of Families of Homicide Victims and Missing Persons, in 2003, I had been subscribing to the organization's newsletter and participating in some of their activities. In March 2005, the chair of the sociology department at the University of Colorado, whom I had met at my first meeting, assigned a research project to some of his graduate students. The independent study involved the compilation of a database of current addresses and telephone numbers of family members of Colorado's unsolved homicides. Although the group primarily was focused on post-1970 murders—too late for Jane Doe—I offered to help. In fact, I plunged right into the *Daily Camera* archives and put together background files on each of the twenty victims from Boulder County.

It was sobering to read about the other unsolved homicides, especially that of twenty-year-old Susan Becker, a hitchhiker who had been stabbed—also in Boulder Canyon—one mile west of Boulder Falls. Her body was found by fishermen in 1982 not far from the site where the college students had found Jane Doe. The mountains held other murders, as well. Hunters found the skeletal remains of Vaughn Everett near Meeker Park, in the northwestern part of the county. In addition, the skeletal remains of fourteen-year-old Margaret Hillman showed up in a shallow grave in Lefthand Canyon, nearly ten months after the young girl attended a party. Christine Jones and Carol Murphy were strangled (and Christine also was shot) a decade apart, in that same canyon. In Carol's case, Boulder County sheriff's investigators had, in 1989, drafted an arrest warrant against her husband, but the authorities had no evidence to directly link the accused murderer to the victim. At the time I read of her homicide, I had no way of knowing that a year later—twenty years after Carol's murder—a DNA breakthrough would make it possible for officials to finally make their arrest.

Prior to doing the research for FOHVAMP, I had no idea that these other murders had occurred. Equally shocking was the realization that Lefthand Canyon had the highest number of homicides. This was the route I drove—and continue to drive—every time I go between my mountain home and Boulder.

In April, Dr. Bob called to say he had recused himself from the Jane Doe case. I felt as if I had lost my closest advisor. Meanwhile, Lieutenant West began to plan for a June press conference at which Frank Bender would unveil his sculpture of Jane Doe. With Frank would be Dr. Richard Froede, who had directed the exhumation, and Dr. Walter Birkby, who had removed many of the remains and had reassembled the skull. Vidocq Society board chairman Frederick Bornhofen said he would be coming, too. The Jane Doe Fund, which I still oversaw, paid for the men's plane tickets. The film crew from *America's Most Wanted* was expected, but neither the lieutenant nor I had heard from the show's producer in months.

Before the Vidocq Society men arrived, Frank Bender had emailed photographs of the Jane Doe sculpture. Initially, I was thrown off by her nearly straight and very blonde hair—made of plaster and a part of the sculpture. I had expected her hair to be light brown, not blonde, and in the form of a wig, soft and curly as was the style in the early 1950s. When Frank called me to see if I had received the photographs, I told him that bobby pins had been found in her hair. I appreciated him painting one on each side.

Lieutenant West, Detective Ainsworth, and I all had our hopes up that the case would practically solve itself as soon as *America's Most Wanted* got Jane Doe's facial reconstruction on the air. Even Frederick Bornhofen wrote in an email, "Things will happen fast now."

10

While Frank Bender sculpted Jane Doe's facial reconstruction, he was also working on others. One of the busts, of an unidentified child from Kansas City, captured the interest of Drew Griffin, a CNN anchor working on a television story about unsolved homicides. The next thing I knew, Drew was on the telephone asking to interview me about the Jane Doe case. A few days later, in mid-May 2005, I met Drew, his producer, and a photographer in the *Daily Camera* parking lot. The crew had flown in that morning from Atlanta, Georgia. We took off in their rental car and visited Columbia Cemetery. A stake still marked the site where Jane Doe had been exhumed and, next to it, someone unknown to me had recently left a fresh bouquet of yellow and pink chrysanthemums.

Then we drove up Boulder Canyon to the crime scene. Drew was wearing a blue-striped shirt, khaki pants, and dress shoes and looked picture-perfect for the camera, but he still climbed down the steep embankment to the rocks at the edge of the creek. His photographer followed behind, effortlessly lugging a heavy television camera. The dark-haired and dark-skinned young man had a great time filming the rivulets in the rushing stream, even though only a few seconds were needed in the final editing of the program. Drew said his cameraman had just come back from Baghdad, Iraq, and was overjoyed to be in a place where no one was shooting at him.

We returned to the newspaper office, where I took the CNN crew upstairs to the *Daily Camera*'s archives. As I had done for Pauline, the Associated Press reporter, I pulled open the drawer of brittle old Jane Doe clippings that first got me hooked on the case. Then Drew and his crew wanted some local color, so we walked part of Boulder's famed Pearl Street Pedestrian Mall, followed by a visit to my favorite hangout, the Carnegie

117

Branch Library for Local History. Reflecting back on the leisurely day I had spent with Pauline, I started to think where I would suggest we go for a late lunch. Before I could make a suggestion, however, the visitors piled into their rental car and drove back to the airport.

The CNN interview was Jane Doe's, and my, first exposure on national television. Drew combined the segment with an interview he did in Tennessee with the Doe Network's Todd Matthews, the identifier of the "Tent Girl." To lead into the part on Todd, Drew asked me, on camera: "Were you surprised to learn how many cases like this are out there? "Yes, absolutely," I replied. I told him that when I first had become interested in researching the Jane Doe case, I had no idea that other people in the rest of the country were doing the same thing. Indeed, his question was a revelation, and I felt that it was a turning point for me. Drew actually reported the National Crime Information Center (NCIC) statistic—at the time, Boulder's Jane Doe was one of nearly six thousand reported and unidentified homicide victims in the United States.

In reality, the National Institute of Justice (NIJ), an agency of the United States Department of Justice, estimates that the actual number is much higher. It states that more than forty thousand sets of human remains are stashed throughout the country in police department and medical examiner evidence rooms, while only fifteen percent have been entered into the NCIC database. The NIJ calls the staggering number of the missing and unidentified the "nation's silent mass disaster." Helping to sort through the backlog is the NIJ-funded Center for Human Identification (CHI), located at the University of North Texas Health Science Center in Fort Worth, Texas.

The following Friday afternoon, after the CNN crew had visited the *Daily Camera* archives but before the segment was shown on television, I got the following message on my cell phone: "If you're still in town, come down to the *Camera* office right away." It was from Carol Taylor, the newspaper's librarian, who was well aware of my research in the Jane Doe case. She added that she had been doing some filing and just discovered a white envelope with large-format negatives of Jane Doe's corpse in the bottom of her "to-be-filed" basket!"

When I entered the empty archives room, the white envelope with "Unknown Murder victim and officers at body site" typed on front was sitting on Carol's desk. On the envelope's upper left-hand corner was the word "Sheriff." On the upper right-hand corner was the date, "4/8/54." There was no doubt they held negatives of Jane Doe. On the front was a note that read "Sylvan Center." It meant nothing to me so I tossed it in the trash, then later thought I should have saved it for its fingerprints.

As soon as I held the first of six four-by-five-inch negatives up to the light, I realized they had never been meant for publication. So, why were they there? The victim's legs and genital area were not included in the photographs, but the rest of her body—what had not been eaten away—was exposed. She lay on a white porcelain table in the morgue at Howe Mortuary, the same mothballed embalming room the mortuary's receptionist had shown me when she took me into the basement on the day that we found the "unidentified girl's" flower cards. The unknown murder victim was photographed from the front, as well as from her right and left sides. Three additional negatives showed police, including the elusive Detective Roy Hendricks, at the site in Boulder Canyon where the students had found Jane Doe's body. The Boulder Canyon photographs were similar, but not identical, to one that had been taken of the detectives and published in the newspaper, but I had never before seen any of the others.

The layout department at the *Daily Camera* did not have the capability to scan negatives, but I knew that the sheriff's office would need copies and I did, too, so I took the negatives home. Without even thinking about cooking dinner, I scanned the first one, then after dinner I scanned the others and was amazed at their quality. I was able to zoom in and compare some of the victim's injuries with the original autopsy report. Even her appendectomy scar was clearly visible. The next day was a Saturday, and I spent hours mesmerized with the photographs, realizing how important their sudden appearance was to the Jane Doe case. I called the sheriff's dispatcher and asked him to contact Lieutenant Phil West, who called me right back; we set a time of one o'clock in the afternoon on Monday for me to bring in the scans.

First, however, I went back to the newspaper office and returned the negatives to Carol, along with all scanned images on a disk, hard copies of all the photographs, and a cover letter explaining my part in the Jane Doe case. Following protocol, I filled out a permission form and paid twenty dollars for each image. Then I went to the sheriff's office for my appointment. Lieutenant West was running late, but I was met by Captain Dennis Hopper. I told him the morgue photographs of Jane Doe would probably interest him, too. He immediately escorted me into the conference room, where we started looking at the prints. When the lieutenant came in, I explained to them both how the negatives had mysteriously surfaced at the newspaper office. The captain then went out to get Sheriff Joe Pelle, who returned with a smile and asked, "What have you brought us now?"

The sheriff officials and I discussed the fact that, most likely, birds and mammals had eaten away at her face, neck, and most of her fingers. Her left eye and right ear were missing. It also was obvious that her body had suffered a lot of soft-tissue damage and parts of her skin had dried out, or mummified, rather than decomposed. The men also commented that she was slender, small-breasted, and had long wavy hair—the same hair I had touched at her exhumation.

At the *Daily Camera*, Carol Taylor sent an email to the newsroom staff. No one admitted to having any knowledge of the photographs, but Carol showed them to retired editor Laurence Paddock, and he confirmed that they were the photographs that he had taken at the request of the coroner. We also were aware that no one from the public had access to the room where they were found. I wondered, but never knew, if the mysterious discovery was somehow related to my recent escorting of the CNN crew through the *Camera*'s newsroom. After all, when I was being interviewed, I had made it clear that within a few weeks, forensic artist Frank Bender would be unveiling Jane Doe's "likeness"—the face that the reporters and the public were anxious to see.

Maybe someone at the newspaper office was cleaning out his or her desk and realized, for the first time, how important the photographs would be to the Jane Doe investigation. At a later date, when Lieutenant West and I were discussing the photographs, he asked me, "Do you think God had a hand in their return?"

My husband Ed and I still enjoyed living without television, and I had no idea when the CNN show would air, so I was surprised two weeks after the film crew was in town when the telephone started ringing with people I knew who called to say they had seen the five-minute "Spotlight" on *Headline News*. Other news of the day included singer Michael Jackson on trial and the one-week-old mystery of Natalee Holloway's disappearance in Aruba. A few days later our segment was repeated on *Paula Zahn Now*. The nationwide airing of Jane Doe's story meant that millions of television viewers now knew of her, too. As always, I was hoping for new leads.

In June 2005, the Vidocq Society men were back in Boulder. Visiting with them was like attending a reunion, but without Dr. Bob's commentary and sense of humor. In addition to Dr. Richard Froede and Dr. Walter Birkby were forensic artist Frank Bender and the Vidocq Society board chairman Frederick Bornhofen. On the day before the sheriff's office's scheduled press conference, I found Frank and Frederick in the Corner Bar of the Hotel Boulderado, which, again, had provided complimentary rooms for the forensic consultants. The two men had flown in together from Philadelphia. Drs. Froede and Birkby were still on a plane from Tucson.

I recognized Frank right away, as a few months earlier, Alan Cass had taped and given to me a video of a CBS *60 Minutes* program that included a segment on Frank. The Philadelphia native looked just the same and was dressed in his usual dark T-shirt and blue jeans. He looked younger than his sixty-three years, despite his balding and close-cropped hair, glasses, white mustache, and goatee.

Frederick, a couple of years older than Frank, was dressed in a blue shirt and khaki slacks. When I asked him how I would recognize him, he said he was "six foot four inches, three-hundred pounds, and extremely good-looking." The former counterintelligence agent had gone into industrial security and had managed many complex investigations, so he was well-suited as the Vidocq Society's case manager. Currently, he heads Frederick A. Bornhofen Associates, a firm that serves the needs of the federal government and major corporations, specializing in product counterfeiting and product diversion. He also is an expert witness in security-related matters.

I joined the men at their table, where Frank explained that he had brought both Jane Doe's actual skull and the facial reconstruction wrapped in Bubble Wrap in his carry-on luggage. "I had to do a little explaining," he said, "to get the skull through airport security." Frank invited Frederick and me to his hotel room so I could see the skull and the bust for myself.

Frank was staying in one of the few small remodeled attic rooms on the hotel's fifth floor. We rang for an elevator operator to take us upstairs in the building's original 1908 Otis elevator, then walked down the hall and around the corner to Frank's room on the west side, where he had a spectacular view of the mountains. In order to show the sculpture in the room's natural light, Frank took it out of his black canvas carry-on bag and set it on an antique glass-topped dresser. As I looked at Jane Doe's face perched there in front of flowery Victorian wallpaper, I was struck by the sadness that Frank had portrayed in her mouth and eyes. Next to his bed, on his nightstand, he placed Jane Doe's actual skull, with a little of the clay still attached.

We left the skull and reconstruction in Frank's room, and I drove Frederick and Frank to Boulder Canyon, as they wanted to see where the students had found Jane Doe's body. After we viewed the crime scene, we walked across the highway to Boulder Falls and took in the mountain scenery. Then we were back in Boulder in time for another dinner hosted by the sheriff's office. As in the previous year, I joined several members of the sheriff's office and their Vidocq Society guests at one long table on the porch of Q's Restaurant, the hotel's main and most elegant dining room.

While we waited for drinks, I showed Frank the photographs Jennifer Kitt had sent of Twylia May Embrey, as well as the recently surfaced morgue photographs of Jane Doe. Frank immediately saw similarities between Jane Doe and Twylia, especially in their eyebrows and hairlines. "It's her!" he exclaimed. "If it looks like a duck and quacks like a duck, it's a duck." Then Frank grabbed my cell phone and called Twylia's great-niece in Nebraska, asking Jennifer a lot of questions about Twylia's build and physical appearance. I knew that forensic anthropologist Dr. Todd Fenton had ruled out Twylia as Jane Doe based on his superimposition of the skull photographs, but Frank was also an expert. Like a juror, I had no idea which expert to believe. With Jennifer and Micki, I had been searching for a living Twylia. Could she be Jane Doe after all?

That night, high winds—and an unsettled feeling—kept me up into the early hours of the morning. I kept thinking about the victim's skull sitting on Frank's nightstand. Then, too, the severe weather reminded me of the rain, thunder, and lightning of the previous year, on the first night of the exhumation when only half of her bones had been removed from her grave.

The next day, on June 13, 2005, at the press conference in the jury assembly room in the Boulder County Justice Center, television cameras from every network and program except *America's Most Wanted* lined up in a row in the middle of the large room. Members of the Boulder Parks and Recreation Department displayed Jane Doe's gravestone—removed for a few hours from its temporary quarters in storage. The press conference was open to the public and included several donors to the Jane Doe Fund.

Sheriff Joe Pelle, in uniform, presented background information on the case. Then Frank, wearing a dark dress shirt and dark sport coat with his usual blue jeans, lifted a black velvet cloth from Jane Doe's sculpted face, allowing the media and the public to view her for the first time. Seated next to the podium were Dr. Froede, Dr. Birkby, and Frederick Bornhofen. When the press conference was opened to questions, a reporter asked the sheriff if he thought he would ever discover who murdered Jane Doe. I assumed that Lieutenant West and Detective Ainsworth still wanted to bring the murderer to justice, and even though they both were present, neither of them spoke. Said the sheriff, "It would be highly satisfactory to simply identify this young lady and give her family some closure."

The new publicity, meant to make a "big splash," said Lieutenant West, brought in a few leads but nothing that helped identify Jane Doe. One contact that came directly to me was from a family member of a woman named Naomi who, in 1954, had left her three-year-old twins

Dr. Richard Froede, Dr. Walter Birkby, Frederick Bornhofen, and Frank Bender, left to right, listened as Sheriff Joe Pelle spoke to the media and public at a press conference at the Boulder County Sheriff's Office in June 2005. Jane Doe's gravestone is on display in the foreground, and her sculpted facial reconstruction is on the table to the right of the sheriff.

with her parents in Phoenix, Arizona. No one in the family had ever heard from her again. The father of the out-of-wedlock twins was rumored to have been the late country western singer Marty Robbins. When the twins were two years old, Naomi married a man who was abusive, and the family believed she was fleeing him when she left. I explained that our experts believed that Jane Doe had never been a mother.

Then a cousin of a woman named Patsy emailed me to explain that, sometime in the 1950s, Patsy and her husband had traveled from Detroit, Michigan, to visit her sister in Boulder. Patsy disappeared, and her husband returned to Detroit bragging that he had beaten her. I sent off for the couple's marriage license and found that they married in 1958, proving that she, too, could not have been Jane Doe.

Another lead came from a Kansas woman who was following Jane Doe's story and wrote to tell me that she believed her aunt Edna had been murdered by her uncle, who dumped her where the couple were last known to have lived—in Colorado. A few days later, the same woman wrote back and said that she had just heard that a cousin had hired a private investigator and recently found the missing aunt. She, too, could not have been Jane Doe, but her story was tragic and showed the too-frequent pattern of sexual abuse. Edna's husband had, apparently, pushed his wife out of their car with only the clothes on her back. She then slept on park benches and ate out of garbage cans and claimed that she could not go home because her father had raped her. To keep her husband and father from finding her, Edna supposedly changed her Social Security number six times.

Edna's niece told me that she believed her aunt had not wanted to be found—by any of the family. The niece had read the recent newspaper articles about Twylia May Embrey and said Twylia may not have wanted to be found, either. Edna's niece suggested that if, in my research, I did find Twylia, not to tell her family until I, myself, had talked with her and respected her wishes. "People leave their families because they hurt," she told me. "There are reasons."

Around this time, I also corresponded with a woman in Oregon who had recently been reunited with her sister, whom she had not seen or heard from in fifty years. She told me that she was one of three children in her family, that both of her parents had been heavy drinkers, and that her father was violent when drunk. She and her siblings were separated and sent to foster homes in the Midwest. After a few years, she lost contact with her mother, as well. The Oregon woman told me that during all of the intervening years, she searched for—and just recently found—both her sister and her mother. When she did, she had to deal with her own resentment that neither her mother nor her sister had looked for her. The mother is now deceased, and of the sister, the woman wrote, "I have some reason to believe she may not have wanted to be found." I began to understand that not all reunions have happy endings.

As I followed up even the unlikely scenarios, I continued to share all of my information with the sheriff's office, but when I asked Lieutenant West if he would share his information with me, he said, "If we're comfortable sharing the material with you, we will. If not, we won't." I had to accept the fact that by remaining guarded, he was protecting the integrity of the case.

Frank's gut feeling that Twylia was Jane Doe pumped new enthusiasm for the case of the missing Nebraska runaway into the minds of the sheriff officials. Within a day or so of the press conference, Detective Ainsworth personally drove to North Platte, Nebraska, after quickly arranging his visit ahead of time with Jennifer Kitt. When the detective arrived in the midwestern town, he met with Jennifer and her grandmother, Midge, and swabbed the inside of Midge's cheek for a DNA sample. The women had been told that superimposition had ruled out Twylia as Jane Doe, so they were caught off guard by Frank Bender's and the detective's renewed interest. The detective explained that—at no cost to Midge—her DNA profile would be compared with the nuclear DNA profile extracted from Jane Doe's femur. By comparing the two profiles, we would know, for sure, whether Twylia was Jane Doe.

During the next three weeks, we all anxiously awaited the DNA results, and Jennifer, Midge, and the rest of the Embrey family rode a roller coaster of emotions. The media spread the story across the country. A self-described psychic in Pennsylvania wrote to tell me that she thought Twylia really was Judy Tyler, a glamorous actress who starred with Elvis Presley in the movie *Jailhouse Rock* but had died in a car accident in 1957. No one gave the psychic's presumption a second thought.

When I spoke on the telephone with Jennifer, she said her grandmother wanted closure, but that neither of them could imagine their long-lost relative having been brutally murdered, stripped, and left to die. "I want to find Twylia, but not this way, just not this way," Jennifer confided to me through tears. Traffic on the Jane Doe message board increased. Some readers were sympathetic and some were not. One person callously wrote, "Said the horse thief hanging from the tree, the suspense is killing me." To bide the time, Jennifer, Micki, and I continued our often frustrating search for a living Twylia. Micki called me one day in exasperation. She said she had talked with a woman she was sure was Twylia and told her: "You may be purple for all I know," after the woman said she could not be the Twylia we were looking for, because she was black.

Four weeks after the press conference, Lieutenant West issued an official sheriff's office press release stating that Twylia was *not* Jane Doe. Although I was still intent on identifying Jane Doe, I shared the Embrey family's relief. But even with the DNA results back from the laboratory, the family's ordeal was not over. DNA extraction, I soon learned, is not always completely reliable. One of the experts cited possible contamination and questioned whether Jane Doe's nuclear DNA profile was degraded and/or had been performed under strict quality control conditions. Television viewers who watched football celebrity O. J. Simpson's double-murder trial in 1994 will recall that corruption of samples during testing can be, and was, challenged in court.

As far as the Jane Doe investigation was concerned, and as Lieutenant West explained it to me, there still was a remote possibility that Twylia was the victim. Frank Bender, in particular, insisted on a second DNA profile, and this time he wanted the extraction of mitochondrial DNA. The rest of the Vidocq consultants agreed.

DNA extraction is complicated. Nuclear DNA, as its name implies, comes from within the nucleus of a cell. In Jane Doe's case, the genetic material for her first DNA profile was taken from her femur, or thighbone. Mitochondrial DNA is only inherited from one's mother, meaning that only maternally related individuals can provide reference samples. The mitochondria of cells are structures found in the cytoplasm, outside the nucleus. A comparison of mitochondrial DNA, we were told, would work fine for Twylia's case, as she and her sister Midge both shared the same mother. Jennifer, the great-niece, could not have provided a sample, as she was related to Twylia through her father's side of the family. To pay for the mitochondrial DNA extraction, we needed more money than was in the Jane Doe Fund. After a few months with only small contributions, the sheriff's office generously matched our bank balance. When we were within three hundred dollars of our goal, Frank Bender paid the difference himself.

Detective Ainsworth then contacted Mitotyping Technologies LLC, in State College, Pennsylvania. Its president and director, Dr. Terry Melton, agreed to handle our specialized needs—including the documented chain of custody required in any homicide investigation. Equipped to process samples where DNA is minimal and degraded, she also had a reputation for taking on historic cases. One of her clients was the Smithsonian Institution, which had contacted her about a case called the "Boy in the Iron Coffin." In 2005, the year that Detective Ainsworth contacted the Pennsylvania laboratory, utility workers in Washington, D.C., unearthed a mid-nineteenth-century iron coffin that contained human remains. Two years later, Dr. Melton would positively identify the deceased as a fifteen-year-old boy who died in 1852.

For Jane Doe's mitochondrial DNA profile, Dr. Melton requested a tooth. The victim's reassembled skull—with teeth—initially had traveled from Dr. Walter Birkby's home in Tucson, Arizona, to Dr. Todd Fenton's forensic anthropology laboratory in East Lansing, Michigan. He then shipped it to Frank Bender's studio in Philadelphia, Pennsylvania, and Frank then carried, with him, both the skull and the facial reconstruction on his flight to Boulder, where he left them with sheriff's officials. In the fall of 2005, Jane Doe's skull traveled once again when the Boulder County Sheriff's Office mailed it to Dr. Melton in Pennsylvania, so she could select a specific molar.

While I tried to understand the different types of DNA extractions, I also read up on the maze of DNA-related databases, including the Combined DNA Index System, or CODIS. Like the old-fashioned method of matching fingerprints of individuals to a master file of fingerprints on index cards, CODIS allows law-enforcement officials to enter profiles of DNA found at crime scenes and compare them with their extensive files in a computerized database. This collaborative effort among local, state, and federal law-enforcement agencies was established by the Federal Bureau of Investigation in 1990.

Within days of the September 11, 2001 attacks on the World Trade Center in New York, the National Institute of Justice created a customized version of CODIS to match the victims of the attack with genetic material provided by their relatives. In some cases the evidence supplied was hair from a comb or saliva from the victim's toothbrush. The efforts led to the identification of more than one-quarter of the people reported missing. Four years later, the same system was used to identify more than one hundred victims of Hurricane Katrina whose badly decomposed bodies left no other alternative.

In 1998, two years after I had first visited Jane Doe's grave, the Federal Bureau of Investigation announced the operation of its National DNA Index System, called NDIS, which compares the DNA from crime scenes with that of known offenders. Of specific interest to cold case researchers, the NDIS also includes DNA profiles both from unidentified human remains, including Jane Doe, and those—like DNA from Twylia's sister Midge—voluntarily contributed by relatives of missing persons.

Meanwhile, with help from Micki, I continued to update the spreadsheet of missing young women that I had begun in the spring of 2004. The work was slow and tedious. We spent hours each day searching Social Security death records and marriage and divorce records, reading old newspaper references, calling possible family members, and ruling out the women who had left a post-1954 paper trail. We eliminated one woman, Joeline, after I spoke to an attorney in Oklahoma who confirmed that the woman had recently been listed as next-of-kin to her mother, who was living in a nursing home.

A newspaper account revealed that a Denver woman named Eva had rented a room and then, around the time of Jane Doe's murder, disappeared. Although there was no formal missing person's report, she had left her belongings in her room, leading to a reporter's speculation that she could have been the murder victim. After I read a month's worth of newspapers on microfilm, I found a news brief that said that Eva had also read of her alleged disappearance and contacted authorities. She had been unable to pay her rent and had simply moved in with a friend.

In August 2005, frustrated with a lack of new leads, I called the television show *America's Most Wanted* to see when our Jane Doe segment would run. Neither the producer nor his crew had been to Boulder since the exhumation, but, at the time, they had invested considerable time and expense. I was shocked when the bureau chief told me that the segment had been cancelled—no one had bothered to tell the sheriff's office or me. After a lengthy conversation in which I explained that *America's Most Wanted* owned the exclusive video coverage of Jane Doe's exhumation and it would be impossible to go back and do it again, I was promised yet another producer and a new show.

Fred Peabody, the new producer, called me within the hour and said he would "make good" on publicizing Jane Doe, adding that his production would be complete with a fog machine and a trained raven. His use of the carrion-eater, I figured, was a Hollywood prop. Macabre sensationalism I could do without, but, realistically, ravens are a part of Jane Doe's story, as they most likely had been at least partially responsible for tearing at the flesh on her hands and face. In some cultures, ravens are associated with lost souls, and here I was looking for one. As I worked in my home office, I enjoyed watching both ravens and crows squabble over the suet I put with the birdfeeders outside my window. The shiny black ravens were larger than the crows and had deep-throated gobbles that sounded like turkeys. After a while, when my thoughts and eyes drifted from my work, I found I could recognize a few of the regulars.

While we were waiting for the results of the second DNA comparison with Twylia's sister, the Jane Doe case took another abrupt turn when Cindi Eichorn, a Denver-area resident and the newest researcher to join our team, asked me, almost as an aside, if former Denver resident Harvey M. Glatman had ever been considered a suspect in Jane Doe's murder. I had never heard of Glatman, but I later learned that the name of this notorious serial killer was familiar to many people.

On my next visit to the Boulder *Daily Camera* archives, I halfheartedly looked in the files to see if a previous librarian had ever clipped an article on him. I thought back to my first conversation with Lieutenant West and Detective Ainsworth, when they told me that identifying the victim might lead us to her killer. Working the case from killer to victim seemed backward to me, but I figured I would give it a try. I opened a drawer in a small gray metal filing cabinet, flipped from "Gh" to "Gi" to "Gl," and suddenly came across a small envelope with Glatman's name neatly typed in the upper left corner. Inside were several yellowed clippings.

"I don't believe it!" I yelled to Carol Taylor, the *Daily Camera* librarian who several months earlier had discovered the negatives of Jane Doe's morgue photographs. The articles, from 1958, were written after Glatman had confessed to strangling three young women in California, but they did not dwell on the California murders. Instead, the newspaper accounts gave me exactly what I had wanted—insight into the mind of Boulder County Sheriff Art Everson. I practically devoured each piece as I ran toward the photocopier—and I nearly stopped dead in my tracks when I finished reading. We did not yet have an identification for Jane Doe, but we might have stumbled on the trail of her killer.

11

The *Daily Camera*'s crime reporter—probably Bob Looney, but no by-line was given—outlined why Sheriff Art Everson considered Glatman "a good suspect in the mystery slaying of 1954." The sheriff's reasoning included the following: Glatman was familiar with Boulder, he had previously been arrested for abducting a woman in Boulder, and he had been arrested for "terrorizing women" in Denver, thirty miles away. A further parallel was that the Boulder County victim had been disrobed, as were the three women Glatman admitted to murdering in California.

The articles mentioned that Sheriff Everson had sent a copy of his file on the 1954 homicide to the Orange County, California, sheriff's office, asking that Glatman be questioned in the case. Then in custody, Glatman had been arrested in Orange County after the last of his assault victims managed to escape from his parked car. Just maybe, I thought, the California agency might still have the long-lost file. If so, it would answer many of our questions. But my hopes were quickly dashed after I corresponded with an Orange County sergeant who told me that even after consulting with the Santa Ana Police Department and the local district attorney's cold case team, no one could find our file—or anything at all on Glatman. That seemed strange to me, as his arrest had been high-profile. Files on him must have been kept by someone, but where were they?

Without going into any detail, one of the *Daily Camera* articles mentioned that a lie detector test "apparently cleared Glatman of three Colorado murders about which he was questioned." If Jane Doe's murder was one of them, what were the other two? Sheriff Everson emphatically stated, however, that he was not convinced of Glatman's innocence. The Boulder County sheriff had urged the California authorities to use a "more effective lie detector test," but if one was found, no one bothered to tell the press.

Sheriff Everson had reason to be leery of lie detectors. At the time, his department probably did not own one, but only a year before, in 1957, Boulder Police Chief Myron Teegarden had purchased the first lie-detector device in Boulder. The fifteen-pound electronic Burns and Wilhelm model cost $330 and originally had been put on the market in 1949. While conducting an interrogation, the investigator placed a curved metal band against one finger on each of a subject's hands. Electrodes in the bands led to the machine, which recorded changes in the static electricity on the person's skin. The person giving the test set the dial of the "electronic psychometer" to the number fifteen. A wide swing to the right, up to fifty, indicated that the subject was lying.

To try out Boulder's new device, the city manager, a radio announcer, and newspaper reporter Bob Looney all showed up at the downtown police station for a "susceptibility test." Each subject was asked to chose a number from one to five and write it on a piece of paper, then answer "no" each time the operator asked: "Did you pick number —?" The subjects lied successfully but, in another session with twelve questions, the chief, who asked the questions, misinterpreted the correct answers on two and was uncertain on one. He was quick to point out that the lie detector was not as expensive or as accurate as a polygraph, which neither department had, either. It was also pointed out that the tests were not admissible in court, and they would not work on people who were uncooperative or pathological liars.

Like finding the crime scene, I believed that by discovering Sheriff Everson's stated opinion that he considered Glatman a suspect, I had uncovered another major piece of Jane Doe's puzzle. I hurried home to email Cindi, the researcher who initially contacted me about Glatman, and tell her of the possible connection.

The Glatman breakthrough spurred me on. I called Sheriff Art Everson's daughter, hoping that her late father might have confided his theory to someone in the family, but she said he had never discussed the case at home. Despite the considerable coverage in the Boulder and Denver newspapers, cops were tight-lipped, and the public did not have the information at its fingertips that we, in the internet age, have today.

This was made clear to me when I got an email from Dave Frederick, another new member of the research team who had reached me through the Jane Doe website's message board. The Billings, Montana, hardware store manager had good internet skills, a passion for genealogy, and a real interest in identifying Jane Doe. "You won't believe this," he wrote, excitedly, then explained that he had been googling Glatman's name and found a "Harvey M. Glatman Memorial Scholarship" at the University of Denver.

According to the private university's website, the endowed scholarship had been started with a bequest from Glatman's mother, and it supported students of junior or senior standing who were majoring in accounting or business administration in the Daniels College of Business.

After I recovered from the shock, I wondered if Jane Doe could have been a University of Denver student. I gave the school a call to see if its administrators knew of any missing female students in 1954. They did not have any missing-student records, but imagine my surprise when no one I spoke to was aware that the school's scholarship was named for a serial killer! Needless to say, all mention of the scholarship was removed from the website by the following day. I tried to find out what the students were told when they received the money, but no university authorities would return my telephone calls—at least not at the time.

The best source of information, I figured, would be the Denver Probate Court, so I went there and read through the probate records of Glatman's mother, Ophelia. I found that she had willed nearly her entire estate—approximately ten thousand dollars and some stocks—to "perpetuate the memory of my son Harvey." This was not just strange, I thought to myself, it was despicable. In 1958, at the time of her son's arrest for two of his admitted three California murders, Ophelia was quoted as saying: "Oh my God in heaven. Not my boy? Not my boy! He was always so good. He never hurt anybody. He was always good and always dependable. There must be some mistake."

On the second floor of the sprawling Denver City and County Building, across the Civic Center from the Colorado State Capitol, I continued to read through Ophelia Glatman's probate file. I learned that she had written her last will and testament in January 1960, four months after her only child had been executed in the gas chamber in San Quentin State Prison in Marin County, California. Her husband, Albert Glatman, had died in 1952, so Ophelia named a nephew—the son of her sister Rosalie Gold—as the executor of her estate. He was to inherit her home, but she ended up selling it before her death in 1968. Her will specified small donations to Boys Town, in Nebraska, and to the women's Zionist organization, Hadassah.

The rest of the estate was put in trust as the Harvey M. Glatman Fund, administered by Ophelia's nephew, whom I felt fortunate to have reached on the telephone at his Denver home. The ninety-three-year-old man—Glatman's cousin, and fourteen years his senior—told me that it had been his decision to carry out his aunt's wishes by using the fund to start the memorial scholarship at the University of Denver. Of Glatman's history of sexual assaults and killings, the family relative said, "He was sick. That's all there was to it."

With a newfound interest in Glatman's parents, I visited Albert and Ophelia's graves in the Mount Nebo Memorial Park Cemetery, in a Jewish enclave off busy Colfax Avenue in Aurora, a few miles east of downtown Denver. The Glatman parents' names are engraved together, under the Star of David, on one pink granite stone. As I stood in front of the joint grave, I wondered if Harvey Glatman had also stood where I was now standing. I also wondered, but never would know, why Ophelia had not claimed her son's cremated remains. If she was so concerned with perpetuating his memory, why did she leave his ashes for prison officials to bury in the San Quentin Prison cemetery?

Meanwhile, Cindi was reading a compilation of true-crime stories, Ann Rule's *Kiss Me, Kill Me,* and forwarded on bits and pieces of information, including the chilling question: "How many victims did Glatman take?" As the author answered, no one knows. "From what we know about serial killers today," she wrote, "they approach dozens of women for every one who falls for their ruses and devices."

One woman who got away in time was Lorraine Vigil, the victim Glatman had attempted to kidnap and sexually assault in October 1958, when he was arrested in Orange County, California. According to the po-

Ophelia and Albert Glatman, Harvey Glatman's parents, are buried in the Mount Nebo Memorial Park Cemetery in Aurora, Colorado.

lice report, Glatman had driven the dark-haired, dark-eyed model southeast from Los Angeles on the Santa Ana Freeway, now Interstate 5. He exited on a road near the then three-year-old Disneyland Resort, drove a few hundred yards, and stopped his 1951 Dodge Coronet on the side of the road. There, he pulled out his Belgium Browning Automatic handgun, set it on the seat, and began to tie Lorraine's wrists with rope in order to, in his words, "get more assured of my control over her." She screamed and struggled and managed to grab the gun, which went off and grazed her leg.

Meanwhile, the passenger side door opened, the interior light came on, and Lorraine tumbled to the ground with Glatman on top of her. Moments later, a California State patrol officer drove by on his motorcycle, then turned around and came back and discovered Glatman struggling with his victim. Lorraine managed to get free, and Glatman did not put up a fight when the officer took him into custody. A search of his car revealed several links of rope, red rubber gloves, and a torn sheet knotted at both ends, apparently intended to be used as a mouth gag, as well as food, water, a camera, and $950 in cash.

The fortuitous arrival of the state trooper no doubt saved Lorraine's life, but three other known assaults by Glatman on California women had ended in their murders. One of the women he met through a "lonely hearts," or dating, club, and the other two through modeling agencies. He made up a story about being a photographer for a detective magazine and had the women pose with their wrists bound and gags in their mouths. Once they were under his control, however, he sexually assaulted them, and then he claimed he had no choice but to strangle them, with rope, to keep them from reporting him to the police.

Books and the internet told us more than we ever wanted to know about Glatman's last victims in California, but what I really needed was primary-source information on his earlier years when he lived in Denver, Colorado. Dave roughed out a timeline with the basic facts, and I agreed to fill in the gaps. I knew from California death records, accessible online, that Glatman had been born on December 10, 1927, in New York. From online federal census records, I learned that his parents were living in Denver when the census was taken in 1930. The same records revealed that the father, Albert Glatman, had been born in New York to Russian parents. The mother, Ophelia, was a native of Poland, and their son, Harvey, was an only child.

The family returned to New York in the early 1930s, but they permanently moved back to Denver in 1937, when Harvey Glatman was ten years old. In his teenage years, he earned spending money working as an usher at the Denver Auditorium, at Fourteenth and Curtis streets in downtown Denver. Ophelia was known to have been rather indulgent, which helps to explain why she would, years later, establish the Harvey M. Glatman Memorial Scholarship.

To research materials unavailable online, I went to the Colorado Historical Society's Stephen H. Hart Library, in Denver, to read through *Denver City Directories*. These annuals were compiled at the beginning of each calendar year and arranged by last names, and in addition to giving residential street addresses, they also listed places of employment. For most of the years, there were separate volumes called householders, or crisscross, directories that were arranged by address.

In the 1940 directory, I found Albert and Ophelia Glatman—obviously with Harvey, but children were not listed—living with Ophelia's older sister, Rosalie, in her home on East Fourteenth Avenue, a few blocks from Denver East High School, where Harvey soon would be enrolled. Then, in 1942, the Glatman family and Rosalie moved twenty-six blocks east to a brand-new two-bedroom ranch-style brick house at 1133 Kearney Street. This rapidly developing section of the Montclair neighborhood was south of Colfax Avenue and west of the Monaco Street Parkway. Although the house was still within Denver's city limits and easily accessible from downtown by bus—via the Capitol Hill neighborhood—it was almost as far east as Lowry Field, where the Army Air Corps was gearing up for World War II.

The Glatman parents and Rosalie most likely rode the bus into downtown Denver, where Albert sold cigars in the lobby of the eight-story Cooper Building, and Ophelia managed her sister's millinery store—the Rosalie Shop. In the years to come, Ophelia continued to work with her sister in the shop, renamed the Hollywood Millinery and located on Sixteenth Street—now a pedestrian mall—near Glenarm Place. By 1945, however, the year of Harvey Glatman's first arrests for robbery and assault, Albert had become a driver—first for Bill's Cab Company, then for Airport Transit, and finally for the Yellow Cab Company. I would learn a lot more about this family before I was through.

Meanwhile, many people interested in the Jane Doe case accessed the website, and many of the viewers posted messages. Whenever a new message was added, I automatically was notified by email. During the summer of 2005, several people asked about Marion Joan McDowell, the young woman abducted from Toronto and ruled out, along with Twylia May Embrey, by photo-superimposition. In the fall of 2005, my thoughts returned to Marion when I heard from her cousin, Susan Ridpath. She thanked all of the researchers for trying to find matches to unsolved cases and added, "Jane Doe's family, wherever they are, can take comfort that all the folks in Boulder have watched over her like guardian angels right here on earth." Of Marion, she wrote: "Not a day goes by that I don't wonder what on Earth happened to her. Even after all this time, I just hope that someday we will finally have an answer to where she is."

I emailed Susan independently of the message board and thanked her for contacting me. She replied that her mother and Marion's father were sister and brother. Susan had never met Marion, however, as she was born three years after Marion disappeared. Susan related that in recent years, her "Aunt Flo" and "Uncle Ross" both passed away, never knowing what had happened to their only daughter. In a subsequent email, Susan told me more about Ross McDowell, her favorite uncle.

"Although he towered over me, every inch of his six-foot-five-inch handsome frame was filled with goodness," she wrote, calling her Uncle Ross an incredibly kind man with a keen sense of humor and a sharp wit. Susan said he was also the smartest person she knew growing up and was always well-informed and well-read, whether the discussion was international politics, investments, or day-to-day goings on. "Over the years he became my soft place to land," she said, "and I miss him terribly."

Susan explained that the one thing she most remembered about her Uncle Ross—Marion's father—was the look he always had in his eyes. "Even if he was in the middle of a good belly laugh or just discussing some unimportant event," she said, "I know now what it was. I have, thank God, only seen it in a few other people since, and I pray I never see it again. I saw his broken heart reflected in those gentle, kind, blue eyes."

Marion's cousin went on to tell me that during the time she was growing up, her uncle never spoke of Marion—except on the fiftieth anniversary of her kidnapping. On that day, he broke down in tears and told Susan's mother that the worst part of the ordeal was that he probably would go to his grave without ever knowing what had happened to his beautiful daughter. That was exactly what happened. Only after the deaths of his parents did Marion's brother, Ross McDowell, Jr., talk with family members about the tragedy. Previously, his sister's abduction had been too painful, even for a sibling. "All of us now have pictures of Marion on our mantels and tabletops," added Susan, "something we would never have done before."

Was Jane Doe's family doing the same thing? In October 2005, I grew more hopeful of someday getting the answers when Fred Peabody, the new

America's Most Wanted producer, brought his film crew to Boulder for that year's "Meet the Spirits" reenactment in Columbia Cemetery. Twylia May Embrey's great-niece, Jennifer Kitt, came, too, from Nebraska, and she was filmed and interviewed, as well. With tears in her eyes, Jennifer watched as the portrayer of Jane Doe continued to draw crowds. Again I acted the role of the Victorian professor—this time captured on camera.

In early November, Detective Steve Ainsworth called Jennifer to tell her that the mitochondrial DNA profile of Jane Doe had been completed, and Twylia was finally ruled out as a match. The result, again, provided comfort to Jennifer and her grandmother, Midge, but my feelings were a little more complicated, as I had hoped to have had Jane Doe identified. If Twylia had been the victim, I envisioned accompanying her remains to the little Maywood Cemetery in Nebraska—even though, in the back of my mind, were the warnings from well-meaning people who told me that sometimes those who leave home do not want to be reunited with their families.

At the same time, I had become emotionally involved with Twylia's family. I was happy for them that—finally—after the photo-superimposition and comparisons with two separate and different DNA profiles, they could rest assured that Twylia and Jane Doe were not one and the same. But we still were faced with the question of what had happened to the runaway Nebraska farm girl. If she was alive, where was she? Micki, Jennifer, and I had not stopped in our search to bring closure for the Embrey family. At home, in the evenings, I continued to listen to the Fleetwoods' song, "Tragedy," which reminded me of Jane Doe, but I also liked to play one of Twylia's favorites—the Roy Rogers tune "Don't Fence Me In." Whenever I was near Columbia Cemetery, I stopped to visit Jane Doe's empty grave and my thoughts went out to both of these young women.

With the very real possibility, again, that Twylia was alive, her family members put aside their nagging doubts about her wishes and set their hearts on a reunion. I, too, continued to work behind the scenes, searching for contact information while Jennifer and Micki called many more women in their seventies named "Twylia." At no charge, forensic artist Frank Bender even provided the Embrey family with an age-progression drawing.

Micki, Jennifer, and I corresponded about Twylia, while I corresponded with Dave, Cindi, Micki, and a new researcher from Michigan, Karen Anne Nicholas, to update our list of missing women and research the twisted life of Harvey Glatman. At this time, I realized I had taken on three mysteries: Where was Twylia May Embrey, who was Jane Doe, and was

Harvey Glatman her murderer? In my mountaintop home west of Boulder, I felt as if I was in an airport control tower as three planes prepared to land at the same time.

Glatman was never far from the top of my priorities. I still had hopes of finding Jane Doe's original case file and/or anything at all that might shed light on her murder. My husband was reading *The Evil That Men Do: FBI Profiler Roy Hazelwood's Journey into the Minds of Sexual Predators*, by Stephen G. Michaud with Roy Hazelwood. The book included a chapter on Glatman, referred to by Hazelwood as "the lonely hearts killer" because of his contact with this type of dating club.

I wrote to Hazelwood, who suggested that I contact Pierce Brooks, a legend in police circles and the man who was the lead investigator of the Los Angeles Police Department in 1958, the time of Glatman's arrest. Brooks had been tracing Shirley Ann Bridgeford, a missing young woman who turned out to be one of Glatman's victims. Brooks's work eventually led to the founding of ViCAP—the Violent Criminal Apprehension Program— put in place by the Federal Bureau of Investigation to identify cases exhibiting similar characteristics.

Brooks was quoted as saying: "Murder is the greatest challenge. You can't close your mind. You have to wonder what kind of person would act like this. You have to get inside the killer's brain." The comment reminded me of the Scotland Yard detective, Robert Fabian, who had traveled to Toronto in the Marion Joan McDowell case and said, "Keep your eyes and ears open and use your brain."

Roy Hazelwood had lost track of Brooks, but he did tell me that the investigator had been a police chief in Springfield, Oregon. In attempting to trace Brooks there, I learned that he had died in 1998, but I ended up talking on the telephone with Sergeant John Umenhofer, who told me that his father and Brooks had been close friends. The sergeant also told me that before Brooks died, he showed up at the Springfield police station one day and gave the officer all of his personal files, including those on Harvey Glatman. The sergeant and I talked several more times on the telephone, and I filled him in on the Jane Doe case. I assumed that the files would primarily be about the murdered California women, but I still thought there was a possibility that they could include the missing Jane Doe file that Sheriff Art Everson had sent to the California authorities.

I asked Sergeant Umenhofer to tell me if he had anything that pertained to our case in Colorado. A few weeks after our initial conversation, he emailed me to say that he had gone through the Glatman files, and they all did pertain to the murders in California but, if I liked, he would box them up and mail them to me. "They need to go where they will do the most good—to a tenacious investigator," he told me. "That's what Brooks would have wanted. Now it's all on your shoulders."

The next time we talked, he commented that he still thought it was amazing that he happened to be the watch commander the day that I called and asked about Pierce Brooks. "No one else would have known about the Glatman files other than me," he said. When the box of police reports and onion-skin-paper copies of Glatman's original confessions arrived on my doorstep, I tried not to get my hopes up that they would help in the Jane Doe case, but I started reading—and I could not stop.

The unusual package arrived during one of the United States Post Office's busiest times—the weekend before Christmas. The more I read, the more angered and shocked I was by the atrocities Glatman had committed, from sexually assaulting women at gunpoint to hog-tying and strangling them. Still, I was unable to set the box aside. Accompanying black-and-white photographs were equally compelling, as they showed extremely frightened women in the moments before their deaths. Glatman was in some of the photographs, too, and he struck me as a creepy-looking, slightly built thirty-year-old with oversized ears.

Finally I had to put the files away, as I had agreed to meet my youngest daughter—and her second child—at a *Messiah* sing-along at St. John's Episcopal Church in Boulder. In previous years, we both had sung in the choir, but this time we preferred to listen, and participate, with the audience. The music lifted my spirits during the performance, but I knew there were horrors waiting for me on my desk at home.

In the midst of page after page of Glatman's transcribed confessions concerning the murders of the California women, he answered a few questions about his life in Denver in the mid-1950s. Here was some Colorado information, after all, and it would prove to be very helpful. I learned that it was while he lived in Denver—*not* after his later move to California—that Glatman began to present himself to women as a detective magazine photographer, even though he did not specify any particular magazine and no photographs of his ever were published. At least part of his modus operandi, or "mode of operation," of tying up women and photographing them was already in place at the time of Jane Doe's murder. Did he murder women in Denver, as well? Did he kill Jane Doe?

The detective magazine angle continued to intrigue me, too, as I was still on the lookout for the article on the "battered blonde of Boulder Bend," recommended by the pathologist, Dr. Freburn L. James. I finally found it as "I'll Be Back in a Coffin," in the July 1954 issue of *Inside Detective*.

The person who went home in a coffin was Bruce Weibel, the man who had been murdered in April 1954 by James W. Hutchins, the absent-without-leave hitchhiker. Weibel was the father of Debbie, the woman who had contacted me at the time of Jane Doe's exhumation. Since Hutchins initially had been arrested for questioning in connection with the Jane Doe case, the *Inside Detective* magazine article contained several pages about her murder, too, specifically referring to the victim as "the battered blonde of Boulder Bend." I mailed a copy to Dr. James, and we talked on the telephone after it arrived. He agreed that it was the story he remembered and said: "I hope you can pull the rabbit out of the hat." One of the main reasons Dr. James had remembered the article was because he had been quoted in it. In a section describing the blow to the victim's head, as well as the fractures on the left side of her body, he had told the magazine's reporter, "She could have been struck by a car."

After Harvey Glatman's arrest, in 1958, his interrogator asked him about the women who had posed for him in Denver, wanting to know what I wanted to know—specifically, were the women dead or alive? Glatman's answer was "Unless they've been run over." In light of Jane Doe's fractured kneecap, which had led to the "bumper theory" that was embraced by the forensic experts who believed the killer may have hit her with his car—and then the original pathologist's very same comment—Glatman's remarks jumped right off the page at me! It was almost as if he had admitted his guilt to running down Jane Doe and leaving her to die.

I dropped off copies of the file for Lieutenant Phil West and Detective Steve Ainsworth. I also left a note asking if they agreed.

12

While I waited for their feedback, I reread the *Inside Detective* article. It echoed Sheriff Art Everson's previously published comments of claiming to have checked out all reports of missing young women whose description was "anywhere near right." I was not so sure, however, that he actually did, and I speculated that he may have conducted a too narrowly focused investigation. Denver resident Katharine Dyer had been reported missing in March 1954—and she was still missing when the detective magazine hit the newsstands four months later—yet the sheriff dismissed her because of her estimated height and Jane Doe's estimated age.

At the coroner's inquest for Jane Doe, a dentist had estimated the victim's age as nineteen to twenty, based on what appeared to him to be a half-grown-in third molar, or wisdom tooth. Katharine's missing-persons report stated her age as twenty-four. The four-year difference was emphasized by the detective magazine writer as enough to disqualify her from further consideration. Similarly, Katharine's height was referenced by a syndicated United Press reporter who quoted the sheriff saying that, at "five-foot-six-inches," Katharine was too tall. Unless the woman's landlady, who initially reported her missing, had measured her tenant herself, how would she know her exact height? Maybe the missing woman had worn high heels when she came home from work or went out in the evening. I questioned both Jane Doe's age and Katharine's height and wondered if the Denver woman had slipped through the cracks.

Every month or so for the previous two years, I had shared my latest findings with Lieutenant Phil West, but instead of embracing me as a partner—as I had naively hoped after our one-day field trip to Denver—both Lieutenant West and Detective Ainsworth kept a professional distance. By December 2005, the lieutenant remained cordial and made time to fit me into his busy schedule, but I rarely saw the detective at all. When I walked into the sheriff's office with the Glatman files, I had hopes of meeting with both men, but the detective was out for Christmas vacation. At the time, I did not think any more about it.

In late January 2006, producer Fred Peabody and the film crew from *America's Most Wanted* again came to Boulder, this time for two days of filming. For the first time in my life I was shadowed. As he followed me around, the producer instructed me to change my clothes five times so it would look as if he had been following me even longer. The camera and sound man tagged along, too, as I stopped at the archives at the *Daily Camera*, went to the Carnegie Branch Library for Local History, visited Jane Doe's empty grave at the cemetery, and looked again at the crime scene in Boulder Canyon. For a few extra sound bites, the men even set up their equipment in my mountain home and filmed me for five straight hours—with and without our two cats, with and without a cup of tea, in my home office, at the dining room table, and in the living room in front of our woodburning stove.

On the morning of the second day, we assembled at the Boulder County Sheriff's Office. The producer seated Phil West—whose title had been changed to commander—Detective Steve Ainsworth, and me around a small round table in the training room. The three of us were placed into the discussion-style setting I had envisioned when I first approached the officers with the case. I assumed that when the show aired, the television viewers would, ironically, think that we casually sat around and debated the case all the time.

At the time of our meeting, both the commander and the detective had read the Glatman files. Commander West had emailed me, calling the new information "fascinating," but I was not aware of the detective's opinion at all. None of our conversation was rehearsed. I was apprehensive that one or the other or both of the men might not consider Glatman a suspect, as I did. In front of the rolling cameras, however, Detective Ainsworth told me that he agreed that Glatman may have been Jane Doe's killer, and that Glatman very likely may have hit her with his car.

The three of us discussed several scenarios, including the possibility that Jane Doe could have escaped from Glatman's 1951 Dodge during a sexual assault, just as Lorraine Vigil, his last assault victim, had done in California. For Jane Doe, however, no passing motorist came along to intervene. She may have started running down the narrow shoulder of the mountain road, and Glatman could have run into her, knocking her down the embankment to the edge of Boulder Creek. She had been found naked, so we gathered that if Glatman had not completely disrobed her in his car, he might have stripped her afterward, so as to remove anything that might lead to her identity.

Commander West said that his initial take was that Glatman was worth pursuing, but he was mystified as to why the man would willingly confess to three murders in California and not to any others that he might have perpetrated. "It's not like Colorado was going to do anything worse to him than California did," he commented. Then the commander surmised that if Glatman had followed the newspaper reports, perhaps he felt guilty about leaving his victim to suffer death by exposure since he had said, in his confession of his other murders, that he had tried to make his victims' deaths as painless and quick as possible. I brought up Glatman's relationship with his mother, interjecting the possibility that perhaps he only confessed to the murders in California—a place where he no longer had been under her supervision. Our conversation became so animated that we almost forgot that our every word and movement was being recorded on film. Which of the sound bites would the viewers get?

At a later date, Commander West told a reporter that a lot of circumstantial evidence pointed in the direction of Glatman as Jane Doe's killer. "If this was a current investigation, a current event," he said, "Glatman would figure very prominently as a suspect."

Sergeant John Umenhofer and I continued to discuss Glatman and Jane Doe, as well. The Oregon officer who had sent me the Glatman files said, "Glatman may well have been the killer. The fact that he had no reason not to confess to additional murders means almost nothing," adding that, in his experience, he had seen a multitude of killers who only confessed to the crimes they thought the police could prove and nothing more. He also related his advice to new patrol officers: "Don't think how you would do something, think how a screwed-up rapist would do it, or a heroin addict. Sometimes they don't make sense in our world."

As the Jane Doe case began to focus on Harvey Glatman, my husband—always an avid reader—went on a Glatman-related publications buying spree on the internet. Some of his purchases were recent books, including Michael Newton's *Rope: The Twisted Life and Crimes of Harvey Glatman*, whereas other more obscure finds included long out-of-print magazines, including two from England and one from France. While other wives were receiving valentines, my mailbox was filling up with serial-killer literature. It was okay with me, as I hoped the written materials would provide some clues as to whether Glatman was indeed Jane Doe's murderer.

Reading through the original files, as well as all the new material, I still did not know much about Glatman's years in Denver, particularly during the late 1940s and early 1950s. To begin, I requested Glatman's arrest record from the Denver Police Department. When the one-page printout arrived in the mail, I first read his description. In 1945, Glatman was five feet nine inches, weighed 160 pounds, and had brown hair and brown eyes. The sheet also gave booking dates and dispositions—two from Denver and one from Boulder. I called the Denver Police Department and asked a records clerk if she had files on these arrests, but she told me that all cases more than ten years old had been purged. To emphasize her point, the woman on the other end of the line said, "There is no additional information available, anywhere."

When I got off the telephone, I noticed the fine print on the bottom of the page which read: "Where disposition is not shown or further explanation of a charge or disposition is desired, contact the county or district court, in whose office a final disposition occurred." I knew from earlier research I had done at the Colorado State Archives that the Denver repository kept records of many old court cases. At the time of Jane Doe's murder, Boulder County—along with Weld, Larimer, and Jackson counties—was part of Colorado's Eighth Judicial District. Maybe records on these cases existed after all. I called the state archives to ask and was told that all I needed were the case numbers.

I thought I would start with the Boulder file, but getting the case number was not an easy task. Boulder County is now its own district—the Twentieth Judicial District—and when I filed a written request at the court's location on the first floor of the Boulder County Justice Center, a clerk told me that she had no record of the case number at all. Then I again called the state archives, and a librarian told me there was no cross-reference within the archives' own system. Without a number, it was impossible to locate a court file. Finally, another of the state librarians said that since the Boulder District Court did not have the index to the 1940s-era cases, there was a possibility that the old leather-bound ledger book might be in the archives' off-site storage in the eastern Colorado town of Simla. Once every six weeks, one of the librarians made the day-long drive to access the archives' least-requested records—housed in a rat-infested former grain-storage building. No one would be going there again, I was told, for at least a month.

While I waited, I stopped at the Boulder Police Department to see if it, like the Denver Police, had an arrest record for Glatman. A clerk found his original "Arrest Card," also from 1945, and after blacking out his name and the name of the victim, as she was required to do, she gave me a copy. From that, I had confirmation that the then seventeen-year-old Harvey Glatman was a single white male and a United States citizen, living with his parents in Denver. His occupation was given as student, and in a place for "nativity" was written "Jewish." His Boulder arrest was for "molesting women," although the rap sheet that had come with the original Glatman files referred to his Boulder charge as "girl trouble." The July 15, 1945 assault occurred in the 1700 block of Thirteenth Street, between Arapahoe Avenue and the railroad tracks that ran on what is now Canyon Boulevard.

I had read a biography of Glatman on Court TV's website, and it listed his Boulder victim as "Norene Laurel." The arrest card, with her name blacked out, gave her address as 954 Marine Street. When I could not find the last name of "Laurel" in the *Daily Camera* files, I looked up her address in the 1945 *Boulder City Directory*. The young woman actually was twenty-four-year-old "Norene Lauer." From then on, for my own research, I resolved to stick to primary sources, rather than often incorrect internet write-ups. From newspaper accounts, I learned that Norene's husband Orville was in the United States Navy at the time, in boot camp at the Great Lakes Training Station in Illinois. The couple had two young children and lived in an apartment in the rear of Orville's parents' home.

From additional articles, I pieced together, as best I could, what had happened on that summer night in Boulder. A headline in the *Daily Camera*'s July 18 edition read: "Boulder Girl Unhurt in Strange Kidnapping Case—Youth Forces Young Mother to Hike into Mountains with Him." While Glatman was free on bail following an even-earlier arrest for assaulting Denver women, he took an hour-or-so bus ride to Boulder, carrying with him a bag with a gun and rope. He got off the bus at Boulder's Union Pacific Railroad Depot, which doubled as a bus station and was located, at the time, on a cul-de-sac on Fourteenth Street. Then he walked west for a block and south for half a block and lurked outside the City Storage Company building—now an art gallery—on Thirteenth Street, across from Boulder's Central Park.

Norene, meanwhile, had been to a downtown movie in one of the two theaters on Fourteenth Street and started to walk home alone. Two films were shown that Sunday evening, so she, perhaps with wives of other servicemen, had a choice of *Hollywood Canteen* or *Bride by Mistake*. If Norene picked the 1944 comedy *Bride by Mistake*, she might have left with what its newspaper advertisements promised—a "risky frisky feeling"—certainly nothing to make her fear walking the few blocks to Marine Street.

Suddenly, Glatman stepped out from an alley, holding his gun and announcing, "This is a stickup." He then forced Norene to walk between the buildings with him, where he bound and gagged her and left her lying on the ground. Glatman then disappeared for a few minutes, but he watched her from the shadows.

The young woman managed to wiggle loose from the ropes on her hands and feet and started to run, but Glatman grabbed her. Norene later told a reporter that her attacker was extremely angry, and he bound and gagged her again. This time he left her for about an hour. No one walked by or saw either of them. About midnight, Glatman returned and loosened the bonds around her ankles, but he kept her wrists tied. Then he forced her, at gunpoint, to walk thirteen blocks to the western city limits and then two miles up Sunshine Canyon Drive, into the foothills of the Rocky Mountains.

Glatman kept Norene captive throughout the night. Later reports indicated that he fondled her but did not rape her. The next morning, according to the *Daily Camera*, he returned her "unharmed," although her hours of fear and the likely endurance of sexual molestation would have been horrific. At a later date, much would be written about Glatman's obsession to control women in order to gain sexual gratification.

In the morning, Glatman walked his victim, at gunpoint, out of the mountains and back into the city limits of Boulder. It must not have occurred to him that Norene or anyone else would turn him in, as he arrogantly hailed a cab and told the driver to take the young woman to her home and to drop him off at the depot to catch the next bus for Denver. Norene, however, did call the police with Glatman's description, and Boulder's Police Chief Art Masters arrested him two days later, in Denver. In addition to kidnapping and assaulting his victim, Glatman had also stolen two dollars from her purse. Anxious to know what happened next, I soon learned that the court case that followed would overlap other arrests and court cases, and the legal entanglements would provide logistical conflicts in the months to come.

Research, at least for me, often has many tangents, and some are serendipitous. On a cold snowy day in early February 2006, I was contacted by a young woman who was visiting Colorado to learn more about the 1948 murder of her great-aunt, Theresa Foster. The family relative approached her research in the same dedicated manner as Jennifer Kitt, who—with Micki and me—still searched for the whereabouts of her great-aunt, Twylia May Embrey. But like the family of Toronto abductee Marion Joan McDowell, part of Theresa's family refused to talk about the once bright and attractive freshman engineering student at the University of Colorado. The murder victim had come from a big family and was the youngest of twelve children of an onion farmer in Greeley, Colorado. Although Norene Lauer's overnight abduction, three years before Theresa Foster's murder, had been described by a newspaper reporter as "stranger than fiction," Theresa's murder was unprecedented in the previously small and quiet community.

On the night Theresa was murdered, she had left a Catholic youth group meeting at ten o'clock in the evening in Boulder's University Hill neighborhood. She disappeared while walking north on Broadway, the city's main north-south street, on her way to a private residence on Spruce Street where she boarded in the home of a psychologist and his family. Her killer must have offered her a ride, as police later determined that she was raped and then strangled with her own jacket on a then-deserted road north of town. She had also been bludgeoned with a "blunt instrument," assumed to have been a .45 automatic pistol. Its grips and magazine clip were found at the scene of the crime.

Two days later, rabbit hunters found Theresa's half-nude and beaten body where it had been dumped on the other side of town—several miles south of Boulder. The rest of the pistol was found at that second crime scene. I invited Alan Cass to meet with Theresa's great-niece and me as we shared information. Alan, I had come to learn, was a walking encyclopedia—not only on the murders of Jane Doe and University of Colorado student Elaura Jaquette, but on Theresa Foster, as well.

A local sheet metal worker named Joe Sam Walker was arrested and imprisoned for Theresa's murder, but his guilt was based on circumstantial evidence and was widely debated by newspaper writers. Walker did admit that he had transported the young woman's body in the trunk of his car from one side of Boulder to the other, but he said she had been killed by a "blonde stocky youth" who got away. Reporters from the *Denver Post* took over a whole floor of the Hotel Boulderado. In November 1948, after Theresa's murder, these Denver newspaper writers even hired fiction writer Erle Stanley Gardner to present the murder scene as it would have appeared to his lead character Perry Mason.

After the publication of Gardner's "The Case of the Shanghaied Coed," a disgusted Boulder resident wrote a letter to the editor of the *Daily Camera* saying that the newspapers were making a sideshow attraction of Boulder's tragedy. "By printing half-truths, theories, and playing up obscure facts that may be sensational," stated the letter-writer, "these newspapers are appealing to morbid curiosity, which probably sells newspapers but is not fair to the victim, to her family, to Boulder, to the University, and to justice." The media situation reminded me of Robert Fabian's intervention in Marion Joan McDowell's abduction in Toronto.

In May 1949, Joe Sam Walker was sentenced to eighty years to life in the Colorado State Penitentiary. After twenty years, however, the Colorado Supreme Court overturned his conviction due to his claims of adverse pretrial publicity. In 1969, Walker left prison and worked as a watch repairman. He maintained his innocence until 1982, when he left a suicide note before he hanged himself in a Waco, Texas, motel room. His wife had long since divorced him, and his only known relative refused to claim his body.

While searching for more information on Jane Doe, I had interviewed the widow of Boulder Police Detective Roy Hill—one of the officers who went to the Boulder Canyon crime scene—and our conversation had turned to Walker. The widow had no new information on Jane Doe, but she told me that her husband believed Walker was "guilty as sin." She reminded me that he had awaited trial in the Boulder County Jail during the 1948 Christmas season. At the time, the jail was on the fifth floor of the art deco–style Boulder County Courthouse, in the heart of downtown Boulder. Sheriff Art Everson and his family also lived on the fifth floor, in an apartment that adjoined the jail. The sheriff's wife cooked meals for the handful of prisoners, and she and her two children slid their trays through small slits in the heavy metal cell doors. The family also was in charge of playing Christmas music, amplified at full volume for the benefit of downtown holiday shoppers. According to the information that filtered back to Detective Hill's widow, the music nearly drove Walker crazy.

Walker's prison term overlapped the date that Jane Doe had been murdered, so he was not a suspect in her case. But his trial fascinated Alan and me, and we combined our unanswered questions on Joe Sam Walker and the murder of Theresa Foster with my search for Harvey Glatman's court records. A month after my initial request for the district court number on the Norene Lauer case, a librarian from the Colorado State Archives informed me that, sure enough, several large, dusty, leather-bound ledgers—containing indexes of all Boulder criminal cases from 1921 to 1960—had been found in the off-site storage facility. A kind employee managed to haul them to the Denver repository.

I met Alan at his home in Boulder and we drove the thirty miles to downtown Denver. By the time we found a parking place and entered the tall brick office building, one block from the Colorado State Capitol, an hour had passed. We were glad we had packed lunches in order to make the most use of our time. Once in the windowless basement, I opened the long-sought index that included the year 1945 and found exactly what I was looking for—"People vs. Harvey M. Glatman, Robbery Case No. 2881." I settled in for a day of reading.

Although the archives were vast, the research room was small, with four basic utilitarian tables, grey metal microfilm cabinets, and a few microfilm and microfiche readers. Seemingly out of place, one whole wall was covered with a large color photograph of a Colorado mountain scene dominated with yellow aspen trees. Also unrelated to the basic and otherwise nondescript décor was a grandfather clock that chimed every hour, with one additional chime on the half hour. Hearing the increasing numbers of chimes forced me to reevaluate how much more reading I needed to accomplish before closing time. Except for a few people who came and left during the day, Alan and I were the archives' only patrons.

While Alan opened and read from one of four boxes of original transcripts of Joe Sam Walker's trial in the murder of Theresa Foster, I dug into the newly found Glatman records, where I learned more about Norene Lauer's assault in Boulder. After Boulder Police Chief Masters arrested Glatman in Denver and then transported him back to Boulder, he turned him over to Boulder County Sheriff Art Everson, who held him for six days on the fifth floor of the Boulder County Courthouse.

At the Colorado State Archives, the author researched documents from Harvey Glatman's district court case in Boulder. Photo courtesy of Alan Cass.

On July 23, 1945, Glatman was moved down to the third floor of the courthouse, where he appeared in district court. Meanwhile, Albert and Ophelia Glatman had retained, as their son's attorney, a short bald man and former Colorado state legislator, Ira L. Quiat. Most likely, he was also a personal friend, as he lived in the Glatmans' Denver neighborhood and was part of their Jewish community.

The deputy district attorney announced that Glatman, armed with a loaded revolver, took Norene Lauer's purse, valued at three dollars, as well as the two dollars in cash. From reading the court papers, I learned, too, that Norene had testified, along with Boulder Police Chief Masters and two of his officers. Instead of an assault charge, however, Boulder's district attorney filed a charge of armed robbery and was quoted, at the time, as saying that the evidence for robbery was the strongest case he could make. Glatman did not stay behind bars, however, even with the sheriff's wife's home cooking. On the day of his hearing, his parents paid the five-thousand-dollar bail and tried to take him home but, somehow, he managed to run off on his own.

A week later, however, Glatman showed up in court again. This time the Honorable Claude C. Coffin wasted no time in signing a court order committing Glatman to the Colorado Psychopathic Hospital for "as long as it takes to determine his exact mental condition." The psychopathic hospital had opened in 1924 and was part of the Colorado General Hospital complex in Denver, midway between the Glatman family's Kearney Street home and the Capitol Hill neighborhood where, I would learn, the perpetrator spent a good deal of his time.

I was pleased to read in the court records the correct spelling of Norene's last name, as I was able to trace her through public records and learn that she eventually remarried and moved to Lafayette, Colorado. She died there, in 1979, at the age of fifty-eight. In the days to come, I contacted her two grown children who still live in the Boulder area, and I gave them copies of the articles and documents on their mother. When Norene's daughter and I met face-to-face in Boulder, she told me that her mother had never mentioned the incident. "I always felt, however, that there was a secret between her and her mother, my grandmother," the daughter told me. "Now I know what it was."

Glatman's doctors knew early on that their patient had mental problems, but they were puzzled as to what they were. On August 24, after he examined Glatman, Dr. J. P. Hilton wrote to attorney Quiat that, in the doctor's opinion, Glatman had schizophrenia, characterized by bizarre thoughts and behavior. The doctor added that his conduct had been abnormal for a number of years, and that he forced women to either undress or to stay with him, but he claimed not to have sexually "attacked" them—using the euphemism, in use at the time, for rape. Glatman talked freely with the doctor about the incidents, but he did not give any reasonable explanation. "It is this disparity between action and thought," wrote Dr. Hilton, "which makes it evident that he has a mental condition since there is no other way to account for these things happening."

Dr. Hilton added that a prison sentence would be of no benefit to Glatman because he would be exposed to the influence of criminals "who would teach him things about sex and robbery which he has never thought of." Instead, the doctor recommended that Glatman be placed under the care of a psychiatrist and kept in an institution for a period of time. "If his condition is improved," the doctor stated, "he can then be discharged. If not, he can become a ward of the state."

In September 1945, Dr. Hilton's colleague, Dr. Charles A. Rymer, acting director of the psychopathic hospital, also weighed in with his own letter to attorney Quiat. Dr. Rymer said that Glatman no longer had any rapport with his parents and particularly resented his father, but he was unable to determine if the father-son hostilities were an underlying cause of Glatman's behavior. The second doctor also agreed that Glatman was unmoved by the seriousness of his crimes, and he was oblivious to the fact that he could straighten out his life. Instead, he simply admitted his guilt and accepted the fact that he should be punished. In his interviews, the doctor learned that the teenager had been bored with high school and started breaking into houses—for the thrills both in anticipating each crime and in recalling them afterward. In his second break-in, he stole the gun which he then used to control his victims, including Norene Lauer.

Dr. Rymer also spoke of Glatman's superior intelligence. "He has an IQ which places him in the very superior group of individuals," the doctor wrote. "One shudders as to the type of crime Harvey may engage in should his genius be used along criminal lines." Dr. Rymer recommended that a competent psychiatrist, "preferably of the Jewish race," needed to "take this boy in toe [sic]."

As I continued to read, I became increasingly curious about Glatman's other assaults. I wanted to read about them, too, but the chimes on the grandfather clock in the archives grew longer as the afternoon wore on. Soon it was time to go home, but Alan and I returned once a week for three weeks. On our drives between Boulder and Denver, we discussed the newly revealed information in Glatman's court records. We commented that the murder of Jane Doe—in 1954—fell right between Glatman's early assaults on women and the three murders to which he had confessed, in California, in 1958.

Jane Doe could easily have been the first woman he killed.

13

In March 2006, I got a sudden jolt back to the present when a Google Alert revealed that Detective Steve Ainsworth had made the same comment on the televised evening news. Months before *America's Most Wanted* would get its program out to a national audience, the detective had gone public with the Glatman-as-perpetrator theory. "We're looking at a serial killer from California from the late 1950s by the name of Harvey Glatman," he told a broadcast reporter, who then explained that Glatman had lived in Denver at the time Jane Doe's body was found, and that he had previously abducted a woman in Boulder. Of that victim, Norene Lauer, Detective Ainsworth added, "I think he was kind of honing his craft."

Next, I read online that a Nebraska reporter announced that the Boulder County Sheriff's Office had identified Harvey Glatman as a suspect. The story read, in part, "Photos of Jane Doe showed ligature mark[s] on the left wrist," and went on to explain that, according to Detective Ainsworth, the possible indentations from a rope were consistent with the way Glatman tied his later victims. This, I believed, was true, but I was surprised that knowledge of the resurfaced morgue photographs and their interpretation had so quickly become public knowledge.

I also learned that Detective Ainsworth had located a 1951 Dodge Coronet—the same kind of car Glatman drove—and had obtained the measurements of the front bumper. In the "bumper-theory" scenario, in which Jane Doe's kneecap could have been fractured by the impact of a car, the horizontal chrome on the Dodge aligned perfectly. When I had measured car bumpers, no Dodge Coronets were available.

On Alan's and my second visit to the state archives, I got bogged down in all of the legal documents and correspondence in Glatman's file and felt the need to make a chronology. I knew a lot about his Boulder

155

arrest, but not his first arrest, in Denver. It was time for me to go to the Denver District Court and start reading the unpublished court records from the beginning. That was when I first learned about Eula Jo Hand—Glatman's first known assault victim—and I knew I had to find her.

The Denver District Court is in the same Denver City and County Building where I had read Ophelia Glatman's will, but the district court office was much more crowded than probate court. Unlike court records from most of the rest of Colorado, Denver's records from the 1940s and 1950s were still housed in their original location in the district court's office. At the Colorado State Archives, however, I had found a slip of paper mixed in with Glatman's Boulder case that read, "Denver case #36756, People vs. Harvey Glatman." This really helped when I went to the Denver District Court, waited in line, and then told a clerk what I hoped to find. When I showed him the number, I was immediately led behind the main desk to a tiny cubicle with a table, a chair, and an outdated microfilm reader. Left alone for as long as I wanted, I cranked a reel of film that, probably, no one had looked at for decades. I also found more documents that Glatman's biographers had missed.

I started with Glatman's first arrest—on May 18, 1945. The "armed robbery" of which he was accused had occurred two weeks earlier, on May 4. As the seventeen-year-old entered into a life of crime, many of his male classmates at Denver East High School had forsaken graduation to march off to war in Europe and the Pacific. According to the court records, Glatman was accused of assaulting Eula Jo Hand, at gunpoint, and robbing her of her purse, eighteen streetcar tokens, and fourteen dollars and ninety-five cents. From what I had learned about the "robbery" of Norene Lauer in Boulder, I assumed there was more to Eula Jo's story.

In reading the court documents, I learned that Ophelia Glatman bailed out her son three days after his arrest. She alone—not Glatman's father, Albert—made the two-thousand-dollar payment in three separate certified checks. While Glatman was out on bond, the court deposed Eula Jo. Other than police officers, the additional "witnesses for the people" were Dorothy Holder, Doris Lukman, Anna Mae Barr, and Rosemary Clement. All, like Eula Jo, lived in or near Denver's Capitol Hill neighborhood. Most were other victims, but one may have been a woman who overheard Eula Jo's attack.

The Capitol Hill neighborhood is one of Denver's oldest. Technically bounded by Broadway on the west, Colfax on the north, Eighth Avenue on the south, and Downing Street on the east, it boasts a number of well-known landmarks, including the Colorado State Capitol, itself, with the building's thirteenth step exactly one mile above sea level. Another prominent building is at 1340 Pennsylvania Avenue—the former home, and now a museum, of "unsinkable" Molly Brown, best known for surviving the *Titanic* in 1912, when the transatlantic ocean liner hit an iceberg and sank on its maiden voyage. Molly and some of her neighbors may have been well-to-do but, by the 1940s, the neighborhood included low-rent apartments as well. Many of the homeowners found ways to use their then-aging late-nineteenth-century homes to bring in extra income. Some rented out extra rooms, while Eula Jo's mother, a nurse, turned her Clarkson Street residence into a convalescent home.

As the bills piled up for Glatman's parents, the teenager was in and out of jail, in and out of court, and in and out of the psychopathic hospital. To make his situation even more complicated, Glatman held up, stripped, bound, and robbed two additional Denver women in September 1945, while he was out on bond for the third time within four months. On the same night as his third arrest, he even admitted to molesting yet another woman, who screamed and ran out of her house. After he was caught, he again was confined in the Denver County Jail.

The third arrest gave Dr. Hilton another chance to examine Glatman, and he soon found himself the sole witness in Glatman's defense in his November 1945 trial in the case of Eula Jo Hand and two other women. In his testimony, the psychiatrist reiterated his diagnosis of schizophrenia and added that he believed Glatman had a chance of complete recovery—if he were to receive shock treatments by insulin injection. This drastic form of psychiatric treatment, repeated day after day, put its patients into one- or two-hour comas. Dr. Hilton commented that Glatman might even "snap out of his present mental condition" without treatment, but he thought it unlikely.

Glatman pled guilty to the Denver assaults and, at the same time, the Boulder court extended the bond in the case of Norene Lauer. A newspaper writer in the Denver courtroom reported that the deposition of one woman was given, along with the testimony of two others. Had Eula Jo been in the courtroom, or was only her deposition presented to the judge? According to the reports, she and two other women had accused Glatman of following them as they alighted from buses and streetcars. He then forced them, at pistol-point, into alleys or their own homes, where he bound, gagged, partially disrobed, and fondled them.

All this reading about Glatman's attacks made me wonder, again, how I would find Eula Jo. I wanted to hear the story directly from her, because I figured that her experience would shed light on the murder of Jane Doe.

I threw my question out to my fellow researchers and, as usual, Dave was on top of my request. He read everything he could online and managed to find a family member of an unnamed survivor of a Harvey Glatman attack. Dave forwarded to me the name of the family member, and I contacted him. Sure enough, he said, Eula Jo, now called Jody, was his grandmother, and she was alive and well in Tucson, Arizona. She had remarried and had a different last name, but he gave me her current name and telephone number, and soon I was talking with the surviving victim herself. "Wow," emailed Dave when I told him, "I feel like we hit the jackpot."

I felt that way, too. My first telephone conversation with Eula Jo lasted for about an hour, and we started with the basics. She was born in Kansas and her father, a conductor on the Santa Fe Railroad, had died when she was a young child. Her mother remarried, and the family moved around the Midwest and West, finally settling on Clarkson Street, in the Capitol Hill neighborhood of Denver.

In May 1945, at the time of Eula Jo's attack, she, like Glatman, was seventeen years old. She, too, had attended Denver East High School but dropped out in her junior year. "I thought I was so smart," the elderly woman told me in that first telephone conversation. "I lied about my age and got a job at Neusteter's, a women's clothing store." A bleached blonde,

Both Harvey Glatman and his assault victim, Eula Jo Hand, attended Denver East High School, located on the esplanade that connects East Colfax Avenue with Denver City Park.

she modeled fur coats, although her main job was an "elevator starter." She was in charge of several individual elevator operators in the five-story building on Stout and Sixteenth streets in downtown Denver. Her job was to tell the operators when to take shoppers up and when to bring them down.

Eula Jo still had on her elevator uniform when she survived the attack by Harvey Glatman. She had gone to the movies after work and was returning home on the bus, alone, at ten o'clock at night. Her bus stop was only a half block from the house she shared with her mother, but Glatman, who also was on the bus, was right behind her. As the bus pulled away, he stuck his gun in her back. Even though sixty-one years had elapsed since Eula Jo's attack, she remembered the incident vividly. At the time, earlier attacks, but no arrests, had already made it into the news. "Are you the guy who is frightening everybody?" she asked him. His response was, simply, "Turn around." Then he led her into a dark alley.

"I don't remember where he tied me up," said Eula Jo. "I was able to walk, and we were in someone's backyard. I heard a lady come to the door of a nearby house, and she said to someone: 'Be quiet. I heard something.' "

Eula Jo said that her attacker hit her hard with the handle of his pistol. Even after so many years, her speech was still slurred from the blow. Glatman ordered her to be quiet, and he put a gag in her mouth. For about forty-five minutes, she wiggled and tried to break loose—still in the backyard of a Capitol Hill neighborhood home. "He took my jacket off and got touchy-feely," Eula Jo told me. He also took money from her leather purse. Eventually, the young victim heard footsteps coming up the alley, and somehow she got the gag out of her mouth. She screamed, Glatman ran off, and a man untied her and took her home. "I have no idea who he was," she said. "Isn't that horrible?" I could not tell Eula Jo who had rescued her, but I was able to tell her the circumstances surrounding her attack. Her past included a large unknown and, like the family of Twylia May Embrey, she needed some closure, too.

Following Eula Jo's assault, her mother called the Denver police, and they came to her house to conduct an interview. An officer asked if she had been raped, and she said no, but she did tell him that she had been molested. She also told police that she did not know her attacker's name, but she had recognized him as a student at Denver East High School. During the next few days, Eula Jo accompanied detectives as they searched each classroom at the high school. Police officers also drove to her mother's home with suspects in the backseats of their cars, asking Eula Jo

The alley behind 634 East Twelfth Avenue in Denver's Capitol Hill neighborhood is the likely location of Harvey Glatman's attack on Eula Jo Hand.

if she could identify any of them as her attacker. She did not know where Glatman eventually was arrested, but she remembered being angry, at the time, because the police ruined her new purse when they covered it with fingerprint dusting powder.

Four days after Eula Jo's attack, the young woman stood on Champa and Seventeenth streets in downtown Denver. Thousands of other people were out on the streets too, as it was V-E Day—the day Americans celebrated the Allied Troops' victory in Europe at the end of World War II. Everyone was kissing everyone, and Eula Jo was swept into the arms of a young Army Air Corps man. Six weeks later they married. The newlyweds moved to the serviceman's hometown of Fort Scott, in eastern Kansas.

Before long, the couple was expecting their first child. The court sent Eula Jo a letter stating that she was to testify at Glatman's trial—on November 19, 1945. As the district attorney in Boulder had claimed after Glatman's assault on Norene Lauer, the strongest charge that could be made was one of aggravated robbery. "I had nothing to be ashamed of," Eula Jo told me on the telephone, "but my mother-in-law said I couldn't go. She said it would embarrass everyone." Now I knew that only Eula Jo's deposition, not her testimony, was given in the courtroom. Even when I talked with her on the telephone, Eula Jo was still upset about her mother-

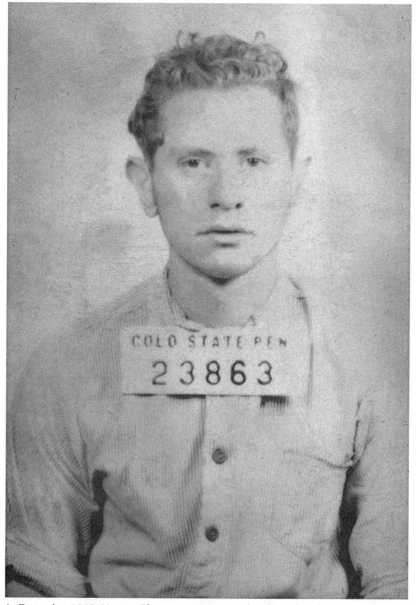

In December 1945, Harvey Glatman was sentenced to the Colorado State Penitentiary for aggravated robbery of Eula Jo Hand and two other young Denver women. Photo courtesy Colorado State Archives, Colorado State Penitentiary Records, PRI-23863.

in-law's decision. She had wanted to testify in person—to see, for herself, that justice was done.

On December 1, 1945, the Denver District Court judge sentenced Glatman to the Colorado State Penitentiary, in Cañon City, "for a period not exceeding five years and not less than one." In announcing the sentence, the judge stated: "There is no idea to punish this boy, but to protect the public." According to the correspondence of attorney Ira L. Quiat, he and everyone involved felt that Glatman would receive better mental health care at the penitentiary than in the Denver jail, as a full-time psychiatrist was expected to be added to the penitentiary staff. The district court judge from Boulder, however, threw up a red flag when he wrote to Glatman's attorney, "I anticipate considerable difficulty in determining whether or not the defendant is cured by psychiatric treatments or otherwise."

Four days later, the prisoner was transported more than one hundred miles from the Denver County Jail to the penitentiary. To learn more about his time there, I went back to the Colorado State Archives to access the Colorado State Penitentiary records. "Prisoner No. 23863" was a few days shy of his eighteenth birthday. Instead of giving his former occupation as student, he said he was a "butcher," perhaps a reference to his part-time employment at Bennie's Meat Market in Denver. His description further indicated that he could read and write, was temperate, smoked tobacco, and had not previously been in prison. His religion was given as Jewish, and his "nationality/race" was "Jewish-American." Although his father, Albert, was still in the home, Glatman only listed his mother, Ophelia, as a parental contact. The Glatmans continued to live in their Kearney Street home in Denver.

The *Daily Camera*, meanwhile, reported on a lecture given by the director of the Colorado Parole Board. Of the prison inmates then currently at the penitentiary, the director said that most of them were first offenders. They still had an opportunity to reconstruct their lives but, he added, there was little to inspire them to a higher effort. He failed to mention, however, the very great incentive of beating the system in order to get an early release. Even before Glatman entered the prison walls, he had learned what to say and what not to say to psychiatrists. What a wealth of information was tucked away in the files of the state archives! As Alan and I continued our weekly research trips, I found more and more Glatman-related correspondence. I kept reading and piecing together the early years of Harvey Glatman and soon was absorbed in his time in prison.

The Colorado State Penitentiary's hoped-for full-time psychiatrist never materialized, but during the time Glatman was incarcerated, he was visited by Dr. Edward Delehanty, Jr., a psychiatrist from the Colorado State Mental Hospital in Pueblo, Colorado. This new, to Glatman, doctor portrayed a much more normal prisoner than had his previous examiners. Completely opposite from Dr. Hilton's diagnosis, Dr. Delehanty wrote in a report, "Rorschach examination shows a good contact with reality and ability to get along with other people." After another one of the new doctor's visits, he summarized, "I can find no evidence of schizophrenia and do not believe shock treatment is indicated." He called Glatman "a somewhat embarrassed and shy boy who has been a model inmate in the Penitentiary and has been made a trustee."

If the Boulder district judge had read these reports, he likely would have shaken in his shoes. According to Dr. J. Paul de River, founder and director of the Sex Offense Bureau for the City of Los Angeles and author of the 1949 text *The Sexual Criminal, A Psychoanalytical Study,* differing diagnoses among psychiatrists was a common problem. Dr. de River compared psychiatrists to philosophers who give their patients a new way of life. "Because there are so many philosophies," he stated, "this disunity and lack of harmony is carried into the field of psychiatry—each psychiatrist holding and wishing to postulate his own ideas."

After Glatman served three months of his prison term, Dr. Delehanty wrote a letter to Ira L. Quiat, Glatman's attorney, stating that he, the doctor, had "never been able to find any evidence of insanity." What he did discover was evidence of what he called "immature sexuality." He also found the "residual" of an Oedipus complex—a Freudian term in which the subject desires sexual relations with his mother while wanting to kill his father. Of Glatman, Dr. Delehanty stated: "It is my opinion that his present sentence and incarceration has been of some benefit in helping this boy realize the seriousness of his past behavior, and we hope [he] has developed a due regard for law and order."

The state mental hospital doctor said he could not guarantee Glatman's future conduct, but he stated that he was firmly convinced that justice would not be better served by another conviction and sentence. "This boy has accepted his present incarceration in the manner in which it was intended," wrote Dr. Delehanty, "and I believe that were he to receive additional sentences, he would become resentful and vindictive and would be more apt to get into further trouble."

On the basis of Dr. Delehanty's upbeat reports, Glatman was paroled early—on July 27, 1946—after serving slightly more than seven months of his one- to five-year sentence. To offer him a fresh start, his mother took him to New York City, his birthplace. According to yet another psychiatric evaluation, he "ran away and went on a rampage." There was nothing that Ophelia could do, so she returned to Denver. Less than one month later, Glatman was arrested for assaulting and robbing a woman in Albany, New York. Within days, a court-appointed New York attorney sent a telegram to Ophelia that stated: "Harvey in custody of Albany, New York, officials since Sunday. Will forward full details." Glatman had proved that he could not stay out of trouble.

Less than three months after his release from the Colorado State Penitentiary, Glatman pled guilty to "robbery in the second degree" and was sentenced, in New York, to "not less than five nor more than ten years." As the district attorney's office in Albany explained to attorney Quiat, Glatman was sent, for classification, to the New York State Reception Center at Elmira, in southcentral New York State. There the director optimistically stated, "We will do our best to understand this lad as fully as possible and will make the best possible disposition in this case." Meanwhile, Quiat forwarded on the director's letter to Judge Coffin in Boulder in the hopes that proof of Glatman's incarceration would get him to release the bond in the Boulder case of Norene Lauer. This the judge refused to do, but he did reduce it again, to five hundred dollars, and he planned for a new trial immediately upon Glatman's release from prison in New York.

When Glatman was examined upon entry into Elmira, a psychiatrist agreed with Dr. Hilton's diagnosis of schizophrenia, adding that sexually perverted impulses were the basis for his criminality. But the new doctor, like Dr. Delehanty, still thought he was a model prisoner. He had been given an IQ test at the Colorado Psychopathic Hospital, but he was given another one at Elmira, and his intelligence quotient of 126 still placed him well above average. Glatman was expected, because of a "conforming attitude and high level of ability," to do well in any program to which he would be assigned. His new psychiatrist, however, seemed to be stating a double message, as he also recommended intensive psychotherapy due to "deep-seated personality difficulties which make him potentially a dangerous individual to be at large."

At a later date, Glatman's mother, Ophelia, would claim that her son could do no harm, but at the time of his New York incarceration, she seemed to have accepted the reality of her son's bizarre behavior. The Elmira report chillingly stated, in part: "Both the mother and father have been seen by the examiner. They are fearful in the event he goes out he may become involved in notorious crime and [they] wished him dead rather than being faced with that kind of destiny."

In February 1947, an Elmira psychiatrist sedated Glatman with sodium amytal, a truth serum then considered safer than the earlier scopolamine given in Boulder to the accused hit man of Officer Elmer Cobb. After observing Glatman under its effects, the psychiatrist related Glatman's criminal acts as "trauma associated with his early experiences with masturbation"—particularly psychological threats made by his father when Albert told his son that if he continued to masturbate, he would "go crazy." The Elmira psychiatrist seemed to get to the heart of Glatman's problems when he described blocked sexual energies that Glatman then transferred to and released as "hostility, fetishism, and impulsiveness."

Glatman admitted to the Elmira psychiatrist that his criminal acts—especially tying up young women with rope—obviated his need to masturbate. In the doctor's further discussions with Glatman's parents, Albert and Ophelia described their son's "pre-crime persona" as sullen and morose, and his "post-crime persona" as a return to his true self. The Elmira psychiatrist added: "He obviously experienced sexual relief through his crimes, although he denies any actual emissions. He also speaks of the guilt he felt, either after his early masturbation practices or his later criminal acts, as the same, and he accepted the fact that he should be punished for both. It seems that in his mind, the two were equal, the latter merely being substituted for the former."

In September 1948, Glatman was transferred—"sent up the river," in prison lingo—to the Mental Department at Sing Sing Prison in Ossining, New York. The facility was named for a tribe of Mohegan Indians known as the Sint Sinck. The initial cellblock of the imposing complex on the banks of the Hudson River had been completed in 1828 by one hundred prisoners who quarried marble on-site, wore striped uniforms, were forced to keep silent, and walked in lockstep. In 1891, the prison boasted the nation's first electric chair, "Old Sparky."

At the time of Harvey Glatman's confinement, conditions had improved, and attempts to rehabilitate sex offenders were very much in vogue. In the July 1947 issue of *American Magazine*, Federal Bureau of Investigation director J. Edgar Hoover published an article titled "How Safe Is Your Daughter?" urging support for psychiatric and medical care of sex offenders. At the time, six states provided funding for psychiatrists to try to explain and prevent sex crimes, and one of the largest programs was headed by the director of the Department of Mental Hygiene of the State of New York, Dr. David Abrahamsen.

In Sing Sing, Glatman was placed under Dr. Abrahamsen's care, and the esteemed doctor spent an hour a week with him, attempting to draw out childhood memories and trying to get him to understand his guilt feelings and to face his emotional conflicts. Dr. Abrahamsen gave Glatman yet another IQ test, at least his third, and this time he scored even higher—130. The psychiatrist rated him "very superior intellectually" but said his prognosis was poor. "[He] should be psycho-educated and if still anti-social," wrote Dr. Abrahamsen, "should be segregated even if schizophrenia does not seem developed."

Glatman's case received so much attention that Dr. Abrahamsen included it in the prison's March 1950 "Report on the Study of 102 Sex Offenders at Sing Sing Prison." By then, Glatman had been arrested three times in Colorado and once in New York, but authorities, after many interviews with him, emphatically stated what I already suspected—"His four arrests represented only a small part of his many offenses."

The Sing Sing report attempted to explain Glatman's compulsion to seek sexual release through overpowering and controlling women. As previous psychiatrists had already done, Dr. Abrahamsen also examined the prisoner's parents. Albert was seen as "hostile and domineering, though well-meaning," telling his son that every time he masturbated his brain would rot, he would get pimples that would reveal his habit to the world, and he would lose the equivalent of a pint of blood. Albert was said to have been dominated by his wife, Ophelia, who in turn controlled their son "in a quiet way." Again the analysis reflected back to the Oedipus complex, and Glatman was said to have felt intense rivalry with his father and to have had a frustrated desire to monopolize his mother's affections. His doctor labeled the inmate "insecure, plagued by guilt feelings, and doubting his own masculinity."

After he had spent two years in Sing Sing, New York authorities began to plan for Glatman's release. In November 1950, according to the Boulder *Daily Camera*, Glatman would soon be up for parole, in Denver, with the provision that he be placed in the outpatient care of Dr. Franklin G. Ebaugh. This colleague of Dr. J. P. Hilton and Dr. Charles A. Rymer—who both had examined Glatman shortly after his assault on Norene Lauer—had returned from war duty with the Medical Corps of the United States Army a promoter of drug induction, or narcoanalysis. He resumed his duties as director of the Colorado Psychopathic Hospital as well as professor of psychiatry at the University of Colorado Medical School. Glatman's parole could not be granted, however, while the two-dollar robbery charge in the Norene Lauer case was still pending in Boulder.

New York's Dr. Abrahamsen had written to Glatman's attorney, Ira L. Quiat, in October 1950, explaining his reasons for advocating the prisoner's release, even though he admitted that it was extremely difficult to predict the way in which Glatman would behave in the future. The New York doctor added, however, that there was no doubt in his mind that additional incarceration "would endanger the favorable results of the treatment he had received." Perhaps anxious to get rid of him, Dr. Abrahamsen wrote, "I trust that this information will suffice in order that the warrant in Boulder may be waived."

Boulder deputy district attorney Horace B. Holmes then filed a motion to dismiss Norene Lauer's case, adding that it appeared, to him, that the defendant may be rehabilitated and that dropping the case would be "in the best interest of society." There was no justice, however, for the sexual assault victim.

Without the Boulder case hanging over his head, Glatman walked out of Sing Sing prison in April 1951. Immediately, however, he was arrested for charges that had been pending in New York State before he had begun his most recent prison sentence. The outstanding charges, from 1946, included first-degree robbery, first-degree grand larceny, and second-degree assault of a woman in connection with a holdup that netted fifty dollars. On the advice of Glatman's psychiatrists, a New York judge then suspended the overlapping assault charge and dismissed the charges of robbery and larceny. In May 1951, Glatman was released again and returned home to Colorado. The *Denver Post* ran a story with the headline "N.Y. Sends 'Phantom Terrorist' Back to Denver."

By this time, Eula Jo and her union carpenter husband had moved back to Denver, too. As her family grew, the young wife and mother tried to put the assault out of her mind and, like Norene Lauer, she did not, at the time, discuss it with her children. Occasionally, however, her mother would clip articles on Glatman from the newspaper and send them to her. Eula Jo told me, too, that in the 1950s and 1960s she often watched *Dragnet*—the televised police procedural drama about cases of the fictional Los Angeles police detective, Sergeant Joe Friday. Eula Jo was shocked, one day, when she recognized that one of the episodes portrayed her then-executed attacker. "I thought about him later," she said. "I couldn't explain it. I just did."

Perhaps the *Denver Post* story announcing Glatman's return to Denver was one of the articles that Eula Jo's mother had clipped for her daughter. If so, reading it must have been frightening for the young woman, as it explained that Glatman had a mental disorder and was homeward-bound. He was a free man and would be walking the streets of Denver once again.

3

CLOSING IN AND CLOSURE

14

Prior to Harvey Glatman's May 1951 homecoming, the twenty-three-year-old ex-convict had spent five and one-half years of his young life in three different prisons. At one of these facilities, he had been trained in television repair. When I first found him as an adult in the 1953 Denver City Directory, he worked as a serviceman for the Valas Motor and Radio Center on Colfax Avenue. The business was located in the northeastern corner of the Capitol Hill neighborhood and a block away from Sid King's Strip Club. The job may have met a requirement of his parole, but it also drew him back into his old haunts, and it may have given him access to women's homes.

As I had learned in the files that Sergeant John Umenhofer had sent me, Glatman also promoted himself as a detective magazine photographer. He paid his Denver models well for the 1950s—twenty dollars per hour—and he bound and gagged them to replicate bondage scenes. He told his interrogator that he had been inspired by the work of Irving Klaw, the New York photographer best known for capturing on film the glamorous black-haired model Bettie Page. Klaw sold photographs of Bettie and other models to Glatman and other customers through mail-order catalogs.

The images in Klaw's photographs showed skimpily dressed pinup models with the same kinds of ropes and gags that Glatman had used on Norene Lauer—his Boulder victim—as well as on Eula Jo Hand, the girl he followed off a bus on Capitol Hill. Scenes provided by Klaw, and probably replicated by Glatman, included women posing alone and also two women whipping, spanking, and tying each other. For Glatman, recreating these scenes with real-life models gave him the control over women that he craved—and most likely fulfilled his pent-up sexual fantasies and desires.

When Glatman first returned to Denver, he lived with his parents in their brick ranch-style house on Kearney Street. After his father died a year later, his aunt Rosalie Gold moved to an apartment on Corona Street, in the Capitol Hill neighborhood, but she and Ophelia Glatman continued to work together at the Hollywood Millinery shop downtown. I wondered, but will never know, if Glatman continued to exhibit what his mother had called his pre-crime and post-crime personas. If so, she may have been well aware of additional crimes he may have committed once he was back in Denver. She must have at least thought it likely, as she and her husband had told two of his previous psychiatrists that they considered him a danger to society. Eventually, Glatman moved to an apartment of his own, at 1531 Clermont, a few steps from Colfax Avenue and its bus line.

At various times in the early and mid-1950s, in addition to radio and television repair, Glatman also worked in a neighborhood grocery store. When he had earned enough money, he bought his 1951 Dodge Coronet. How much outpatient care he received from Dr. Franklin G. Ebaugh is not known, but the learned psychiatrist kept up with the latest research in his field. In the February 1952 issue of the *American Journal of Psychiatry*, Dr. Ebaugh authored an article on sex offenses, referring to Dr. Alfred Kinsey's recent study, "Sexual Behavior in the Human Male." According to Dr. Ebaugh, "Sex talk has slithered from the intimacy of the boudoir and pool hall to the urbane sophistication of living room and public lecture."

Denver's top mental health specialist then raised the question of who, exactly, were the sex criminals, and he answered it himself by stating: "[They are] those impulsive, imprudent, and irresponsible people who get caught." According to popular theory, at the time, as exemplified in the book *The Sexual Criminal, A Psychoanalytical Study*, "no child is actually born a pervert." To coincide with the latest research, Dr. Ebaugh stressed the fact that in order for sex offenders to be cured, they had to want to change and they needed to take responsibility for their actions—they had to have a goal and direct their energies away from sex and toward creative, rather than destructive, ends. We will never know if Glatman told Dr. Ebaugh about hiring women to bind, gag, and photograph, but he and his psychiatrist continued to meet until Dr. Ebaugh retired from the psychopathic hospital in 1953—one year before the murder of Jane Doe.

If Glatman had never gotten into trouble with the law again, one might have thought that that maybe—somehow—he had been rehabilitated, but that was not the case. By 1957, his documented sexual assaults on women had escalated to murder. He managed to avoid arrest from May 1951 to October 1958, but the authors of the Sing Sing report had emphatically stated that Glatman's arrests to date had represented only a small part of his many offenses. He may have picked up skills in prison that helped him elude the police, but it is unlikely that he could have changed his criminal behavior, even if he had wanted to.

As I immersed myself in the strange and depressing life of Harvey Glatman, I tried to remain focused on my initial quest—to learn more about Jane Doe. Around this time, I spoke with a professor who is an expert in the field of DNA research. He offered, at no charge, to read Jane Doe's DNA profile with an eye toward identifying her geographical ancestry. But when I called Commander Phil West to tell him what I thought was the good news, I was told that Detective Steve Ainsworth would not release the profile. Whatever working relationship I thought I had with the detective had become even more strained.

Sometimes even a chilly relationship, however, is better than none at all. In April 2006, seven months after my initial contact with the University of Denver, I was finally granted an interview with the assistant vice chancellor of news and public affairs to discuss the status of the Harvey M. Glatman Memorial Scholarship. I met the university spokesperson in his office in the Mary Reed Building, a handsome 1920s-era brick structure easily identified by its prominent tower. For our brief talk, however, the neatly dressed administrator in his early forties led me downstairs to a nondescript basement room where we sat on either side of a bare wooden table.

First of all, I was figuratively slapped on the wrist for having contacted Ophelia Glatman's nephew, who had complained to the vice chancellor's office about my telephone call. I had not realized that I had stepped on anyone's toes but, by then, the Harvey M. Glatman Memorial Scholarship had become a moot point because the university had simply renamed it the Ophelia Glatman Endowed Memorial Scholarship. Not until my initial telephone call to the university did employees there think that Harvey Glatman was anyone other than the son of a benefactress.

As I was getting ready to leave, the assistant vice chancellor warmed up a little and told me that a lounge in the university's library had been named in honor of two other financial donors—who just happened to be Glatman's late attorney, Ira L. Quiat, and his wife Esther. The university administrator and I laughed over the fact that new students, visiting the library for the first time, often are confused by what they perceive as a misspelling of the word "quiet."

When I got home, I sat, as usual, at the old oak library table that serves as my desk. I watched the ravens, crows, a few nuthatches, and a downy woodpecker outside my window and updated Micki, Cindi, Dave, and

Karen Anne about the latest Glatman-related developments. I told them that I believed Glatman had the means, method, and opportunity to have been Jane Doe's murderer, but the identity of the victim was still uppermost in my thoughts. A little further back in my mind was the constant question of the whereabouts of Twylia May Embrey.

One evening in late April 2006, my computer screen flashed with an email message, and in the subject line was "I think I might have found something." Then, out of the blue, I got a very excited telephone call from its sender—Micki.

My fellow researcher had emailed me so often that she referred to me as "my diary and my friend," but during the four years of our correspondence, we had rarely spoken on the telephone. Micki breathlessly explained that she had recently done a Google search with only Twylia May Embrey's parents' names, and up popped what she believed was Twylia's obituary— three weeks after she died! According to the write-up Micki had found, Twylia had lived for half a century, mostly near Boston, Massachusetts, and under an assumed name.

Each on our own computers, Micki and I compared the recent photograph that accompanied the online obituary with the photographs of Twylia from her high school yearbooks. Even though the portraits were taken a half century apart, there was no doubt in our minds that we were looking at the same woman. I urged Micki to immediately call Twylia's great-niece, Jennifer. After Micki talked with her, she emailed me to say that, like both of us, Jennifer was taken aback. Micki's first email the next morning read: "I am so emotional this morning. It's going to be so hard to be focused today. I haven't cried yet; I am in such shock and filled with sadness, but relieved. I hope to talk to you soon."

That same day, Jennifer broke the news to her eighty-five-year-old grandmother, Midge, Twylia's oldest surviving sister. For the past fifty-four years, Midge had been the one who had worried the most about her kid sister. Jennifer, who spoke for herself and for Midge, wrote to Micki and me, "Grandma is in good spirits. You both have become part of our family." Jennifer called us "two terrific women who have made a difference in the lives of others." She then asked us both to meet her at Twylia's final resting place some day—far from the little cemetery in Maywood. Thinking back to what I had read about Jane Doe's funeral and the gladiolus flowers sent by a stranger, I ordered a spray and had them delivered to the Embrey family.

A few days later, the *Denver Post* sent a reporter to Nebraska. He then traveled on to Boston to flesh out his account. His article, and others on the internet, spread far and wide the story of how the search for the identity of Jane Doe had—in a strange twist—found Twylia. I had not heard from my former mentor, Dr. Bob, in a year, but all of a sudden his deep, familiar voice was on my answering machine. "This message is for the tracker of lost souls," he said. "I've been reading the articles on the net, and I just wanted to let you know that I'm very proud to know what you did. And I'm proud of you."

I was thrilled, of course, that our research—specifically Micki's—had found the long-lost Nebraska farm girl, and I appreciated everyone's warm words, but the revelation was bittersweet. There would be no family reunion with Twylia's sister Midge, great-niece Jennifer, and other Embrey family members after all. I thought back to the Kansas woman who told me that if Twylia ever was found, for me to first make sure that she actually wanted to be reunited with her family before I put them in contact with each other. I also recalled the similar advice from the woman in Oregon who started having second thoughts about her long search for her sister after the sister finally was located. Sometimes, I realized, situations have a way of resolving themselves.

Indeed, Twylia's family, who had been searching for her everywhere between the Midwest and California for the better part of a half century, was more surprised than anyone to learn that Theresa—as the runaway teenager had renamed herself—had been working as a typist in an insurance company on the east coast. From what Jennifer learned from Theresa's longtime friend, the pretty teenager then named Twylia had, at first, traveled extensively so that her father would not be able to find her. Where she got the money, no one knows, although the answer could lie with the unknown man who was said to have driven her away in his fancy convertible. Twylia had married twice but had no children. Her second husband, of forty-five years, had died in 2004.

With a little more digging, we found that, in 1955, shortly after Twylia's first marriage, she—as Theresa—had applied for and received a new Social Security number under new first, middle, and last names. To make the application process easy to understand, the Social Security Administration had, at the time, recently released an informational pamphlet featuring a baby-faced, bow-tie-wearing cartoon character of the era, "J. Wilbur Worker." The instructions specifically stated that if a person changed his or her name by marriage or divorce, the applicant had to request a new card—but he or she must keep the same number. Twylia, however, filled out a new Social Security application form and simply checked "no" in the box that asked if she had ever had a previous number.

On Twylia's new application, she made herself more than four years older by writing in a completely new fictitious birth date. Instead of her actual birth date of October 15, 1934, she told the Social Security Administration she was born on December 3, 1930. Obviously, no one asked her to provide any documentation. She also changed, on paper, her place of birth. Instead of Nebraska, Twylia claimed to have been born in Minnesota. In 1959, when she married again, she kept her newly revised, but incorrect, age, and this time she stated she had been born in California. No wonder her family had not been able to find her!

Months before Theresa's death, at the actual age of seventy-one, Detective Steve Ainsworth had entered her information into the National Crime Information Center's missing persons' database. After Jennifer heard from Micki, she called the detective and told him the news. He then called the woman in Boston who was listed in the obituary as Theresa's close friend. When the friend admitted that the recently deceased woman had talked about her Nebraska family on her deathbed, Detective Ainsworth was able to officially close his missing person's case and confirm that Theresa and Twylia were one and the same. How sad that the Boston friend did not know how to reach Twylia's family, especially when Midge so often thought about her sister and sat, year after year, by the telephone.

Micki's discovery of Twylia made me hopeful that our Jane Doe mystery might soon be solved. Six months earlier, when Micki, Cindi, Dave, Karen Anne, and I started weeding through our list of missing young women, Dave had written, "I'm going to take another look at Katharine Dyer."

All we had to go on for the missing Denver woman was the newspaper clipping from the *Rocky Mountain News* that had been published on April 9, 1954, the day after Wayne Swanson and James Andes found Jane Doe's body. The article mentioned that the discovery had prompted a search of Denver Police Department files, which turned up the names of two missing young women. One, at 140 pounds, was too heavy for us to seriously consider. The other was Katharine Dyer of 1118 Washington Street, in the Capitol Hill neighborhood of Denver. Like the students who found Jane Doe, she had rented a room in a family's home.

The newspaper's report stating that Katharine was missing was published thirteen days after her landlady, the late Marjorie Humbarger, said she had "vanished" between midnight and seven o'clock in the morning on Friday, March 26. According to the published weather report that day, a snowstorm was on the way. When the students found Jane Doe's partially decomposed body, officials estimated that it had been exposed to the elements for a week or more. I still was skeptical about Katharine's stated height of five feet six inches. She was also said to have been 110 pounds, twenty-four years old, and of slender build. Her hair color ranged from blonde to red, depending on whether or not she "tinted" it.

When last seen, Katharine had been wearing "blue slacks," perhaps a reference to the blue jeans that had recently become acceptable clothing for young women in the mid-1950s. Her slacks were definitely not part of the skirt-and-jacket uniform she had to wear in her job as an elevator operator at the American Furniture Company, the large four-story building on the corner of Sixteenth and Lawrence streets with a big electric sign in the shape of an American flag on its roof. According to the newspaper report, "Mrs. Dyer," at the time, was separated from her husband, "James." Our search for Katharine included learning more about him.

I went back to the Colorado Historical Society to look through more *Denver City Directories*. Using the same method as I had when I searched for the Glatman family, I looked for any and all listings for Katharine and James Dyer, a process complicated by the fact that first names are often abbreviated and many names contained spelling errors. I did find, however, in 1951, a "Kath E. Dyer" who was an elevator operator and a "Jimmie Dyer" who worked for the Public Service Company. In 1953, "Jas Dyer," who

Katharine Farrand Dyer disappeared on March 26, 1954, from this Capitol Hill neighborhood home, where she rented a room from owners Leon and Marjorie Humbarger.

worked at Public Service, had a wife named "Cath." In an internet search of names and addresses, we found approximately fifty James Dyers of the right age, but only one was living in Colorado. When I wrote to him and asked if he had been married to a woman named Katharine, he wrote back and said he had not. We crossed him off our list.

Also helping us during this time was a genealogist named Paul who lived in the Denver area. He graciously volunteered for a nationwide organization called Random Acts of Genealogical Kindness. Dave had found the group online and learned that these generous individuals perform library, courthouse, and other genealogically related research in their local areas. Although Paul and I both accessed the *Denver City Directories*, he also checked marriage records and telephone books of the era. We corresponded for several months about an additional listing for a "Mrs. C. Dyer" in the Five Points area of Denver. This was a predominantly black neighborhood northeast of downtown, and Jane Doe had been described in her autopsy report as Caucasian, but maybe she knew someone there or was hiding from her estranged husband. We came up with several different possible scenarios but, ultimately, could find no connection.

In 1954, there were two listings for the Dyer who worked for Public Service—one was for "Jimmie" and one was for "Jas Gyer." After 1954, "Jimmie Dyer" at Public Service was consistently listed with a new wife. If James (or Jimmie) and Katharine had legally divorced after April 1954, when Jane Doe's body was found, Katharine could conveniently be ruled out as Jane Doe. If they divorced before that date, she was still a candidate. In a search for any information on whether she was even dead or alive, I went to the Denver Probate Court, where I had read up on Ophelia Glatman's estate. The court had no records, however, to show that Katharine either died in Denver or was declared legally dead. Of course, if she was an unidentified murder victim, she would not have been recorded as deceased in the first place. There was always the possibility that she resurfaced without any mention in the newspaper and remarried without getting divorced, which would have thrown us off her paper trail. Where did Katharine come from, and what was her maiden name? As usual, we had many unanswered questions.

Three days after learning of Twylia's fate, I received proof of Katharine's maiden name. I shared this coveted piece of genealogical data with my fellow researchers, and it was a big deal to all of us, but the information did not come without a lot of rigmarole. In previous weeks, we had found a brief online newspaper obituary in the *Rocky Mountain News* for Jimmie Dyer. It gave us his wife's and daughter's names, his occupation as an engineer, and his place of interment at Fort Logan National Cemetery, south of Denver. The obituary also told us his date of death—August 7, 2002—only a few months after Micki had answered my first online genealogical query.

With this new information, we found Jimmie—his legal name, not James or Jim—in the online Social Security death records and learned that he was born on June 5, 1925. The death records also showed that he originally applied for his Social Security number in Arizona, so Dave searched online Arizona birth records and found a copy of his birth certificate. It had a June 4 date, but we knew that it was possible for official sources to differ. Jimmie's birthplace was ten miles west of Flagstaff in the small railroad and sawmill town of Bellemont, known today for its part in the 1969 film *Easy Rider*, in which outlaw bikers tried to rent a room in the Pine Breeze Motel. Through more online searches, Dave found that Jimmie had served as an electrician's mate in the Navy on the USS *Halford*, from 1943 to 1945.

Again, because Jimmie had applied for his Social Security number in Arizona, I followed a hunch and checked online obituaries on the alumni website of Northern Arizona University, formerly Arizona State College, in Flagstaff. There I found even more information—some that we knew and some that we did not. Jimmie Dyer had, indeed, served in the Navy during World War II, and he had graduated from Arizona State College with a bachelor's degree in physical science in 1950. In college, he was a member of the hiking club. The alumni obituary also mentioned his work as an engineer for the Public Service Company in Colorado. New information included a major achievement—he had climbed all of Colorado's mountain peaks over fourteen thousand feet. Jimmie died on August 7, 2002. The death date agreed with his Social Security record. He was our man, and the new information showing that he had been a student in Flagstaff opened up many new avenues to search.

Our next goal was to find someone who knew Jimmie, and who could, we hoped, tell us about Katharine. Through the university's website, I looked up the names of some of the surviving students in the hiking club, called the ones whose telephone numbers I could find, and wrote letters to others. Several of the alumni told me about a ten-day hiking trip they took with Jimmie through "Indian Country" at the end of the spring semester in 1946. Forty-six years later, in 1992, six of the group, along with their spouses, recreated the trip by traveling in a plush rental van and staying in motels. Jimmie and his wife, Maxine, were part of the group. There was no mention of Katharine, and the individual members I spoke with on the telephone had no recollection of a former girlfriend or wife with her name.

The library at Northern Arizona University confirmed that Katharine was not listed in any of the college yearbooks in, or prior to, 1950.

There was only one way to find out if Jimmie was married to Katharine during his college years and that was to contact the registrar's office at his alma mater, now Northern Arizona University. I wrote the registrar a letter and explained that I was working with the Boulder County Sheriff's Office, trying to identify a murder victim from 1954. I asked if records of former student Jimmie Dyer showed a listing for next of kin. Specifically, I wanted to know if Jimmie was married to Katharine while he was still in school and, if so, what her maiden name was.

My letter must have sat on someone's desk for several weeks. When I followed up, I got a brief response, not from the registrar's office as I had expected, but from the university's police department. The officer who emailed me told me that the information I requested required a subpoena, per the Family and Educational Rights and Privacy Act (FERPA). I had never heard of this federal law that protects students' educational records, but I was not surprised that it existed. However, it seemed strange to me that the police had become involved in what I thought was a simple request to an administrator's office. Then I thought back to my contacts with the University of Denver over the Harvey M. Glatman Memorial Scholarship and realized that correspondence with administrators is not always easy.

The next email I received from the university's police department read: "The information you need is actually listed here at the University, but it can't be released without going through the FERPA restriction. Basically, if Jimmie is deceased, then the restriction no longer applies. Otherwise it takes a court order to get the information."

I wrote back to the officer with Jimmie Dyer's Social Security death record, as well as the obituary from the *Rocky Mountain News* and even the online obituary from the university's own alumni association. The police officer then told me to forward the documentation to the registrar's office. Meanwhile, Commander Phil West emailed me to say that the officer from Northern Arizona University had contacted him for confirmation that I was "legitimate," and that I really was working with him on the Jane Doe case. Only then did the university officer authorize the registrar's office to release the information I had requested on Jimmie Dyer.

The next day I heard directly from the registrar, who told me that he had consulted not only with the university's police department but also with the university's legal counsel. The news was worth waiting for. After confirming Jimmie's dates of birth and attendance, the administrator said that he had graduated on May 27, 1950, and added, "The official NAU transcript lists Mr. Dyer's spouse at the time as one Katharine E. Farrand Dyer." He added, "Best of luck with your research."

My lengthy correspondence with Northern Arizona University had confirmed that Katharine was, indeed, Jimmie Dyer's wife. My fellow researchers and I now knew, too, that the couple had married prior to 1951, when they first showed up in the *Denver City Directory*. Even though Jimmie was deceased, we had hopes of learning about Katharine through her husband's family and friends. We knew Jimmie had at least two more wives—the one who was listed in the 1956 *Denver City Directory*, and the one named in his obituary, who was the same wife mentioned on the re-created hiking excursion. Most importantly, we had documentation that showed that Katharine's maiden name was Farrand. Now, at last, we were ready to start looking for her immediate family, which seemed—at the time—a relatively easy thing to do.

15

Flagstaff lies in Coconino County, in northcentral Arizona. With 18,661 square miles, the county is the second largest in the forty-eight contiguous states of the United States—smaller, only, than San Bernardino County in California. The researchers' and my first thought was that Katharine and Jimmie Dyer likely were married in or around Flagstaff, but a check with the Coconino County Clerk showed that they had not. We decided to expand our search to a wider area. Online, I found the Sharlot Hall Museum in Prescott, Arizona. Its genealogical archives are primarily focused on Yavapai County, but they also extend to nearby areas, including Flagstaff. Thinking that this research facility might uncover something I had missed, I requested records on Katharine Farrand. What a surprise it was to learn that Katharine E. Farrand and Jimmie Dyer had married, not in Flagstaff, but in Prescott, on September 25, 1949. This was the second official documented source that listed the Farrand name.

I sent off for copies of the Dyers' marriage license and certificate. Of most interest to me were the names of their witnesses. One was the wife of Charles Franklin Parker, who married the couple. A quick Social Security death records check showed that both of the Parkers were deceased. The other witness was a man named Hugh Acton. Thinking he might have been one of Jimmie's college friends, I searched online for anyone with his name and in his probable age range—late seventies or early eighties.

There were only a handful of Hugh Actons in the country, and the first one I called was the wrong one. Then I called seventy-eight-year-old Hugh Acton of Blanding, Utah. He had throat cancer and could only whisper on the telephone, but he told me that he had lived in Prescott, Arizona. He remembered the Dyers' marriage ceremony because he thought it was so strange. "I was wearing my Navy uniform," the man told me, "and this young couple came up to me on the street and asked me to witness their marriage. I never saw them before, and I never saw them since." There were no wedding guests at all.

Right after I talked with Hugh, I emailed my fellow researchers and told them about the conversation. I said I believed Jimmie and Katharine's marriage was either an elopement or a spur-of-the-moment romance, adding that, to me, Katharine was looking more and more like Jane Doe—a woman without close family ties.

I then wrote to the Yavapai County Court to see if they had any more documentation on Jimmie and Katharine's marriage. In response, I received a copy of their marriage affidavits. Jimmie had given the clerk his date and place of birth, which we had already confirmed, but Katharine's information was new to us. It stated that she had been born in San Antonio, Texas, on October 14, 1926. If correct, that would have made her twenty-seven years old when she disappeared from Denver—not twenty-four, as her landlady had reported.

Arizona brides were supposed to be at least sixteen years old to be married without parental consent. The clerk told me, however, that it had been common for young women to lie about their age and, often, proof of age in the 1940s was not required at all. No matter how I did the math, though, Katharine was old enough to have married. Maybe, like Twylia May Embrey, she had added three or four years to her age on her Social Security application, perhaps to get a job—then, again, like Twylia— continued to repeat the same misinformation on her marriage affidavit. Eula Jo Hand, too, had lied about her age to get her modeling job at Neusteter's Department Store.

Another possibility was that Katharine may have wanted her new husband to think she was older than she really was and closer to his age of twenty-four. Or perhaps the landlady who reported her missing had simply been mistaken.

Throughout the next few months, the researchers and I used this new—but conflicting—information in our nearly daily search for Katharine's family. Thinking it very likely that Katharine could be Jane Doe, we started looking for a living family member who could tell us whether she had ever resurfaced and who—if she had not—could provide a sample of DNA. The most logical place to find her family would be in the federal census.

Beginning with the assumption that Katharine came from an intact home with two parents and, hopefully, siblings, we started with the 1930 federal census records from San Antonio, Texas. When I first started genealogical research in the early 1980s and wanted to access federal census records, I had to either physically drive to the Denver Federal Center where the National Archives and Records Administration houses a regional division for the Rocky Mountain area, or send off for microfilms through the local library of the Church of Jesus Christ of Latter-day Saints, often referred to as the Mormon church. Now, magically, the exact images of every page of the published census records are available online.

Every ten years, the federal government takes a head count to determine how many representatives each state can send to the United States Congress. When the first census was taken in 1790, there were only thirteen states in the Union. In that year's census, only the names of the heads of the households were listed, along with the numbers of "free" persons and the numbers of slaves.

In the intervening decades, census data has become more and more detailed. It is now a wealth of information for anyone doing genealogical research. A seventy-two-year privacy rule, however, has sealed the most recent information. Assuming that Katharine's birth year was 1926 (as she had written on her affidavit) or 1930 (to correlate with the missing persons report), or somewhere in between, we agreed that it was likely she would have shown up in the 1930 census—released to the public in 2002. Then again, she may not have been in the census if she was born in 1930 and had an October birthday, her birth month as stated in her affidavit. Only children born prior to April 1, 1930, were listed in the census records for that year.

To compile the 1930 census records, a census taker canvassed neighborhoods door-to-door, then filled in the specifics under each household. Some households showed only one or two people, while others comprised parents, children, and extended families. After the head of the household, everyone else was described according to his or her relationship to the head. Among the forty-nine different classifications were the common ones, such as wife, son, and daughter. Others described in-laws, grandchildren, and even lodgers. Children in orphanages were listed as students or inmates, while men and women in prison were either inmates or convicts. Additional information after every name included age, sex, color or race, marital status, state or country of birth, and the states or countries of birth of the individuals' mothers and fathers.

If a person was foreign-born, the census taker wrote the year of immigration, noted whether the person was a naturalized citizen or an alien, and whether he or she was able to speak English. In addition, adults were asked for their ages at their first marriages, if they could read and write, and if they attended school or college. If they were currently employed they were asked to give their occupations. Interviewers also wanted to know if the households included farms and/or if the heads of the households owned or rented their homes. If they owned their homes, the census takers were required to write down the homes' values. People were even asked if they owned a "radio set." What these more detailed questions had to do with determining the number of representatives for Congress, I never figured out. Family historians, however, are grateful for the information so as to flesh out a name when a name is all that is known.

One of the pitfalls in accessing census records, however, is the spelling of a person's name, and this kind of detective work lies with the person who is deciphering a particular census taker's handwriting. Some census takers wrote neatly and distinctly while others scribbled the information, probably thinking that no one would ever look at the pages again. When I tried to read hard-to-figure-out handwriting, I usually found that the letters began to make sense after a few pages, but by then another census taker invariably took over with a completely different writing style. Online indexers may not have the leisure of distinguishing an "a" from an "e," for instance, in a particular census taker's handwriting style, so the looked-for name in today's indexes may be under any number of spelling variations. For instance, Texas resident Wallace Farrand was spelled correctly in an index of the 1920 census, but his name had been misspelled, or misinterpreted, as "Wellace Harrand" in 1910.

The National Archives and Records Administration, the Mormon church, and many individual libraries maintain microfilmed copies of the actual census records, making it possible for researchers who are not online to look directly at the handwritten entries themselves. Internet researchers can, and should, go past the indexes and read the original documents, too. When the researchers and I took into consideration every likely spelling and misspelling for the name Farrand, only one couple—Richard and Emma Farrand—were found living in San Antonio in 1930, and they had no children at all.

Our census search expanded to all of Texas and then to all of the United States. No one named Katharine Farrand was listed as having been born anywhere in the country during that time period. Three names, however, were close. The first was Kathryn Violet Farrand, born in Oklahoma, in 1922, to Stephen and Juanita Farrand. Now deceased, Kathryn married John Reis and had at least one child by 1942. Another Kathryn Farrand was born in 1922, but in Oregon. She was the daughter of Merrill Farrand.

I confirmed that she was not the Katharine we were looking for by talking with her on the telephone.

We also ruled out Kathryn Farrand, known as "Ruby Cathrin Powell" when she was born in April 1924 in Williamson County, Texas. She married John Arthur Farrand, and they had a child born in Texas in November 1949. At that time, "our" Katharine had been married for two months to Jimmie Dyer and was living in Flagstaff, Arizona.

My fellow researchers and I concluded that if Katharine Farrand was born before April 1, 1930—and thus in the 1930 census—she must have had a different name. She could have been an orphan whose parents changed her name, or she could have changed it herself, as did Twylia May Embrey. The only other possibility was that she was born after April 1, 1930. If so, Katharine easily could have been twenty-four years old, as her landlady had stated when she reported her missing.

A search of Texas birth records was equally unrevealing. A thorough correspondence with the San Antonio Metropolitan Health District's Office of Vital Records, the Bexar County Clerk's Office, and the Texas Department of Health, Bureau of Vital Statistics confirmed that there was no birth certificate for Katharine Farrand, no matter how her name was spelled. We did find another San Antonio–born Katharine, with a birth date just two days later and with a different last name, but when we sent off for her obituary, it clearly was not her, as the other Katharine had never lived in Arizona or Colorado. If the Katharine we were seeking was born at home and her birth was not recorded, she may not have gotten a birth certificate immediately, but a check of "delayed" birth certificates—applied for by individuals at a later date—did not turn up any documentation, either.

Before long, we began to doubt not only the date of Katharine's birth, but also the place. In long group emails, I updated Micki, Cindi, Dave, and Karen Anne about our collective progress and lack of progress. They responded with new leads that we all checked out on our own and then debated. Some looked promising at first, including online Texas birth records that showed an unnamed female baby, born to a single mother in San Antonio in October 1926. When the 1930 census listed the mother still living in the city—but without the child—we assumed, at first, that she had given up the child for adoption and thought that perhaps the child had been adopted by a family with the last name of Farrand. A check of online Texas death records, however, showed that the baby had died when she was only four days old.

One day, Karen Anne wrote: "This just puzzles me to no end. Is someone out there saying, 'What happened to —' and we have not connected the dots? I mean, how does a person go missing, with no sibling, no parent—no friend—nothing—no one to say a word?"

Together, the researchers and I started compiling a list of Farrand families from all over the country. The name is relatively unusual, and a very prominent Farrand family actually had lived in Boulder at one time. From 1914 to 1919, Dr. Livingston Farrand was president of the University of Colorado. Toward the end of his term, however, he and his wife and children moved to Paris, France, where he directed the anti-tuberculosis commission for the International Health Board of the Rockefeller Foundation during World War I. After that, he oversaw the transition of the American Red Cross as it adapted from times of war to peace.

When Dr. Farrand's overseas work was done, he accepted the presidency of Cornell University, in Ithaca, New York, where he remained for the rest of his career. His name has since been given to a dormitory at the University of Colorado, Boulder, as well as to the adjacent Farrand Field, in the national news once a year when it is descended upon by masses of marijuana smokers. My fellow researchers and I scrutinized all familial connections of this family, but we found no one named Katharine and no one missing.

As Micki had done when she called women named Twylia, I started calling members of various Farrand families to see if their family trees included any missing young women. When I told the people who answered the telephone that my purpose was to try to trace a missing person who I believed was a murder victim, and that my intention was to return the victim's remains to wherever they belonged, some people were very interested. Others were not. Two separate women patiently listened to my story and then asked me the same question: "Why would you want to do that?" I explained that I believed no one should be buried as an unknown, but in each case I met blank silence on the other end of the line.

I also returned to the Colorado Historical Society's library, in Denver, and compiled lists of every Farrand—in the appropriate time period—that I could find in the *Denver City Directories*. I found and confirmed a few intact families, then looked for a single woman of the right name and age who could have been Katharine's mother. I soon found myself corresponding with the nephew of a now-deceased woman named Marion E. Farrand, who, as a child, had been in and out of Denver-area orphanages and foster homes. She could have—speculated the nephew—given birth in 1927 to an illegitimate child. That possibility opened up communication with homes for unwed mothers, but no one found any records of the woman having given birth to a child, illegitimate or otherwise. Social workers and others I talked with, however, explained that birth mothers often gave assumed names, and some births went unrecorded.

In continuing to scour the Denver directories, I surprised myself when I found a Katharine Farrand listed in 1948. I had missed her before, when I was only looking for Katharine Dyer. Katharine Farrand worked at the soda fountain of Republic Drug Company, in the Enterprise Building at Champa and Fifteenth streets in downtown Denver. Now I knew that Katharine—but not her future husband—had lived in Denver for at least a year before her marriage in Arizona. Had she been raised in Denver, too, perhaps by parents with a different last name? Was she illegitimate, orphaned, or adopted? Had her mother remarried a man with the last name of Farrand, or had Katharine, herself, been married to a Farrand before she married Jimmie Dyer? The more I learned, the more questions I had.

In an effort to rule out the possibility that Katharine was Jane Doe, the researchers and I also tried to find her alive. We entered her stated date of birth—in various combinations of the month, day, and year—in every search engine we could find. At Commander Phil West's request, Detective Steve Ainsworth searched his sources, too, available only to law-enforcement officials. Even he came up empty-handed with the source that I considered our greatest hope and our greatest hurdle—the Social Security Administration.

After people are deceased, copies of their Social Security applications, like the one I obtained with Twylia's fictitious name, are available, for a small fee, to anyone who requests them. With the living, however, there is no way to pry the information from government files. Unidentified murder victims do not fit into either category. They are not officially deceased, so they are still considered alive—even when they are not. I found it extremely frustrating that we were unable to read what Katharine wrote on her application, if indeed she did apply for a Social Security number. If she told the truth, we would have a second documentation for her birth date and place, and—what we needed the most—the names of her parents.

We also needed, and this time received, a member of law enforcement to initiate a search of Colorado birth records. Unlike the state of Texas, which allows the public to access any vital records more than seventy-five years old, the Colorado Department of Public Heath and Environment prohibits public disclosure of birth records until they are one hundred years old. A simple faxed request from Detective Ainsworth, however, confirmed that no one named Katharine Farrand had a Colorado birth certificate.

Again I looked at the address in Denver where Katharine had lived in 1954, before her landlady reported her missing. This time I found a possible connection between Katharine Farrand Dyer and Harvey Glatman. After Glatman moved to California in 1957 and was arrested there, in 1958, he was dubbed "the lonely hearts killer." The reason was because he admitted that in trolling for victims, he had frequented dating clubs, and he ended up murdering at least one of the women he met through a California club. Denver had lonely hearts clubs, too.

From *Denver City Directories*, as well as classified newspaper advertisements on microfilm at the Denver Public Library, I found two Denver clubs in business in 1954. One was the Get Acquainted Club, at 2239 East Colfax Avenue, and the other was the Clara Lane Friendship Society. The Clara Lane club was in a large old house at 1046 Washington Street, in Denver's Capitol Hill neighborhood. The building was within two blocks of the alley where Glatman had assaulted Eula Jo Hand. It also was within one block of, and on the same street as, the house where Katharine had rented a room—the room from where she disappeared.

I knew the club was no longer in operation, but I wondered if the houses were still there, so I drove to Denver, where I found both residences. In 1954, after Katharine had separated from Jimmie, it would not have been out of the question for her to have walked down the street and signed up for a date. Or Glatman, with his Dodge Coronet parked on the street, may have spotted Katharine, at night, when she got off a bus—and then forced her into his car at gunpoint. In California, Glatman drove his victims long distances—with their wrists tied together—taking them from cities to remote desert areas. He easily could have driven Katharine from Denver to the mountains west of Boulder.

Even before Glatman had his car, however, he had become familiar with Capitol Hill. Not only had he assaulted Eula Jo and at least two other women there, but the neighborhood was on the bus route between his parents' home and downtown Denver. When he was in high school, he most likely rode the bus to his job at the Denver Auditorium, only one block from the Republic Drug Company where, two or three years later, Katharine was known to have made malts and sundaes. The auditorium also was within walking distance of the American Furniture Company, where Katharine was working when she disappeared.

The late Clara Lane, I learned by reading old newspaper articles about the dating club's owner, was an Iowa native who had franchised similar dating clubs all over the country. Today's generation can sign up on the internet to be matched to, hopefully, compatible persons, but lonely Denver men and women in the 1950s answered the advertisements published by businesswoman Clara Lane. One of the come-ons I found in a Denver newspaper read, "Lonely? My specialty is helping others with their problems and finding the right companion." In return, the proprietress charged a fee. Lane admitted, in a magazine article, that extroverted men and women can meet in taverns and ballrooms, then asked, "But what about the quiet, re-served ones?" The matrimonial matchmaker stated that she hoped the quiet, reserved ones would come to her. Glatman would have fit right in.

He also fit into the *America's Most Wanted* program, still under way. Finally, near the end of June 2006, producer Fred Peabody told me that our segment was scheduled to be shown in eleven days, and I was expected in the Bethesda, Maryland, studio on July 8 for the show's debut. As I scrambled to get a last-minute plane ticket, I was told that Detective Steve Ainsworth would be a guest that evening, as well.

As luck would have it, Micki, the researcher who had been with me the longest, lived in Woodbridge, Virginia, within an hour's drive of the *America's Most Wanted* headquarters. She drove in to meet me at my hotel. With dark brown wavy hair and bright blue eyes, Micki was in her thirties and almost young enough to be my daughter. I was overjoyed to finally meet the person I had been corresponding with for four years, and we im-mediately talked liked old friends—about Jane Doe, Twylia May Embrey,

Researcher Micki Lavigne, left, and the author, right, met face-to-face for the first time in Bethesda, Maryland, on the afternoon of the America's Most Wanted *show.*

and our families. I gave her a copy of the compact disc containing the song "Tragedy," and she gave me a rhinestone-studded pen to take notes with that evening. I wished that she could have stayed, but there was no studio audience and no way to slip her through the door. I told her I was anxious about the show.

A few hours later, in the lobby of the Marriott Hotel, I found myself in a social setting with Detective Ainsworth. He was holding a newly released copy of the book *Cold Case Homicides*, by Vidocq Society member Richard Walton, who had used our Jane Doe case as a textbook example. I asked to see the book and told the detective that I looked forward to finally getting some new leads and sharing my subsequent research with him when we got back to Boulder. Then the detective and I were wined and dined, along with several other guests, all in law enforcement, who represented their own cases to be covered in the three other ten-minute segments of the upcoming show. After dinner, a producer ushered us into the television studio where all viewers in the eastern time zone—including all of us—watched the program for the first time.

The Jane Doe segment began with a reenactment of the two students who found her body, as well as actual footage of the recent "Meet the Spirits" event—similar to the one in 1996 at which I first became aware of the unidentified victim's story. The coverage also included our search for Twylia, but not the recent information on how Micki had tracked her down. Frank Bender and Vidocq Society board chairman Frederick Bornhofen were interviewed, and Frank's sculpted facial reconstruction of Jane Doe finally was shown to a national audience. In addition, viewers were told that Harvey Glatman was Jane Doe's probable killer. A plea, by host John Walsh—himself a parent of a murder victim—was made to the audience to call the show with any leads on Jane Doe's identity.

There was no mention of Katharine, as all of the filming for the program had been completed far in advance. I was eagerly hoping, however, that a member of Katharine's family would recognize her and call the show. I was uncomfortable and a little embarrassed that the segment had so much footage on me. On air, both of the Vidocq Society men had complimented my work, and even Boulder County Sheriff Joe Pelle had been interviewed and jokingly said that he might have to deputize me and put me on the payroll, but nothing was shown of the hours that the crew had filmed Commander West, Detective Ainsworth, and me sitting in the sheriff's office training room discussing the case. The program did not credit any of their work. Except for a brief scene at Jane Doe's exhumation, neither of these sheriff officials were in the program at all.

In the control room at America's Most Wanted, *an operator takes a telephone call from a viewer and types a synopsis of the call onto her computer.*

When the show was over, Detective Ainsworth and I went into a windowless control room, where twenty or so operators sat behind computer terminals, ready to answer viewers' calls as they came in. During the next four hours, the show was repeated in the Central, Mountain, and Pacific time zones. I watched as the telephone operators typed up their conversations. Although most of the calls were about the other cases on the show, I was nervous and excited, thinking at any moment we might get some real answers on Jane Doe. Then a staff member came up to me and told me that I could look at the screens over the operators' shoulders, but when their information was printed out and placed in the "tip folder" on the table, only Detective Ainsworth and other law-enforcement professionals were allowed to read it.

This command that I could look but not touch—a policy with which the detective agreed—seemed extremely illogical to me. If it had to do with protecting the integrity of the case should the murderer go on trial, then why was I allowed in the control room in the first place? As the evening wore on, I found myself getting more and more exasperated. At one point I used Micki's pen to scribble notes on a napkin, then I sat on it so that no one would be able to see what I had written!

16

Disappointed, I left the *America's Most Wanted* studio late at night and did not get much sleep. In the morning, I got in my rental car and headed to Cherry Hill, New Jersey, to visit friends. To stay awake at the wheel, I stopped at every rest area along Interstate 95 through Maryland and Delaware. My attitude improved, somewhat, when I reminded myself that even though the hours I spent in the studio and my interaction with Detective Steve Ainsworth had not gone as I had expected—he did not allow me to leave with copies of the "tip sheets"—I had never before worked with law-enforcement professionals and, to my knowledge, they had not worked with a layperson like me. I had no idea that Sheriff Joe Pelle would, one day, present me with an award for being the "driving force" in revisiting the Jane Doe case.

The next day, I had an appointment in Philadelphia with Frederick Bornhofen and Frank Bender. Since excerpts of interviews with all three of us had aired on the show the night before, I knew we would have plenty to talk about. Frank told me to come directly to his art studio.

Although a native of southeastern Pennsylvania, I had not been in Philadelphia for forty-one years. On several of my childhood birthdays, my mother had driven my friends and me from our hometown of Lancaster to the Philadelphia Zoo, the first zoo in the country. During my high school days, I always considered it a treat to go to into the city by train and shop for clothes at Wanamaker's, a twelve-floor department store that encompassed an entire city block. In addition to selling nearly everything imaginable, the store was known for its marble-clad atrium, which held the world's largest pipe organ and a huge bronze eagle from the St. Louis World's Fair, as well as elaborate Christmas displays.

Driving on the Schuylkill Expressway into the city by myself, in July 2006, was a different experience, but once I turned off on the South Street exit, I felt at home in the midst of the historic and predominantly redbrick buildings. When I stopped my car in front of Frank's combined residence and studio, I found him tending a few flowers in a postage-stamp-size plot in the sidewalk. He looked just the same as when I had met him a year earlier in Boulder.

Divided display windows, now covered with blinds, covered the front of the former commercial building, which was once a butcher shop. When we went inside, I found myself in a narrow eighty-eight-foot-long room with a high ceiling, white walls, and a paint-splattered gray floor. Shelves lined part of the walls, and each one was jam-packed with supplies and eclectic objects of art. Frank had a clay sculpture in progress, while busts of other murder victims, lined up in rows, stared down from high shelves. Stacked against another wall were painted canvases, mostly of people, including one self-portrait discreetly hidden behind the others. In addition to the art, there were books, compact discs, family photographs, and all sorts of other items practically oozing off the shelves.

One flight down, in a small section of the basement that was open to the studio above it, Frank kept a track for a model train. Only instead of railroad engines and cars, he had toy trolleys. He proudly showed me his collection and explained that running the trolleys around the track was the way he liked to relax.

At the end of the studio was a kitchen, of sorts, with a refrigerator, microwave, hot plate, and sink. In the very rear of the building was Frank and his wife's bedroom, a bathroom, and a small living and computer area. Frank had recorded the *America's Most Wanted* program, so we watched it together. As planned, Frederick Bornhofen came by and drove us to a Chinese restaurant for lunch. On the way, we discussed the show. The men commented that the sheriff had made us all look good, and they felt that the focus on me—the "Grandma angle," as they called it—had made the story easier to relate to for the average person. In addition, we were pleased that the contributions of the Vidocq Society had been acknowledged.

I told Frederick and Frank about watching the operators take calls in the control room. They quizzed me about new leads, but I could only tell them what I knew and that was not much. I had seen enough of the operators' computer screens, however, to know we had not had a breakthrough, and I was sure there was no mention of Katharine Farrand or Katharine Dyer. Frank, particularly, was interested in any feedback on the bust he had sculpted of Jane Doe. I told him about my scribbled notes on the napkin—about a man who thought the facial reconstruction resembled Agnes, a classmate he knew in a California orphanage in 1953. The man said the girl had been mistreated, but he did not even know if she was missing or if there was any connection with Colorado. I promised to let the Vidocq men know more—if and when I learned more myself.

At home, I was pleased to get another email from Susan, the cousin of Marion Joan McDowell, who had disappeared from Toronto in December 1953. Susan, a Canadian resident, had also watched the *America's Most Wanted* program, and she said she hoped it brought in new leads. "Unless a family has had a tragedy such as ours," she said, "they do not understand how the dynamics of your family remain changed forever, even if it is fifty years. I know if the girl had turned out to be Marion, it would bring so much comfort just to know where she is, even if the answer to finding her creates more questions."

The very next day, two Jehovah's Witnesses knocked on my door. My husband and I live in a remote mountain location and never before, or since, have we had a visit from representatives of this religious organization. When I answered the door, one of the women asked, "Wouldn't it be nice if we could bring the dead back to life?" Astounded, but not wanting to get into a prolonged conversation, I agreed with her and let the women go on their way.

Three weeks after our *America's Most Wanted* program aired on television, Detective Ainsworth did release the "tip sheets" to me. At that point, it did not matter what hoops I needed to jump through, I was just glad to finally be able to read them. With Commander West's permission, I summarized the information and emailed it to my fellow researchers. Two of the show's callers were psychics. One thought Jane Doe's name was "Susan" and the other said it was "Josephine." Another well-meaning person suggested that "all the lady detective needed to do was to go to Jane Doe's grave and listen."

Another viewer thought the victim looked like Harvey Glatman and suggested we check to see if he had any missing relatives, which he had not. A woman called to say she had a neighbor in Georgia whose daughter was a writer and had run off, in 1954, with a man who had a connection to a crime magazine. The man's name was Harvey.

Focusing on the more likely scenarios, my fellow researchers and I eliminated a young woman named Lucille whose paper trail extended past April 1954. The only other information I could find out about Agnes, the girl that a male caller had known in a California orphanage, was that the owners of the "Mountain Home for Contented Children" had ended up in prison. Only one lead was specific to Colorado, and that was from a woman in Mississippi who called to say that the bust looked like her childhood friend, Maxine. The two had gone to school together in Denver while Maxine was living in the Colorado Christian Home. The caller told me that she had been thinking about her friend for a week or so. Then, after watching the *America's Most Wanted* show, she said to herself, "I hope she's a grandma somewhere like I am."

The Christian home is still in operation as a treatment center for abused, neglected, and at-risk youth. I contacted the director who found a group photograph that included Maxine. I had already emailed him Jane Doe's facial reconstruction, and he said there was "a resemblance of sorts." The treatment center's records also confirmed that Maxine had lived there for two years, then was released to the care of a family member. There was no report of her having been missing. What was of most interest to me, however, was that at a time when so many public and police records have vanished, this private facility found records of four specific dates within a two-week period in the 1940s that Maxine had gone to a dentist. She had dental work on her teeth, but Jane Doe never even had a filling. Maxine was not Jane Doe.

Dental work also ruled out another possible Jane Doe—Connie Smith. Several people writing to the Jane Doe website's message board had suggested Connie's name, but the researcher most interested in the twelve-year-old girl was Sandy Bausch, a Connecticut resident and both the daughter and wife of Connecticut state troopers. She worked as an auditor for armored car companies and became the sixth member of our core research team. Connie's story had been high profile when the young girl vanished in 1952, as her grandfather had been the former governor of Wyoming, and no resources were spared in her search. Connie had lived in Wyoming, but she walked away from summer camp in Connecticut after saying she was homesick and wanted to go back home.

No confirmed trace of Connie has ever been found, but on October 31, 1958, northwest of Flagstaff, Arizona—south of the Grand Canyon—in Coconino County, two deer hunters found the skeletal remains of a five-foot to five-foot-three-inch teenage girl. They notified police, who called her "Little Miss X." She had lain naked and prone on the ground for more than a year, and her clothing was found nearby. Coconino County sheriff's officials presumed she had been murdered, but they did not determine the manner of her death.

Ironically, the very day that this victim's remains were discovered was the day that California officials arrested Harvey Glatman for murder. The popular east-west route, United States Highway 66, ran nearby, and it was the likely route that Glatman would have driven—via Albuquerque, New Mexico, and Flagstaff, Arizona—to travel between Denver and southern California. After his move to the Los Angeles area in 1957, he made frequent trips back to Denver to visit his mother. Little Miss X, who had been stripped and dumped in a remote area, could easily have been one of his victims. If I had been the one to interview Glatman, there were a lot of questions I would have liked to have asked.

According to the Arizona State Department of Health's official death certificate for Little Miss X, her remains were buried in the Coconino County section of Citizens Cemetery in Flagstaff, adjacent to the college campus where Katharine Dyer's husband, Jimmie, had been a student. In 1958, the Coconino County sheriff sent out more than one thousand circulars describing the victim's remains, and he received missing-persons reports from all over the country. The only one who pre-dated Jane Doe, however, was Evelyn Hartley, a teenage girl who was abducted from La Crosse, Wisconsin, while babysitting in 1953. I had read everything I could on Evelyn and told Commander West about her, but the young Wisconsin woman's description did not fit either Jane Doe or Little Miss X. Evelyn was larger-boned than Jane Doe and wore larger clothing than that found with Little Miss X. Evelyn was listed on my spreadsheet of missing young women, but she—like Connie Smith and Marion Joan McDowell—has never been found.

In the mail that poured in to the Coconino County Sheriff's Office following the discovery of Little Miss X's remains was a movie magazine on which the name of actress Dana Wynter had been circled. The German-born dark-haired beauty had starred in the 1956 science-fiction film *Invasion of the Body Snatchers*, in which a small-town doctor is overrun with patients accusing their loved ones of being imposters. Instead of mass hysteria, as the fictional doctor had first thought, humanity was being overrun by "pod people"—creatures from plantlike pods who looked exactly like the people they replaced but were devoid of emotion and who killed and disposed of their human victims. Whether this was supposed to be allegorical, helpful, or just a crank suggestion is not known, but the actress lived to star in many more movies.

In 1962, Little Miss X's remains were exhumed so that a pathologist and dentist could compare her teeth with dental records of Connie Smith, still missing after a decade. Clarke Cole, who was Coconino County under-sheriff at the time, took Little Miss X's jaw and teeth and drove to Wyoming to visit Connie Smith's father. Then the under-sheriff continued on to Connie's former dentist in Spearfish, South Dakota, before visiting with a pathologist in Denver. Both the dentist and a pathologist noted similarities, but they were not enough to make a positive identification between Little Miss X and Connie Smith. In addition, as was the case with the girl in the Colorado Christian Home, Connie's dental records showed that she had fillings—proving that she could not have been Jane Doe. There was still a possibility, however, that she could be Little Miss X.

Sandy, the researcher who initially contacted me about Connie Smith, explained that there was new interest in the case because DNA from a member of Connie Smith's family had recently become available for comparison with DNA that could be extracted from one of Little Miss X's bones or teeth. The only problem is that no one has been able to find her remains!

Newspaper reports from 1962 stated that Under-Sheriff Cole returned to Flagstaff, Arizona, with Little Miss X's jaw and teeth, but no records in the Coconino County Sheriff's Office or the Coconino Superior Court give a clue as to the current location of her remains. The county section of the Citizens Cemetery, where the victim was initially buried, is a wide-open field with no grave stones or markers. Cemetery officials admit that the area is "full of bodies," but they are as baffled as everyone else as to the precise location. Perhaps the sheriff and under-sheriff were present at Little Miss X's original burial and simply dug her up and reburied her remains in the same place. Both men are now deceased. No wonder the National Institute of Justice calls the desperate situation of the missing and unidentified the nation's silent mass disaster. Not only have records been lost, but so have remains.

Flagstaff may not have been able to help its unknown victim, but the people of Prescott, Arizona, remembered theirs. In 1960, the community buried the remains of a seven- to nine-year-old girl they called "Little Miss Nobody." A rock-hunting schoolteacher found the partially decomposed body half-buried along the side of a creek. A knife was found nearby, and sheriff officials declared it a homicide. The girl was dressed in white shorts and a checkered blouse, and had nail polish on her fingernails and toenails. No one came forward to claim her.

Just as it had been important to the Boulder community that Jane Doe have a Christian burial, so, too, did the people of Prescott insist on Christian services for Little Miss Nobody. Plans were initiated by a radio announcer, and townspeople, a monument company, florists, and others answered his pleas for private donations. More than seventy people turned out for the service, led by the First Congregational Church's Reverend Charles Franklin Parker.

According to a write-up in the *Prescott Evening News*, the Reverend Parker had tears in his eyes as spoke. "Here is a little wanderer who has been in our midst," he said. "We don't know her name. We can only guess her age. It occurs to me we may not know, but God knows. There are no unknowns, no orphans in God's world." The young girl's pale blue casket was adorned with a large spray of pink and white carnations, while four baskets of flowers and several additional floral arrangements were set on the ground nearby. An anonymous writer left these words: "Forgive us, child, for the weakness of men; and, in turn, when in your final home, pray for us."

Sandy, the other researchers, and I corresponded about these unknown victims as well as Jane Doe. Although the *America's Most Wanted* program had not brought in the hoped-for leads, contributors to the Jane Doe message board added tips of their own. One concerned a report in a January 1954 Modesto, California, newspaper of a sixteen-year-old, blonde, epileptic hospital escapee. Could she have been Jane Doe, the reader wanted to know? I was struck with how far all of us—who I continued to call Jane Doe's extended family—had come in our combined quest for her identity. It had all started with her gravestone, generously donated by a caring community. How tragic that the Flagstaff community had not done the same for Little Miss X.

Harvey Glatman was often on my mind, too. In July 2006, I made an appointment with Richard Nelson, an alumnus of Denver East High School, to see if I could find any more information on the notorious former student. The Jacobean-style redbrick building with terra cotta trim dates from 1924 and is located on the esplanade that connects busy East Colfax Avenue with Denver City Park. On a hot summer afternoon, Richard and I climbed the stairs of the spacious building. As our voices echoed off the walls, I tried to imagine what the hallways were like filled with students. Richard took me into the clock tower where the school's alumni association stored its collection of old yearbooks. From the outside, the tower is reminiscent of Independence Hall in Philadelphia. Because of the building's architectural significance, the Denver Landmark Commission and the Denver City Council granted it landmark status in 1991.

I was hoping to find Glatman's photograph, but it was not included in the annuals that we searched. It was not unusual, said Richard, as in the 1940s not all students submitted individual photographs for the yearbooks. My alumni contact was a former student and also a retired teacher at the school, but he had never heard of Glatman. Like the administrators at the University of Denver, he was not thrilled to know of East High's connection with a serial killer. We discussed some of the other notable alumni, from silent screen actor Douglas Fairbanks, Sr., to folk singer Judy Collins.

After I returned home, Richard emailed me information he later found on Glatman's high school registration card. In addition to the basic information I already knew, it stated that the former student had ranked in the upper seventh percent of his class—correlating with his later psychiatrists' statements indicating his high IQ. School records also mentioned that Glatman was a member of both the high school orchestra and band. At a later date, in the Denver Public Library, I looked at the yearbooks again

Bus routes through Denver's Capitol Hill neighborhood with sites for Harvey Glatman, his known Denver victims and Katharine Farrand Dyer.

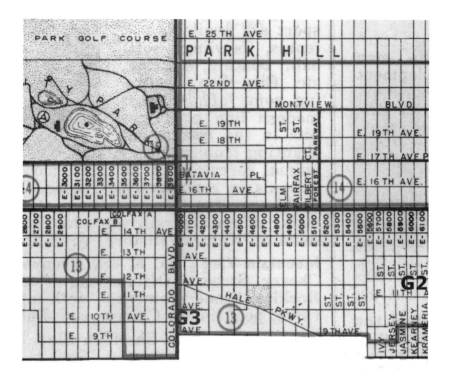

Key: **G1** = *Denver East High School, where both Glatman and Eula Jo Hand went to school.* **G2** = *1133 Kearney Street, home of Glatman and his mother, Ophelia.* **G3** = *Colorado Psychopathic Hospital, Colorado Boulevard and Ninth Avenue.* **G4** = *1045 East Colfax Avenue, Valas Motor and Radio Center, Glatman's employer in 1953.* **G5** = *Glenarm Place and Sixteenth Street, Rosalie Shop (renamed Hollywood Millinery) owned by Glatman's aunt, Rosalie Gold, and employer of Ophelia Glatman.* **G6** = *1010 Corona Street, home of Glatman's aunt, Rosalie Gold, in 1954.* **G7** = *1046 Washington Street, Clara Lane Friendship Society in 1954.* **V1** = *1230 Clarkson Street, home of Eula Jo Hand in 1945 at the time she was assaulted by Harvey Glatman.* **V2** = *Sixteenth and Stout streets, Neusteter's Department Store, Eula Jo Hand's employer in 1945.* **V3** = *624 East Twelfth Avenue, home of Rosemary Clement, a victim/witness in Eula Jo Hand's 1945 court case, and probable location of Eula Jo's attack.* **V4** = *1170 Logan Street, home of Dorothy Holder, a victim/witness in Eula Jo Hand's 1945 court case.* **V5** = *1540 Washington Street, home of Anna Mae Barr, a victim/witness in Eula Jo Hand's 1945 court case.* **V6** = *1703 Vine Street, home of Doris Lukman, a victim/witness in Eula Jo Hand's 1945 court case.* **K1** = *1715 Vine Street, home of Katharine Farrand in 1948.* **K2** = *Fifteenth and Champa streets, Republic Drug Company, Katharine's employer in 1948.* **K3** = *1624 Tremont, Evans Investment Company, Katharine's employer in 1951.* **K4** = *Sixteenth and Lawrence streets, American Furniture Company, Katharine's employer in 1954.* **K5** = *1118 Washington Street, home of Katharine when she was reported missing in 1954.* **K6** = *1282 Lafayette Street, home of Jimmie Dyer, Katharine's estranged husband, in 1954. Composite map based on Denver Convention and Visitors Bureau Map of Denver 1954, modified by Silvia Pettem.*

and found him, in his junior year, as one of seventy-three musicians in the school's concert band. In crisp white slacks and a dark double-breasted jacket, with a cornet in his hand, he sat with the band on the stage of the 1,800-seat high school auditorium. In that setting, Glatman blended in with his classmates—and appeared to fit into the norms of society—most likely for the last time. In Richard's correspondence, he added, "I did talk with a 1945 graduate, and he did not know the boy [Glatman] personally, but he said that everyone was abuzz about his arrest."

During the summer of 2006, I continued to talk on the telephone with Glatman's surviving victim, Eula Jo Hand. She was pleased to know I had visited Denver East High School, as it had been her high school, too. She told me that the reason we were unable find any records of Glatman's graduation was because, in May 1945, when he should have graduated, he was in jail following his arrest for assaulting her.

All of the discussion of Glatman's activities in various Denver locations made me eager to look them up on a map. I went back to the annual Rocky Mountain Antiquarian Book Fair—where I had met the book dealer who provided me with a copy of *Dood* magazine—and decided to see what else I could find. This time I came home with a 1954 transportation map of Denver, showing all of the downtown bus routes. On it, I plotted where Harvey Glatman lived and worked, as well as where Eula Jo Hand (and a few other victims), and Katharine Farrand Dyer had lived and worked. I found the lives of these people so intertwined that they could easily have ridden the same buses, followed each other off the buses, or run into each other on Denver streets.

My telephone conversations with Eula Jo Hand spanned August 2006, when the nearly ten-year-old case of JonBenét Ramsey was back in the news following the arrest of murder suspect John Mark Karr. I reflected on the fact that the little girl's death on Christmas night 1996 occurred just two months after I had first viewed Jane Doe's gravestone in Columbia Cemetery. In recent years, former Boulder County district attorney Mary Lacy, of Colorado's Twentieth Judicial District, had taken charge of the Ramsey case. News accounts revealed that even though she was flying in—first class, no less—the suspect from Thailand, her office had been unable to place Karr in Boulder at the time of the crime. The suspect's own family insisted he had been with them, in Georgia. I had lived in the community during and after the six-year-old's murder, and my own opinions did not support the intruder theory. Talk show hosts tended to agree and were having a field day. A Denver station played a parody of the Beatles' song "Baby,

You Can Drive My Car . . ." substituting the words "Baby, It's Not John Mark Karr. . . ."

I went to the district attorney's press conference out of curiosity. If nothing else, I figured it would be entertaining, and I was not disappointed. The event was held outside, in the parking lot of the Boulder County Justice Center. The crush of media—with rows of tents as well as double-parked satellite trucks—was overwhelming, obvious proof that JonBenét was one murder victim who would not be forgotten. A platform was set up for the district attorney officials. The former district attorney, herself, with coiffed light-brown hair and a pale green suit, stepped up to the podium and addressed an international crowd of print and broadcast journalists and a very long bank of television cameras.

Seated among the seasoned veteran reporters were others who had been in high school at the time of JonBenét's murder. I overheard one of the young reporters say she "never thought she would see this day," adding, "There really was a killer on the loose." I urged her to wait and see. In murder investigations, things are not always as they seem.

Former district attorney Lacy began her remarks by stating that on the previous day, Karr had been arrested in Bangkok, Thailand, for the murder of JonBenét Ramsey. In a carefully phrased media release, Lacy explained that the thin forty-one-year-old schoolteacher was arrested because a judge had found probable cause. Specifically, Karr had recently been identified as the writer of four years of previously anonymous emails that culminated in his self-described sexual involvement with the six-year-old victim. Included in the former district attorney's remarks was the advice given to her office on the previous day by the victim's father, John Ramsey. "Do not jump to judgment," he said. "Let the justice system take its course."

News anchors reported live and satellite trucks sent the breaking news around the world. Within days, Boulder authorities released Karr, whose DNA did not match the DNA at the scene of the crime. All that could be pinned on him was an expressed fascination for young girls and his previous convictions that included charges of possessing child pornography. In many people's minds, the former district attorney arrested him first and investigated him second, and she received more criticism than praise for her efforts.

When I was asked by a *Rocky Mountain News* reporter what I thought of Karr's arrest, I said that although we all long for justice for JonBenét, life is sacred and all murders—not just the high-profile ones—have equal significance. Without explaining the cases of Jane Doe, Little Miss X, or even Little Miss Nobody, I said that even unidentified murder victims deserve the same amount of attention and resources.

By the fall of 2006, my fellow researchers and I shared a belief that Jane Doe may have been Katharine, but the search for justice for the murder victim had taken on a life of its own. Karen Anne, the researcher from Michigan, philosophized in one of her emails: "What we find on our way to other things may actually be the reason we are looking."

17

I was feeling particularly proud of the fact that Twylia May Embrey's great-niece, Jennifer Kitt, was the keynote speaker at the Nebraska Press Women's annual fall conference, held in 2006 in North Platte. At the time, the young wife and mother was studying to be a radiologist and had never given a public speech in her life. I wish I had been in the packed room when she tearfully explained to the assembled seasoned journalists that the search for Jane Doe had finally brought her family the answers they had sought for more than half a century.

To me, personally, Jennifer had written: "Even without a name, Jane Doe has helped my family. Thanks for your friendship, hard work, and positive attitude that keeps my head up. You are an inspiration to the people around you, and I am proud to be your friend." The gratitude from Twylia's relatives was what I had hoped to hear from Jane Doe's family. Now I was starting to doubt that she had any family at all.

Katharine, too, was as elusive as ever, but my fellow researchers and I had amassed a large amount of information on her husband, Jimmie Dyer. Katharine had been his first wife, but through in-person courthouse research and diligent searches on the internet, we found that he also was married to wives number two, three, and four. Any or all of them, we figured, might know something that could help us. I found wife number two through the couple's divorce records. I called her on the telephone, and she invited me her home.

On the prearranged day, Jimmie Dyer's second wife, Joan, greeted me at the patio gate of her modest single-story condominium, a one-and-a-half-hour drive from my home. She gave me a warm smile, and I knew right away that I would like her. She had short gray hair and looked relaxed in shorts and a T-shirt. I knew that she had to be about seventy-five years old, but she looked younger. I sat down on the living room sofa in her un-cluttered and tidy home. My visit went surprisingly well given that I asked some rather intrusive questions.

During the course of two hours, Joan told me that she and Jim—as she had called her ex-husband—had met while skiing, in the spring of 1955. I explained that this would have been one year after Katharine was reported missing. I asked Joan what she knew of Jim's first wife. "On the night Jim proposed," she said, "he told me that he had been married before and had no children. He and I were married for fifteen years, and he never spoke of her again. I never even knew her name." When I asked if she thought it odd, she said that she was so much in love she would have married him no matter what he said. The only other information Joan had about Katha-rine came from Jim's deceased half sister Emily Starr. Joan had asked Emily about Jim's first wife, and Emily had called her a "falling-down drunk." Apparently, Jim was quite a drinker, too.

Later, with Joan's permission, I sent off for her marriage license with Jim. On it, he declared that he was divorced, but a search of the Denver District Court—the jurisdiction where both Jimmie and Katharine lived—proved fruitless. In the newspaper account that stated that Katharine was missing, it said she was "separated" from her husband. Perhaps he skipped formality and simply moved on with his life. Proof of divorce was not re-quired at the time.

At the Public Service Company, Jim had been what was called a "results engineer." He was responsible for the outcome, or results, of the power plant—making adjustments in the steam boilers and other equip-ment in order to keep the costs down and the machinery running as ef-ficiently as possible. Joan also mentioned that Jim had brought to the mar-riage his 1949 Mercury.

Joan was very open and seemed genuinely happy to tell me about her marriage, even though she admitted that it was not all rosy, and it had ended in divorce, prompting the paper trail that had led me to her. She spoke frankly—which pleased me—and we even discussed the possibility that Jim could have been Katharine's murderer. Joan thought it unlikely, however, noting that even though he had been a rugged outdoorsman and climber and was big and strong, he had never been abusive to her. I explained the theory, shared by the sheriff's office and me, that serial killer Harvey Glatman was Jane Doe's likely killer. Still, I took note of the fact that two years earlier, when I had followed up on the "bumper theory" and measured bumpers in a car collector's warehouse, a 1949 Mercury was the only car available to me with a bumper at the same height as Jane Doe's knee. Now we had two cars that fit the scenario—Harvey Glatman's 1951 Dodge Coronet and Jimmie Dyer's 1949 Mercury.

In the weeks that followed my visit with Jimmie Dyer's second wife, I reflected on our conversation and realized that Joan had given me a new lead—that her husband had been an active member of the Colorado Mountain Club. I had already tried to contact a couple of Jimmie's Public Service Company coworkers and found them all deceased, so I thought I would follow up on Colorado climbing buddies. I went to the club's archives in Golden, Colorado, to look for the names of anyone who might have known Jimmie in the early 1950s. It was possible, I thought, that his friends might be able to tell me some new tidbit of information about Katharine.

Woody Smith, the club's archivist, took me into the dingy, unheated basement of the mountain club building. The room was so cold that we kept on our winter coats. Woody, an intense man in his twenties with short brown hair, said that instead of leaving me there on my own, he would help me search for Jimmie's name if I would agree to watch a video he took of unidentified flying objects in Moab, Utah. It was a deal, and we set to work.

File cabinets lined the walls, and the room's only table was cluttered with papers. From the Colorado Mountain Club's minutes, we found that Jimmie—but not Katharine—had become a member of the Denver group between October 1950 and January 1951. I knew from the registrar's records at Arizona State College (now Northern Arizona University), that Jimmie had graduated in May 1950, so the date that he joined the Colorado Mountain Club showed that he, and presumably Katharine, had moved to Denver before the end of the calendar year. Since both Jimmie and Katharine had been listed in the 1951 *Denver City Directory*, the time frame made sense. The Colorado Mountain Club's Denver group, with more than six hundred members, was by far the largest in the state, although the Boulder group had one hundred members, and smaller groups met in Fort Collins, Colorado Springs, Walsenburg, and on Colorado's western slope.

The archivist explained that when climbers reached the summits of Colorado's fourteen-thousand-foot peaks, they normally signed registers giving their name, address, and date. This practice, to prove that a climber had made it to the top, was started in the 1920s, when conscientious climbers kept the brass cylinders in place and filled them with paper and pencils. Periodically, when the lists were full, they were removed and filed by date under the names of the individual peaks. With fifty-four Colorado "fourteeners," there were a lot of files for us to go through. Joan said Jimmie eventually climbed all of the peaks, but we only looked for his name in the early 1950s, during the time he was married to Katharine.

Woody and I found records of Jimmie's climbs on Mount Belford, Mount Bross, Crestone Peak and Needle, Huron Peak, and Mount Oxford, among others. When he climbed Mount Antero, in 1955, he added the number twenty-nine, in a circle, indicating that Antero was his twenty-ninth fourteen-thousand-foot peak, and he was more than halfway to his goal. Then, all of a sudden, I found Katharine's signature. Although she was not a Colorado Mountain Club member, she must have been a good hiker, as she accompanied her husband to the summit of Quandary Peak on August 26, 1951. The mountain is south of Breckenridge and is the highest point in Colorado's Ten Mile Range. Jimmie signed the register first, then Katharine, both giving their addresses as 952 Downing Street in Denver. Climbing with them was a man named Bill Perkins of 470 Lafayette Street. The Dyers and their climbing partner all lived on Capitol Hill.

I wondered what Katharine's life was like when Jimmie went on climbs without her. Second wife Joan had told me that she was often home with the couple's young children while her husband took off on strenuous weekend climbs, then disappeared for a week or more at a time during the summers. She said that she was envious of other couples with children who did activities together as a family. Katharine had no children. Perhaps her work schedule interfered, she had different interests, or Jimmie did not want her along.

When I got home, I began an internet search for Bill Perkins. I found fourteen current telephone listings for Bill and William Perkinses in Colorado alone. I called a few who turned out to be the wrong men. Finally I found the right Bill Perkins, in Boulder, and he remembered Jimmie Dyer, adding that they had also climbed Longs Peak together. Jimmie's former climbing partner then said they went their separate ways in 1953. I asked Bill Perkins what he knew about Katharine, hoping against hope that he would have some new information. The young woman must not have made much of an impression on him, however, as all he remembered was that Katharine was "an average female." He had no idea what had happened to her.

Meanwhile, Woody had taken a particular interest in the search for Katharine. In order to try to get more information, he asked if I minded if he approached a psychic. I told him he could do what he wanted but to leave me out of it—that I preferred to stick with facts. Little did I know that my husband Ed and I would, after all, end up attending a séance.

Woody made an appointment with a middle-aged woman he had picked from a classified advertisement and talked with several times on the telephone. The two set up a time to meet in her high-rise apartment building in Denver. On the appointed day, Ed and I had already planned to visit friends in Denver. Just before we left our home, Woody called to say that the clutch had gone out in his truck, and could we please pick him up and drive him to the psychic's apartment? Timewise, his request fit into our plans, and by the time we took him there, we were curious enough to tag along.

The three of us took the elevator to the eighth floor, where the psychic met us at the door to her apartment. It was small but sunny and bright, with white walls and a white couch. The woman's hair was nearly white, too, and she had on navy blue slacks with a navy blue sweatshirt over a red turtleneck shirt. After we were seated in her living room, Woody handed her the original register from Quandary Peak that contained both Jimmie's and Katharine's signatures. The woman placed one hand under the penciled page and the other hand over it, explaining that—from the original document—she was able to feel the couple's spiritual energies. From the heat given off by Katharine's signature, she said, she could tell that Katharine was very much in love. Jimmie's signature must not have given off the same amount of heat, as the psychic told us that Katharine was more in love with him than he was with her.

Our hostess then announced that she was going to go into a deeper level of awareness. While Ed, Woody, and I kept complete silence, she sat on the couch and meditated. For several minutes, the woman remained seated with her eyes closed and her palms up. When she opened her eyes, she told us that Katharine had been angry. "I heard her screaming 'no, no,' and then I think she was killed." Of Jimmie, she said that he was capable of her murder, but Katharine might not have been killed by him.

Ed and I agreed that, most likely, Woody had provided the woman with too much background information. Still, I welcomed their interest and looked for any way to advance Jane Doe's case. That opportunity came in November 2006, when Dr. Richard Froede asked my help in the preparation of a poster session on Jane Doe to be displayed during the conference of the American Academy of Forensic Sciences scheduled for the following February in San Antonio, Texas. I was excited at the prospect of sharing Jane's story with the academy's six thousand members—among them physicians, attorneys, dentists, toxicologists, physical anthropologists, document examiners, psychiatrists, engineers, physicists, chemists, criminologists, and educators.

To plan our poster session, Dr. Froede and his wife, Sue, graciously invited me to visit them in their home in Tucson. The trip also made it possible for me to meet with Eula Jo Hand, the Glatman assault victim who got away.

Denver International Airport was cold and snowy when I took off, so I soaked up the warm climate in Tucson while picking up my rental car and driving to the Froedes' southwestern-style home. From our vantage point overlooking the city and surrounding mountains, Dr. Froede and I got right to work, selecting photographs and working on the accompanying text for our presentation. The following morning, he and I went to the Pima County Medical Examiner's Office and reviewed the material again with Dr. Walter Birkby. The morgue was an eye-opener to me, especially when Dr. Birkby pointed out a refrigerated tractor trailer that held an overflow of dozens of bodies—many unidentified. Most of the corpses were those of illegal aliens who had crossed the border from Mexico and perished in the heat of the desert.

After the three of us were happy with our selection of photographs and text for the forensic conference, we had lunch in the nearby Ajo Café. Then I was off to see Eula Jo. I had been in contact with her daughter, who had set up our appointment. She was going to meet with us, too, but circumstances intervened and I went to see the Glatman assault victim on my own. At the time, she was recovering from surgery to repair a broken femur and was in the Healthsouth Rehab Institute on the northwestern outskirts of the city.

As I entered Eula Jo's small, sterile, semiprivate room, the first thing I noticed were her sparkling eyes, framed by a pair of glasses with molded plastic rims that included every color of the rainbow. Her shoulder-length gray hair was held back with a black plastic headband, and she was wearing a black T-shirt and royal blue sweatpants that hung loosely over her slender frame. She asked me to wheel her into a sitting room across the hall so that her roommate would not be able to listen to our conversation. I got the feeling that neither of them had many visitors. We spent a few minutes talking about her family and mine before getting to the subject we both planned to discuss. Our telephone conversations had already made us friends.

It was clear from the beginning of our conversation that Eula Jo was hungry for information on her long-ago attacker. I had brought along a copy of the *America's Most Wanted* video featuring the ten-minute segment on Jane Doe, so I popped it into a video recorder, and we watched it together. When Harvey Glatman's mug shot appeared on the screen, Eula Jo immediately recognized his jug-like ears. Just seeing his face brought back horrific memories, but she managed to stay calm. She told me again how he followed her off the bus and then bound, gagged, robbed, fondled, and beat her in an alley. From my Denver bus route map, we determined that she had ridden the bus that ran on East Thirteenth Avenue, within a block of her mother's home.

The night of Eula Jo's assault was a Friday, and she had just been paid. After work, she had gone to a movie, just as Norene Lauer—Glatman's Boulder victim—would do a few weeks later. Eula Jo did not remember which movie she saw, but of the new releases in downtown Denver at the time, one was *The Affairs of Susan*, a romantic comedy starring Joan Fontaine. The other starred Fred MacMurray in a musical comedy titled *Where Do We Go From Here?*

I told Eula Jo about Katharine and explained that she had also disappeared on a Friday, which likely had been her payday, too. Glatman's known victim and his possible victim also had something else in common. As Eula Jo had told me in one of our telephone conversations, she had worked both as a model and as an elevator "starter." Katharine had, a few years later, worked as an elevator "pilot"—the term used to describe young women elevator operators at the time. Eula Jo filled me in on elevator operator uniforms of the era, explaining that Katharine's would have been similar to hers. They included knee-length skirts, short tailored jackets, and, most likely, pumps or high-heeled shoes.

When Glatman forced Eula Jo at gunpoint into the alley off East Thirteenth Avenue, they walked for a block and probably ended up in the backyard of 624 East Twelfth Avenue, the address of one of the women listed in connection with Glatman's November 1945 trial. If the woman at the East Twelfth Avenue address was a witness, rather than a victim, she may have been the woman Eula Jo overheard telling a companion that she thought she "heard something" outside.

At the time, Eula Jo was still wearing her elevator operator uniform, but not for long. Glatman stripped off her jacket, gagged her to keep her from screaming, and tied her to a telephone pole. He must have fondled her then, before bludgeoning her with his gun. Then, keeping her gagged, he bound her again and forced her to lie down on the ground. Except for the pistol-whipping, Glatman's method of carrying out his crimes was nearly identical to what he would do during his next assault—on the Boulder mother, Norene Lauer. No wonder he had been easily apprehended after the young Boulder woman gave his description and told of being bound and gagged and molested. No one else apprehended in the area at the time had his same modus operandi. As a criminal, Glatman was one of a kind.

While Eula Jo writhed on the ground, Glatman stayed in the shadows and watched. His psychiatrists' reports, to be written in the months and years to come, would explain his unusual method of achieving sexual satisfaction. "He tied me up so tight my arms were numb for a day," Eula Jo said to me. Even though I had heard most of her story on the telephone, she felt the need to relate it to me again. When she, somehow, managed to get the gag out of her mouth, she screamed and a passerby found her, untied her, and took her home. I knew that just by listening, I had helped her deal with this difficult part of her past.

After two hours of intense conversation, Eula Jo fought back tears as I got ready to leave. She told me that she was very grateful to be alive, and that my visit had made her feel like a survivor. I knew I was parting with a friend I would probably never see again. By then I was calling her by her nickname, Jody. I told her I wanted to take her photograph, and I asked where she wanted to pose. She said she wanted everyone who would see her photograph to know she was a survivor. So I typed "Jody, you are a survivor" on my laptop and set it next to her on the table when I took her picture. When I walked out of the room, I knew that the time and expense I had put into flying to Tucson had been more than worthwhile.

The following morning, I again visited Dr. Walter Birkby at the Pima County Medical Examiner's Office. He and I talked about his work

Eula Jo Hand, who goes by the nickname of Jody, posed next to the author's laptop computer with the words, "Jody, you are a survivor." Sixty-one years after being assaulted by Harvey Glatman, she finally felt closure.

in reassembling Jane Doe's skull, which, at the time, was boxed up in the evidence room of the Boulder County Sheriff's Office. Our discussion of her skull led to mention of the rest of her skeletal remains. I asked where they were, and the forensic anthropologist replied, "Why they're right here in my office." I said that I thought, and he agreed, that all of Jane Doe's bones, teeth, and hair should be stored together. I was anxious to get her back underground.

After my return to Colorado, I talked on the telephone with Eula Jo's daughter, who appreciated my answers to some tough questions. "I always wanted to know what I feared the most," she told me, "and that was—did Glatman rape my mother?" The daughter added that she did not want to ask the question for fear that the discussion would be too traumatic for Eula Jo. Although she knew more about her mother's attack than Norene's daughter knew about her mother's, both daughters finally learned the truth about their respective family secrets. Horrible as the assaults were, neither included rape, nor did they escalate to murder. Before Eula Jo's daughter hung up, she thanked me for coming into her life. I was glad the Jane Doe case could put her mind to rest, too.

The next time I met with Commander Phil West, I gave him a report on my trip to Tucson. I told him about Jane Doe's remains in Dr. Birkby's office, and he made arrangements to have them shipped to Boulder. I also told him of my visit with Eula Jo. In addition, the commander and I went over the poster session that the forensic specialists and I had finalized for presentation to the American Academy of Forensic Sciences conference in San Antonio.

In preparation for my trip and hoped-for new information on Katharine, I contacted the San Antonio Public Library and began a correspondence with Jim, a genealogical volunteer. Like Paul, in Denver, he donated his time, in his hometown, to assist the organization Random Acts of Genealogical Kindness. Neither of these men asked for any money, and I never knew their last names. I explained to Jim that my researchers and I had not found an appropriate Katharine Farrand in the 1930 census, nor had we found her birth certificate in city, county, or state records. We also had ruled out another San Antonio Katharine with a birth date that was close.

Jim picked up the search in the library, going through *San Antonio City Directories* and telephone books from the 1920s and 1930s. He found Richard and Emma Farrand, the childless couple who had also turned up in our search of census records. From copies of their obituaries, we learned that the couple remained childless throughout their lives. Just to make sure, however, I called a cousin mentioned in an obituary, and he confirmed that the Farrands had not even had foster children. Jim even read microfilmed birth announcements in three different historic San Antonio newspapers, starting on Katharine's stated birth date of October 14, 1926. He looked every day for the next several weeks, but he did not find any babies born—during that time period—to anyone named Farrand.

Shortly before Christmas, my youngest daughter and I again attended the annual *Messiah* sing-along. The previous year, the music had given me a spiritual and much-needed break from reading the files that Sergeant John Umenhofer had sent on Harvey Glatman. Sitting again in Boulder's St. John's Episcopal Church, where the *Messiah* choir and orchestra continued to perform the sacred oratorio of Christ's birth, death, and resurrection—culminating in a resurrection for all—I was moved not only by the words and the music but also by choir director Robert Arentz's words.

Before conducting the overture, the director spoke briefly on G. F. Handel's connection with a foundling hospital in eighteenth-century London. Initially, Handel's first *Messiah* concert had been performed as a charitable event in Dublin, Ireland. Then, in 1749, the composer gave the oratorio as a benefit for the Hospital for the Maintenance and Education of Exposed and Deserted Young Children. At the time, orphaned babies and children died in the streets, and their unidentified bodies were thrown in the Thames River, where they floated away downstream. That first London concert attracted a wide audience, including the Prince and Princess of Wales. Handel's *Messiah* was performed for years to continue to raise money for the care of abandoned children.

As the orchestra began to play, followed by a tenor solo and the choir's first chorus, "And the Glory of the Lord," my thoughts turned back to Jane Doe. The soprano, alto, tenor, and bass vocal parts reminded me of the diverse layers of interest and support shown to her case from the many people involved—sometimes alone and sometimes in harmony. Vidocq Society board chairman Frederick Bornhofen had made a similar comment when he once told me that the Vidocq Society members "work together like a clock." My combined efforts with the forensic community and law-enforcement officials were not always that smooth, but all of us, including the other researchers, had a common bond. We worked toward the same goal—to obtain justice and restore dignity to a nameless murder victim.

18

December 2006 also brought the death of seventy-two-year-old Wayne Swanson, one of the two students who had found Jane Doe's body. When I stumbled upon his birth and then death dates on the internet, I was hit with the realization that the last of the people associated with Jane Doe are, themselves, slipping into the past. I was glad I had interviewed Wayne when I did, and I was pleased that Dr. Richard Froede had agreed to post the photograph of the students in the poster session at the upcoming forensic conference.

During the holiday season, I printed out hard copies of all of the photographs that we had selected. They included the detectives who searched for clues and almost always wore their soft felt hats, a couple of April 1954 newspaper headlines, part of a page from the original autopsy report, Jane Doe's gravestone, and the mourners at her burial. Additional photographs showed scenes from the exhumation, Jane Doe's reassembled skull, her sculpted facial reconstruction, the press conference at which Frank Bender unveiled his sculpture, the "dummy toss" mannequin, and the crime scene in Boulder Canyon as it looks today. Finally, we chose a mug shot of serial killer Harvey Glatman, a photograph of one of his California victims with her wrists tied, and two of the never-published morgue photographs with close-ups of the wrist indentations that we believed came from a similar kind of ligature. In conclusion, we added a paragraph about Katharine Farrand Dyer.

In preparation for the conference, I volunteered to work eight hours in whatever sessions I would be needed in order to pay off my registration fee. Also, I lined up a roommate to stay with me at a bed-and-breakfast, within walking distance of the city's famed Riverwalk, the King William Historic District, and the Henry B. Gonzales Convention Center, where the conference would be held. Before I left home, I had spoken with a crime reporter from the *San Antonio Express-News* in the hopes that she could write a story on the forensic conference that would tie in with our search for Katharine in her stated hometown. The reporter responded enthusiastically, and the night after I arrived in Texas, we met in person and hashed out the details that tied the two stories together.

On the appointed day of our presentation, Dr. Richard Froede, Dr. Walter Birkby, Frederick Bornhofen, and I assembled the photographs and text on a large freestanding panel. I was pleased to be welcomed as a colleague on the home turf of the forensic community, and I helped Drs. Froede and Birkby, as well as Vidocq Society board chairman Bornhofen, tell our victim's story to a group of like-minded individuals. The *Express-News* reporter showed up with her photographer. The next day, we all were amazed to see our story above the fold on the front page of the large-circulation newspaper. If Katharine had any friends or family members at all in San Antonio, we expected to hear from them—but we never did.

In addition to being a room moderator for a couple of sessions, I browsed through a huge sea of vendors. I met with Dr. Terry Melton, president and director of Mitotyping Technologies, who had done the mitochondrial DNA profile of Jane Doe which emphatically had ruled out

In February 2007, Dr. Walter Birkby, left, and Frederick Bornhofen, right, explained the role of the Vidocq Society in the Jane Doe investigation to attendees of the American Academy of Forensic Sciences conference in San Antonio, Texas.

Twylia May Embrey. She told me of her continuing interest in our case, adding that Jane Doe's profile was "fairly unusual" and that her maternal line was closest to European types, possibly Swiss-German.

I also attended lectures on topics of interest to me. One evening's talk was on the role of the forensic scientist in controversial and politically charged international death investigations presented by Dr. Henry Lee, chief emeritus of the Connecticut Forensic Laboratory of the Connecticut State Police. With him was Dr. Cyril Wecht, a forensic pathologist, attorney, and medical-legal consultant from Pennsylvania. I remembered when Dr. Lee gained national prominence during the O. J. Simpson double-murder trial, then went to Boulder as a consultant on the JonBenét Ramsey murder case. Dr. Wecht, also well-known in high-profile cases, had authored the book *Who Killed JonBénet Ramsey?* giving his opinion that the child's murderer was a family member.

The session I liked best was called the Last Word Society, consisting of ten fifteen- to twenty-minute slide presentations, most with a historical slant. One included the well-known London serial killer, Jack the Ripper. Another was "The Saga of Willie Bryant's Winchester," presented by Richard Walton, the Vidocq Society member and author who had included Jane Doe in his textbook on cold case homicides. He told of the case of an innocent Native American man convicted of murder in 1928, then wrongly imprisoned for twenty-six years. Because of Richard's own steadfast historical investigation, the man was granted a posthumous pardon on the grounds of innocence in 1996. In his presentation, Richard made reference to Edward O. Heinrich, the California criminologist who had served, briefly, as Boulder's first city manager.

Unfortunately, my husband could not attend the conference, but Ed is a Texas native, so I knew that while I was in San Antonio I had to go to the Alamo. As I built in some free time to learn more about Texas history, I also tried my best to see what else I could find on Katharine Farrand. I spent a morning in the Texana genealogy section of the San Antonio Public Library reviewing my research with Jim, the volunteer from Random Acts of Genealogical Kindness.

Then I spent several more hours at the Bexar County Courthouse going through district court records that ranged from 1910 all the way to 1972. The imposing late-nineteenth-century Romanesque-style building of Texas granite and red sandstone was a treat in itself, but I left with the name of only one new Farrand—a young serviceman who had died in 1950 when he was hit by an airplane propeller. At first I thought there might have been a family connection, but I traced him through census records to his home in Wisconsin. When I found and talked on the telephone with his brother's wife, she told me that the serviceman had never married, nor did he have any relative named Katharine.

Back in Boulder, I asked Commander Phil West if he would authorize a comparison of Jane Doe's second—and more reliable—DNA profile with DNA from Marion Joan McDowell's surviving brother, even though the missing woman from Toronto had previously been ruled out by photo-superimposition. West agreed that in order to fully concentrate on Katharine, we needed to confirm that Marion was not Jane Doe. Dr. Terry Melton was called into service again and in March 2007, she officially stated that Marion was not a match. The results came to me in a brief email from Commander West, who simply wrote, "Back to Katharine Farrand."

By this time, two additional researchers had joined our core research team. One of them started a website on which we posted dozens of Farrand family trees, making it easier to keep track of Farrand families from different states, as well as individuals descended from the same ancestors. We also decided it was time to contact Jimmie Dyer's third and fourth wives. His second wife had given me their names, but she did not know how to reach them. She did, however, put me in contact with her daughter, who connected me with a male friend of Ann, wife number three.

I talked on the telephone with Ann's friend. He had known Jimmie, too, and described him as "a quiet, silent guy—big, tall, burly, rough and tough, and a cross between actor John Wayne and president Lyndon Baines Johnson." Ann and Jimmie had met on a Colorado Mountain Club hike to the summit of Mount Evans. Ann's male friend also told me that she would not talk with me but, on my behalf, he would ask her about Katharine. When the man called me back a few days later, he said that Ann told him that Jimmie had never spoken to her about Katharine. Only Jimmie's half sister Emily—who had once mentioned Katharine to Jimmie's second wife—had again mentioned Katharine to Ann, the third wife. Ann's comment, passed on to me through her friend, was that she only was aware that Katharine had been Jimmie's first wife—she did not know any more about her. If only Emily were alive. I learned from her obituary that she died in 1977, in Flagstaff, Arizona, at the age of forty-six.

My fellow researchers and I then found Maxine, wife number four, through an internet search. When I talked with her, she was both interested and friendly. Maxine also said that Jimmie never talked about his family, and she never asked. She had, however, accompanied him to the college hiking club reunion, and she told me that he had kept in contact with a man he knew in the Navy—Clayton Donton.

My next telephone call was to the elderly Navy buddy, and he, too, was interested in what I had to say. He told me he still had every Christmas card that Jimmie Dyer had sent him since 1947. Like Sergeant John Umenhofer, who boxed up and mailed me the Glatman files, Clayton mailed me a stack of Christmas cards and said I could keep them all. Except for a big gap in the 1970s and 1980s when Jimmie was married to Ann, the cards provided an intact record of his addresses and activities. Jimmie's old friend wrote, "I'm hoping this meager info I'm furnishing helps you in your attempt to find out what happened to Katharine."

In 1947, Jimmie wrote Clayton that he was in college in Flagstaff and driving a 1936 Chevrolet Standard. He had just taken up skiing and said he got "a freshman sweater in football." Although Jimmie only signed his name in 1948, he had much more to say the following year. His card depicted two cowboys and a horse in a desert landscape and a message that read, "Season's Greetings from the Great Southwest." In December 1949 Jimmie wrote, "Been married three months now." He then told his friend about his new 1949 Mercury—complete with heater, radio, and overdrive. He called it the "finest car ever made" and added, "Wife working and making payments." This was the same car that Jimmie was driving when he met and married Joan in 1955.

I wanted to know where in Flagstaff Katharine worked, so I contacted the Flagstaff Public Library, and a librarian mailed me photocopies of pages from the *Flagstaff City Directory*. While Jimmie was in his senior year of college, Katharine was a waitress at Bushey's Fountain Café. The popular college hangout was half a block off United States Highway 66, more commonly called Route 66, which ran right through the center of town. In closing, Jimmie told his friend that he had a new hobby—taking color transparencies with a "German 120 camera." Most likely, the high-end camera was a Rolleiflex, with twin lenses, well accepted at the time by both professional and semiprofessional photographers.

Beginning in 1950, Jimmie's Christmas cards included Katharine's name, and the addresses on the cards were the same ones that I had found in the *Denver City Directories*. All were apartments in large homes, and the couple had a different address each year. I knew from the newspaper account of Katharine's disappearance that she and Jimmie had been separated prior to March 1954, but I did not know until I got Clayton's cards that the separation occurred in 1953. On Jimmie's card that December he simply wrote, "I am a single man," without any explanation. Clayton must have written to him of the birth of a child, as Jimmie replied, "I hope to be a happily married man with a son someday." He told his friend that he liked his job as a results engineer, and that he enjoyed basketball, skiing, ice-skating, and square dancing, and that he had climbed, so far, twenty-eight of Colorado's fourteen-thousand-foot peaks. It was eerie to read that and know something Jimmie did not know at the time—that Mount Antero would be, for him, peak number twenty-nine.

I had stayed in contact with Jimmie's second wife, Joan, and I remembered that she had talked of her former husband's interest in photography. In August 2007, after I read the Christmas cards and learned that Jimmie's interest in color transparencies had begun in 1949—the year that Jimmie and Katharine were married—I emailed Joan to ask if she still had his slides. "Your timing is impeccable," she wrote. "I'm on a house-cleaning spree and have the slides in the garage, ready to get rid of." Explaining that I hoped they might contain a photograph of Katharine, I quickly arranged with her a time to pick them up.

A few days later, we carefully loaded three heavy brown and tan leather-bound cases and more than a dozen additional boxes of two-and-one-half-inch-square glass-mounted slides into my car. Joan said she thought they were mostly landscapes but I was welcome to have them anyway. Jimmie had started his photograph collection when he was married to Katharine, then expanded it when he was married to Joan, and he kept it with him through his marriages to Ann and then Maxine, who then hauled the hefty boxes back to Joan after Jimmie died. Now they were in my possession, and I could not wait to get home. As soon as I did, I started laying out the well-traveled slides on a large light table—and I held my breath.

Suddenly, there was Katharine! I stood, transfixed, and stared at a very attractive young woman in rolled-up blue jeans, brown and white saddle shoes, and the "A" letter sweater that Jimmie had earned in football. Inside the lid of the slide case that held the oldest photographs, in Jimmie's writing, was "Grand Canyon—Katharine," with a line running through all of the words. Did he rearrange his slides at a later date and cross off her name, intending to throw away her photograph? If so, how come he never did? I wondered what had happened between the outdoorsman and his pretty wife.

Since Katharine and Jimmie were married in September 1949, and he graduated from college in May 1950, he must have taken Katharine's photograph during the 1949–1950 school year. Appearing happy and carefree, the slender young woman stood on the very edge of the Grand Canyon's South Rim, an hour-and-a-half drive from the newlyweds' home in Flagstaff.

Katharine's wavy hair, parted on the left side of her head and pinned back from her face, was typical of the era and fit my fantasized ideal of the

Jimmie Dyer took this photograph of his first wife, Katharine, at the Grand Canyon during the 1949–1950 school year. Photo courtesy of Jimmie's second wife, Joan.

hairdo I would have liked to have seen on Jane Doe's facial reconstruction. The colors in the decades-old slide, however, had become distorted through the years—the blue of the letter sweater looked almost black—so it was impossible to tell Katharine's hair color. The landlady who later reported her missing, however, said she had blonde hair that she frequently tinted red. In the months to come, I would meet a woman who knew Katharine in 1949 and 1950, and that woman's recollection was that Katharine's hair was light brown. Jimmie's bride did have one unchanging and defining feature, and that was her beautiful smile—with even, but slightly protruding, teeth.

I hurriedly searched through the remaining three hundred slides in that first case, easily identified by its broken leather handle. Joan had been right. Jimmie was an avid hiker and climber, and most of his photographs were of landscapes. Nearly a third of his Arizona scenes were of a hike he took with a couple of male companions to spectacular Havasu Falls, within the depths of the Grand Canyon. The crystal-clear blue-green pool at the base of the falls has long been popular with bathers, and Jimmie and his friends had joined in. The photographs at the back of the case were taken after the couple's move to Colorado and included some of his other climbs. Katharine occasionally showed up in non-mountain-climbing scenes, but her placement was solely for composition or perspective. In Colorado, she always had her back to the camera.

During the next few days, I looked at hundreds and hundreds of slides, but I did not find any more of Katharine. Jimmie's notation of her name in his slide case, however, added yet another consistent documentation of the correct spelling of her first name. My initial knowledge that "Katherine," mentioned as missing in the 1954 newspaper, actually was "Katharine"—with a "K" and two "a's"—was from Jimmie Dyer's records at the registrar's office of Northern Arizona University. Then came her signature on her marriage affidavit, as well as the typed transcriptions on both her marriage license and certificate. Katharine signed her own name, again, as "Katharine Dyer" on the Colorado Mountain Club register, while Jimmie signed Katharine's name on his Christmas cards.

At home, I scanned the one and only slide, taken at the Grand Canyon, that showed Katharine's face. The quality was so good that I zoomed in for a close-up, then took both images, in hard copy and on a disk, to Commander Phil West. We discussed the photo-superimpositions that Dr. Todd Fenton, of Michigan State University, had done with the photographs of Twylia May Embrey and Marion Joan McDowell. Commander

West suggested that Dr. Fenton be contacted again about doing a similar comparison with the photograph of Katharine. I thought it was a great idea, and I sent the original photograph to Dr. Fenton, then emailed my fellow researchers that we might have the results within weeks.

Commander West said he hoped that Dr. Fenton had taken enough photographs of Jane Doe's skull when he did the comparisons of Twylia and Marion that he would not physically need the skull again, but it turned out that he did need it in order to view the skull from the same angle that Katharine used in posing for her photograph. When sheriff officials took the skull off their evidence room shelf to repackage and send it to Dr. Fenton, however, they noticed that it was so fragile that it had cracked into several large pieces. Beth Conour, now Beth Buchholtz, the forensic anthropologist who had assisted Dr. Walter Birkby at the exhumation, then reassembled the skull for its second time. Instead of mailing the well-traveled and twice-reassembled skull, Detective Steve Ainsworth contracted with a local artist who spent two months replicating it with a plaster cast.

While biding my time, I attended another annual meeting of FOHVAMP—Families of Homicide Victims and Missing Persons. My first visit with the group had been at its potluck dinner in Castle Rock, at its second annual meeting in 2003. By the time of its sixth annual meeting, in October 2007, the event had grown into a daylong session that swelled several conference rooms of the Four Points Sheraton Hotel in southeast Denver. In addition to families and friends of the murdered and missing, I was pleased to see that the meetings now included law-enforcement officials who led workshops on crime labs, coroner duties, victim assistance, and cold case investigations. Again I heard the frustrations of the families who were concerned that the cases of their loved ones had been forgotten, but this time I also heard from police officers who told of equal frustrations when witnesses refused to talk. In a plea for murder witnesses to come forward, one officer stated, "For evil to flourish, all that's needed is people to fail to act." I was glad to see a growing bond between family members and law-enforcement officers as they verbalized the joint commitments that drew them together. As one of the cops on the panel of cold case investigators stated, "We are better together than apart. We are advocates just like you."

In my constant search for any new information on Katharine, I posted her photograph and a plea to anyone who might recognize her on the Northern Arizona University's alumni website. I also convinced the editor of Flagstaff's newspaper, the *Arizona Daily Sun*, to run an article on the missing young woman who once lived in the college town. The only response came from Lieutenant Rex Gilliland of the Coconino County Sheriff's Office, who called me on a Sunday morning. He said, "Volunteers like you are the only way to solve cold cases," and he suggested I contact his mother, Pat Crawley. When I talked with her, the former longtime Flagstaff resident told me that she remembered Jimmie from Flagstaff High School, and that her late husband had graduated with him in the same Arizona State College class. Pat did not, however, know anything about Katharine.

Shortly before Christmas, in December 2007, Detective Ainsworth put the cast of Jane Doe's skull in the mail to Michigan, but fitting the superimposition into Dr. Fenton's busy schedule took time. Wanting to learn more about the process, I called Dr. Walter Birkby, as he had been Dr. Fenton's anthropology professor at the University of Arizona, and he knew all about Jane Doe's skull since he had initially glued it together. Dr. Birkby explained that there could not be a perfect match with Katharine's or anyone's photograph because of the slight distortion—called "warpage"—that occurred while the skull had become waterlogged in the wet soil in her grave. Dr. Birkby also told me not to get my hopes up, as he had found a few gaps when he assembled the skull's many pieces. Even the weather was depressing, as the winter seemed never-ending, with cold, wind, and snow. The waiting—through January, February, and March—was excruciating. Every morning I got up and said to myself, and often to Ed, "Is this the day I will hear about Katharine?"

I got most of my news from the *Daily Camera* and continued as the newspaper's history columnist even as their circulation, like that of newspapers everywhere, began to drop. I emailed my stories from home, but whenever I did visit the newspaper office, I found the once-busy newsroom strangely quiet. Occasionally I would still lose myself in the endless files of the archives, but Carol Taylor, the librarian who had taken such an interest in the Jane Doe case, had moved on to another job. She was not replaced, and the archives were mothballed. As long as the building remains unchanged, the room will always draw me toward it, as it is where I first read of Jane Doe's murder, first saw her mysteriously resurfaced morgue photographs, and first read that Sheriff Art Everson, in 1958, considered Harvey Glatman a likely suspect. I held on to my job as a columnist mostly to keep open my access to these and other files. Instead of an orderly retreat where my interests in Boulder history were invigorated, however, I found the room in disarray, with piles of newspapers and files on every tabletop, and even more on the floor.

On April 1, 2008, I got an email from Commander West, who forwarded comments from Dr. Fenton saying that his graduate student had been working all week on Jane Doe's superimposition. They would have the results soon, he said, but he did not want to rush to judgment. Dr. Fenton also had mentioned to the commander that the superimposition with Katharine was not like the ones he had previously done of Marion Joan McDowell and Twylia May Embrey. Those two young women he had easily ruled out, and he was pleased that the subsequent DNA comparisons had confirmed his results. Katharine's superimposition, he said, was "very close," and he needed a few more days to get the opinion of a colleague.

Three days later, on a Friday afternoon, I heard from Commander West again. I knew that photo-superimposition had only two possible outcomes. If one or more of several specific facial and cranial reference marks on Jane Doe's skull did not align with Katharine's photograph, she would be "excluded" as Jane Doe—meaning that she would be ruled out as a match. Only if the five reference marks he used matched or were very close could the official forensic result be "failure to exclude." In our case, Dr. Fenton's results showed four reference marks that matched and one that was very close, indicating that Katharine and Jane Doe could, indeed, have been the same person. I thought back to Hollywood's forensic expert—Dr. McAdoo—in the film *Mystery Street*, in which the search for the identity of a murder victim was narrowed by the dramatic alignment of a photograph of a missing woman with a photograph of a victim's skull. I remembered the professor's words: "If the skull does fit, it may not prove it's the right girl, but if it doesn't fit, it certainly eliminates the wrong one."

In Jane Doe's case, Dr. Fenton said that the cast of her skull displayed a "similar facial proportionality and a similar overall face shape" to Katharine's photograph. He also remarked on the "rather good fit" of the teeth. The placement and shape of Katharine's right eye, however, did not fit precisely into the orbit, or eye cavity, of the cast of Jane Doe's skull. Dr. Fenton added that if the photograph and the skull were of the same person—if Katharine and Jane Doe were one and the same—there were, however, two possible explanations. The oblique angle of Katharine's photograph could have thrown off the comparison, or the slight distortion could have been due to the warpage that Dr. Walter Birkby had observed when initially reassembling the skull.

Dr. Fenton pointed out what I already knew—that, even at its best, photo-superimposition is not a positive identification. Only DNA could provide that, and only if the DNA were properly profiled. Considering the fact, however, that the skull was reassembled twice, and all the specialist had to work with was a plaster cast, I was amazed that the superimposition was close at all. The result—"failure to exclude"—combined with all of the circumstantial evidence that my fellow researchers and I had compiled for more than two and a half years, convinced me, in my heart, that Katharine was Jane Doe.

19

As the revelation sank in, I experienced a mixture of sadness and relief. I wanted to mourn rather than celebrate, as I had grown to care about the beautiful young woman who had become a real person to me. At the same time, I was relieved that we were closing in on the end of a long journey. In more than two years, no other credible leads had come in, and despite plenty of publicity, no blood relatives of Katharine had come forward. If I believed in symbolism, I would have thought of an appropriate interpretation for the temporary disappearance of the raucous ravens and crows at my suet feeder, replaced instead by a large flock of red-winged blackbirds whose songs always heralded—for me—the beginning of spring. I hoped our victim's soul was at peace.

That evening, I emailed Micki, Cindi, Dave, Karen Anne, and Sandy and told them the news. Soon afterward, I talked on the telephone with forensic artist Frank Bender. We discussed the similarities—particularly in the cheek-to-chin line—between Katharine's photograph and his bust of Jane Doe. He also believed they were one and the same.

A few days after Commander West got the results from Dr. Fenton, the commander issued a press release calling the new forensic evidence "promising" and asked the media to circulate Katharine's photograph in the slim hope that a blood relative might still come forward to provide DNA for a positive identification. When none did, I made plans to fly to Michigan to see the photo-superimposition for myself. Karen Anne lived a half-hour's drive from the Michigan State University campus, so I called my fellow researcher, and she invited me to stay in her home. We had never met face-to-face but I considered her a close friend, as I did Micki, whom I had met for the first time before the *America's Most Wanted* program.

On May 7, 2008, Karen Anne, who had short, light-brown hair and was close to my age, picked me up at the Flint, Michigan, airport, then took me to her home. The landscape was lush and green, and lilacs and fruit trees were in full bloom. As we sat out on her deck overlooking a lake, we had plenty to talk about, as she had joined the Jane Doe research group back in the days when we were still searching for Twylia May Embrey and just beginning to learn about Harvey Glatman. Karen Anne described her dedication to Jane Doe as her "Sunday case." Although she had recently taken a new job with a propane company, she often spent several hours a week sharpening her genealogy skills, which she had learned by tracking deadbeat dads and helping women collect child-support.

The following morning, Karen Anne and I headed toward East Lansing, where we had arranged to meet with Dr. Fenton in the Michigan State University Forensic Anthropology Laboratory in East Fee Hall, a redbrick former dormitory that is now used as an academic building. The second we stepped off the elevator, we were greeted by the man we had come to see—Dr. Fenton, a short-haired man with glasses, in his midforties, wearing a gray-and-white striped dress shirt and dark slacks. With him was Carolyn Hurst, his graduate student.

The next two and a half hours went too quickly for Karen Anne and me. We were ushered past boxes of human remains—all related to other cases that Dr. Fenton worked on for various law-enforcement agencies—and then into a room with a table full of video-monitoring equipment. A camera pointed down at Jane Doe's plaster cast, set on a black cloth–covered stand, while the close-up photograph of Katharine's face filled the screen of a monitor. I will never forget walking into that room and seeing, for the first time, the double image of the cast of Jane Doe's skull superimposed onto Katharine's photograph.

I was grateful that Dr. Fenton took the time to explain the procedure in detail. He and Carolyn had begun the process by placing Katharine's photograph—adjusted to the same size as the cast of the skull—under a video camera. Then they inserted wooden tissue-depth markers into each ear opening of the skull cast and placed, on the cast, five green dots as reference markers to correspond with bony facial landmarks. The cast was then placed under a second video camera. Carolyn held it in her hands and adjusted it to the same orientation as Katharine's photograph, manipulating the images so that one was on top of the other.

When the photograph and the skull cast were overlaid as closely as possible, both Carolyn and Dr. Fenton compared the reference marks. Specifically, they showed the distance from the outside of one eye to the

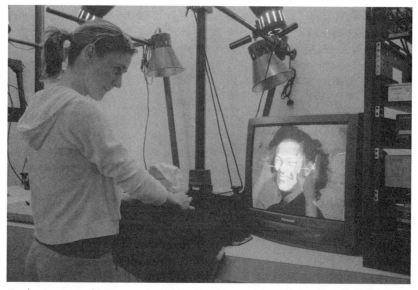

To demonstrate photo-superimposition, Dr. Todd Fenton's graduate student, Carolyn Hurst, aligns the cast of Jane Doe's skull with the photograph of Katharine Farrand Dyer. The images were so close that Katharine could not be excluded as Jane Doe.

outside of the other eye, the distance from the bridge of the nose to just below the nose, and the distance from the base of the nose to the chin. Dr. Fenton and his student also compared the outer edges of the eye sockets to the middle of the ears and, finally, individual teeth in the photograph to the teeth in the skull cast. As Carolyn related to me, she found the work really exciting and had a "Eureka moment" when the two images aligned so closely. We discussed the possible distortion due to warpage, and we lamented that I had no other photograph, particularly straight-on from the front, that might have provided an even better match.

After Dr. Fenton finished showing us his laboratory, he took Carolyn, Karen Anne, and me into a conference room where I opened up my laptop and showed my small but attentive audience the latest version of a Power-Point program that I had prepared on the Jane Doe case. Both Carolyn and Dr. Fenton asked a lot of questions, and they told me that the story behind the skull really piqued their interest. I asked Dr. Fenton for statistics on the comparisons of facial characteristics between two random people, and he said that even though about ten percent of the population would have the same basic bone structure as Katharine, the results of the comparison—especially between Jane Doe's and Katharine's teeth—were "compelling." His scientific training, however, would not permit him to be pinned down as to whether or not he, personally, thought Jane Doe and Katharine were one and the same.

When I got home, I found my thoughts on Katharine difficult to separate from my thoughts from Jane Doe. I wanted to see what, if any, additional pieces of Katharine's life I could find, so I decided to drive to Flagstaff, Arizona. I had kept up my correspondence with Pat Crawley, the mother of the sheriff's deputy and, when I called her, she was enthusiastic about my upcoming visit and promised to show me the town.

In August 2008, I headed west on Interstate 70, traversing the Continental Divide and admiring the scenery of Glenwood Canyon. I continued all the way through Colorado into Utah, where I turned south to Moab and then on to the small town of Blanding. There, I had arranged to meet Hugh Acton, the man who had witnessed the marriage of Katharine Farrand and Jimmie Dyer. All I knew from corresponding with him was that I would find him at Huck's Museum and Trading Post, a big log building on the south side of town.

After driving all day, I knocked on the door of the trading post close to five o'clock in the afternoon, hoping that the man I came to see would still be there. Immediately I was ushered inside by a short, slightly stooped, elderly man in work clothes and a tattered cap. Despite his age—he said he was eighty—his eyes sparkled, and he bubbled with youthful enthusiasm. He told me to call him "Huck," a nickname given to him by his siblings, who likened his appearance to Mark Twain's fictional character, Huckleberry Finn. We got acquainted while he showed me his vast collection of artifacts from the Anasazi, the Native Americans who, two thousand years ago, inhabited the Four Corners region of Utah, Colorado, Arizona, and New Mexico. Huck had purchased many of the arrowheads and pieces of pottery in his collection during the early 1950s when uranium strikes brought swarms of prospectors to the area, all trying to raise money to mine their claims.

Not wanting to take up too much of his time at the end of what, for me, anyway, had been a long day, I checked into a motel room and we made plans to meet at Yak's Center Street Café for breakfast. Over bacon and eggs, Huck told me, again, that on September 25, 1949, he was home in Prescott, Arizona, on a ten-day leave and walking down the town's main street in his Navy "blues." He said he did not have any civilian clothes at the time and, admittedly, Navy uniforms of any color were a little out of the ordinary in the Arizona desert. Huck, then twenty-one years old, explained that a man—later identified as Jimmie Dyer, a Navy veteran—yelled: "Sailor, would you be our witness? We want to get married."

I had assumed that the exchange of marriage vows, with no other witnesses or guests present, had taken place at the Yavapai County Courthouse, but Huck said it was in a church or a building associated with a church. I got out my copies of Jimmie and Katharine's marriage documents, and Huck immediately recognized the name of Charles Franklin Parker who performed the late afternoon or evening ceremony, explaining that he was the pastor of a church. I had read Parker's name several times before, but it finally clicked in my mind that he was the same Reverend Parker who had presided at the funeral of Prescott's unidentified murder victim—Little Miss Nobody. I told Huck that I would be visiting the town, so he drew me a map showing the courthouse and, two blocks away, Reverend Parker's church.

After breakfast, I followed Huck back to his trading post, as it was on my way out of town. He showed me more of the artifacts he had collected. Then, before I left, he handed me a bottle of orange juice to drink on my journey; some Huck's Trading Post trinkets, including a pen, flashlight, keychain, and tape measure; and a twenty-dollar bill. "This is to help you find Jane Doe," he told me. He was so compassionate and sincere that I was nearly in tears when I got in my car and headed south.

The second day's drive was not as long as the first. I savored the majestic sandstone formations of Monument Valley, well-known to viewers of John Wayne films and other Westerns, and arrived at the Quality Inn Motel in Flagstaff in the early afternoon. I tried to imagine the current city of approximately fifty-eight thousand people as it was in 1950 when there were little more than seven thousand in this commercial and travel center of northern Arizona. The town was situated in a pine forest, and the local economy was based on its lumber industry. Even the name "Lumberjacks" was given to the athletic teams of Arizona State College, where Jimmie Dyer was one of seven hundred students.

Passenger and freight trains between Chicago and Los Angeles ran right through the center of town, as did Greyhound and Continental buses on the two-thousand-mile-long Route 66. The town got a boost in 1946 when rhythm and blues singer Nat King Cole celebrated the romance and freedom of automobile travel with his hit song, "Get Your Kicks on Route 66." Today, trains and buses still go through town, and a new tourist industry caters to nostalgia buffs who enjoy following the old highway.

Pat Crawley, the sheriff's deputy's mother, met me for dinner, and we plotted our schedule for the next two days. White-haired but energetic, she had driven from her home in Cottonwood and was eager to be my tour guide. I told her I would be glad for her company as I searched for anything that had to do with Katharine.

First on our list was to pick up Katharine's paper trail. From the pages I had photocopied from the *Flagstaff City Directory*, we found the house where, in a small apartment, Katharine and Jimmie spent the first few months of their marriage. The address was near the railroad tracks and immediately west of downtown and was conveniently located within walking distance of the college campus, for Jimmie, and also a few blocks from Katharine's job at Bushey's Fountain Café. Instead of walking to the former lunch and ice cream shop, however, we drove into downtown, parked at the railroad station, and then walked half a block up San Francisco Street. The cinder-block building that once was the café now houses a retail clothing store, but Pat remembered booths on one side and a soda fountain on the other, with sandwiches and malts on the menu.

The highlight of our day, however, came later in the afternoon, when we visited the Special Collections department in the large brick building known as the Cline Library on the Northern Arizona University campus. Ever since I had read in the April 9, 1954 issue of the *Rocky Mountain News* that Katharine's landlady had described her as five feet six inches— causing Sheriff Art Everson to dismiss her as "too tall" to be Jane Doe—I had wondered about Katharine's height. The photograph Jimmie took of Katharine at the Grand Canyon did more than show a pretty face. It also showed his letter sweater, complete with the "A" for the school's name at the time—Arizona State College. I figured that if I could measure the letter, I could extrapolate Katharine's height from her photograph. In advance of my Arizona trip, I had contacted the library director and asked if she could find me a letter sweater like the one Katharine was wearing.

When Pat and I walked into the Special Collections department, the letter sweater was waiting for us in a box on the table. With it was a photocopied page out of the 1950 college yearbook, and one student's photograph was circled. Pat took one look at the yearbook page and asked me why her late husband's photograph and name were in the box with the sweater. Then it dawned on us both—the sweater had been his. To prove it, we even found his name embroidered inside. Like Katharine, who wore Jimmie's sweater, Pat had often worn her husband's sweater—the very same sweater set on the table for us to see. Pat was teary-eyed and thrilled, and I told her to try it on. When she did, the years slipped away from her face, and she looked like the wife of a college student once again.

Since I still had not measured the "A," I took out the tape measure that Huck had given me at his trading post. From top to bottom, the letter measured six-and-one-quarter inches. When I did the math, I was able to determine that Katharine was approximately five-feet-two-and-one-half-inches, within a half inch of the height of Jane Doe as estimated by Dr. Freburn L. James, the pathologist who had performed her original autopsy. Katharine's height also correlated with Jane Doe's estimated height as determined by Dr. Richard Froede and Dr. Walter Birkby when they had examined and laid out her skeletal remains.

Although I could congratulate myself on resolving the question of Katharine's height, I still did not know—and may never know—Jane Doe's exact age. I reflected on two previous, and possibly conflicting, contacts. Dr. Birkby had told me that after examining her bones, he and Dr. Froede had leaned toward a twenty-or-younger age estimate, but he pointed out that there was always room for individual variation.

I had also emailed photographs of the victim's skull, with teeth, to Richard M. Scanlon, DMD, in Lewistown, Pennsylvania. He is a former chief deputy coroner of Mifflin County, but I found him as a volunteer with the Doe Network, in the field of forensic dentistry. Dr. Scanlon explained that the root formation of Jane Doe's upper right third molar was complete and added that it was easy to see in the photograph because the bony plate that normally covers the tooth was missing from the reassembled skull. "It's clear that the tooth—from the apex to the tip of the root—is completely formed and is impacted," he explained, "indicating that Jane Doe was, at the minimum, twenty years old, and likely older."

The morning after Pat's and my trip to the library, we met at the home of one of her longtime friends, Billie Ruth Hubbs. She and her husband Jay lived in Camp Verde, an hour's drive south of Flagstaff and more than three thousand feet lower in elevation. Billie Ruth told us that when she was a student at Flagstaff High School, she had been a close friend of Jimmie Dyer's half sister, Emily, whose name I first heard from Jimmie's second wife, Joan. Billie Ruth and Emily had stayed in contact until 1977, when Emily died of cancer, but Billie Ruth had cared for her throughout her illness. "I know for sure," she told me, "that if Emily knew anything about Katharine's disappearance, she would have told me."

Billie Ruth was the woman who told me that Katharine's hair was light brown. She said she met her through her friendship with Emily, and she knew the rest of Jimmie's family, as well. His now-deceased half brothers also lived in Flagstaff, and their mother, a grocery store clerk, did psychic readings in her spare time and lived with the newly married couple for at least part of the 1949–1950 school year. The close proximity of Jimmie's family in 1949 made me wonder why none of them had attended his wedding. Billie Ruth did not know, but she said that other than being at work or with her husband's family, Katharine kept to herself. Emily lost track of both of them, as she temporarily moved to California with her second husband, and by the time they returned to Flagstaff, Jimmie and Katharine had moved to Denver. After that, he only returned once to visit the family, and that was after he had married again.

As Pat and I continued to talk with Billie Ruth, she remembered more tidbits of the past that provided additional information. Emily's first marriage was when she was quite young, and her first husband, now deceased, was in the Army Air Corps, stationed at Lowry Field in Denver. When I got home, I looked up the couple in the *Denver City Directory* and found them, in 1947, on Vine Street, practically next door to where Katharine had lived the following year as a single woman. I also found Katharine and Emily working together as waitresses at the Republic Drug Company in downtown Denver. Through Billie Ruth, I contacted an Army friend of Emily's late husband. He reminisced on the telephone about bus rides from Lowry Field to the downtown drug store where both Katharine and Emily worked.

The Army friend then put me in contact with Emily's late husband's kid sister, Shirley Ostrander. When we talked on the telephone, she remembered more about Katharine than anyone else. In the late 1940s, Shirley was a young teenager, living in Denver with her mother. Her brother (Emily's husband), Emily, and Katharine often came by bus to picnic in Shirley's back yard. Of Emily and Katharine, Shirley said, "I just adored them." She remembered how they dressed—fashionably, in skirts, with colorful scarves—as well as Katharine's light-brown hair and infectious smile. Shirley's family thought she was so beautiful that they compared her to the actress Katharine Hepburn, remarking that the two Katharines even spelled their names the same way. Shirley never saw Katharine with any friends other than Emily, and she added that Katharine never spoke about her own family. She did, however call herself "Tex."

I had often wondered how Katharine met Jimmie, and now I knew that the connecting link was Emily. In 1948, Katharine was single and lived near Emily and her first husband on Vine Street, in Denver. Katharine and Emily worked together at the Republic Drug Company. Billie Ruth and Shirley both explained that, by 1949, Emily had left her first husband and returned to Flagstaff. Katharine, most likely, went with her, as she and Jimmie married that same year in Prescott, Arizona.

The central Arizona town of Prescott was nearly one hundred miles from Flagstaff. Even though Katharine and her future sister-in-law were friends, perhaps the marriage really was as spontaneous as Huck, the witness, had related. After Pat and I visited with Billie Ruth for a couple of hours, I drove on to Prescott to see what I could find. Huck's hand-drawn map was very helpful. I traced his steps on East Gurley Street to the First Congregational Church of Prescott, a handsome brick building that had been placed on the National Register of Historic Places. Sure enough, when I entered the green frame house next door that had served as its parsonage, the church secretary explained that the late Reverend Parker's twenty-eight years of service included 1949. He had married many couples, even without wedding guests, in the parsonage itself. Jimmie and Katharine Dyer were duly recorded, on a Sunday, in the church records. Their address was a post office box in Flagstaff.

On my way home, I spent a few hours at the Grand Canyon, marveling at its grandeur and clutching a copy of Katharine's photograph in my hand. From the background that faintly showed the South Kaibab Trail, I was able to confirm that Jimmie took Katharine's photograph at Yaki Point, off Desert View Drive, approximately five miles east of Grand Canyon Village. I liked thinking of her standing there.

The new contacts I made on my trip to Flagstaff added at least a dozen more people to the hundreds who have donated their time, money, and expertise to the Jane Doe case. Through the national media, thousands more have followed its many twists and turns. Years ago, when my initial curiosity led to indignation that a murder victim had been buried without a name, I never foresaw that her violent death would reach beyond the grave and touch the lives of complete strangers.

My contacts at the sheriff's office found her exhumation a valuable learning experience. Both Commander Phil West and Sheriff Joe Pelle told me that they were appreciative of the opportunity to network—for the first time—with the nation's foremost forensic authorities. In addition, Detective Steve Ainsworth said he liked the return to "old-fashioned police work." Forensic anthropologist Todd Fenton was pleased to have played his part, and Dr. Richard Froede, Dr. Walter Birkby, Dr. Robert Goldberg, forensic artist Frank Bender, and Vidocq Society board chairman Frederick Bornhofen—all working pro bono—added to their combined knowledge and discussed Jane Doe in their meetings. Richard Walton even made our investigation into a textbook case. Donors, both in 1954 and 2004, found satisfaction in helping a less fortunate person than themselves, and my fellow researchers and I formed friendships we will keep for the rest of our lives.

I have tremendous respect and admiration for all of these contributors, including the researchers who—as regular citizens of diverse backgrounds and with their own lives and family responsibilities to tend to—were will-ing to give up hours of their time, every day, to help in the search for answers. With no badges or doctoral degrees, they worked behind the scenes, and will continue to do so, while making a difference in the lives of others. The researchers and everyone involved in this quest have displayed deep empathy for those whose family members have been murdered or are missing.

By simply living and dying, Jane Doe—a woman with few friends—will be remembered for the compassion she brought out in all of us, as well as the closure she brought to others—particularly to the families of Twylia May Embrey and Eula Jo Hand. Families of murder victims, I have been told, prefer the word "resolution" to closure, but for Twylia and Eula Jo's families, closure is the appropriate word, as it denotes the end of one chap-ter of life, allowing a person to move on to another.

Twylia's sister Midge no longer sits by the telephone, waiting for a call that will never come. Now in her late eighties, the Nebraska farm woman has moved on with her life and is finally at peace with her long-lost sibling. In Arizona, Eula Jo had kept her questions about her attacker to herself for sixty-one years, ever since her former mother-in-law prevented her from testifying at Glatman's trial. Then, in recent years, Eula Jo's daughter

Twylia's sister Mildred "Midge" Garner credits the Jane Doe investigation for ending her half-century search for her long-lost sister.

was afraid to ask her the hardest question. Now that the assault has been brought out in the open, the victim who got away is proud to tell the world that she's a survivor.

In discussing Jane Doe, Micki—the researcher who has stuck with me on this case for more than seven years—expressed the victim's legacy well when she wrote, "I want her to be remembered, not just for the injustice that has happened to her, but for what she DID presently—more than fifty years later—connecting friends and people who care. How special is that!"

Most people in Jane Doe's age range do have friends and people who care, and many have children and grandchildren as well. Our murder victim's life was cut off in 1954. She missed the harmonious ballads of the Fleetwoods and never even heard of the Beatles. She died violently and alone, probably without the opportunity to reflect at all. She was never allowed the privilege of looking back on a full life of accomplishments, or even disappointments, that she could call her own.

A few weeks after I returned from Flagstaff, the time had come to re-inter her remains. Boulder had changed a great deal since 1954, when sheriff's officials buried the victim in Columbia Cemetery. The city's politics had shifted from conservative to liberal, and its population more than tripled. Although the lighted star still glows every Christmas season on Flagstaff Mountain, the Easter cross is long gone. In the fall of 2008, when plans were under way for another "Meet the Spirits" reenactment in Columbia Cemetery, Eleanor Wedum, the portrayer of Jane Doe, revised her comments to bring tour-goers up to date. Jane Doe will always be remembered at the biannual event, but the quest to acknowledge her life and seek justice for her death was nearing an end. Initially, I had hoped to return her remains to her family, but through the decade-long search and the involvement of so many people, I slowly came to realize that she had acquired an extended family—and it was all of us. She belonged with us. She belonged in Boulder.

As evidenced by the donors and others who responded in recent years, Boulder people are still compassionate. No doubt many of them would have attended her reburial, but Commander West chose to make it dignified and private, only inviting representatives from the sheriff's office, Crist Mortuary, the Boulder Parks and Recreation Department, sheriff's office chaplain Reverend Andy Wineman, my husband Ed, and me. Also included was Alan Cass, who, in addition to his interest in Jane Doe and other murder victims, had personally organized a memorial service and erected a bronze plaque on the University of Colorado campus for murder victim Elaura Jaquette—forty years after that student's murder.

On the day before Jane Doe's scheduled reburial, I contacted Frederick Bornhofen to keep him informed on the case. His response set off a flurry of last-minute telephone calls to Commander West and to me. Even though the sheriff's office has the victim's mitochondrial DNA profile and the cast of her skull, Frederick asked the commander to withhold a tooth and some of Jane Doe's hair. "New methods of identification are coming up all the time," he said, mentioning the latest research involving the analysis of oxygen and carbon isotopes in tooth enamel. "We don't want to be caught empty-handed."

September 9, 2008, was warm and sunny. The leaves on the trees were green, and the graveyard that holds so much of Boulder's history had a late-summer look rather than one of early fall. By the time Ed and I arrived, Crist Mortuary employees had dug Jane Doe's grave, as they had done more than four years earlier for her exhumation. The same shiny black hearse was parked nearby, but this time it held a new casket, identical to the blue-cloth-covered one that had turned into splinters underground. That part of history would not be repeated, though, as the groundsmen had lowered into the grave a concrete vault—modern-day protection from the seeping water of the nearby irrigation ditch.

Mortuary General Manager Michael Greenwood again donated his time, materials, and services, and he opened Jane Doe's casket so I could look inside. Except for the one tooth and a lock of hair removed after Frederick Bornhofen's request, the victim's cleaned and dried skeletal remains were carefully packaged into five white boxes that included typed inventories of every bone. Her twice-reconstructed skull had been carefully placed in yet another box that was cushioned with pillows. I had hoped against hope that her bones would not be thrown back in the dirt, and I was gratified that, instead, her remains were treated with the utmost respect.

Shortly before eleven o'clock in the morning, Commander Phil West, Detective Steve Ainsworth, Michael Greenwood, and an employee from Crist Mortuary acted as pallbearers and carried the casket from the hearse to the scaffolding above her open grave. Then, without needing any prompting, our small group assembled around the casket. Reverend Andy Wineman opened his remarks by saying: "On April 22, 1954, a group gathered at this same place for the same purpose as we gather today—to lay to rest the body of a young woman and ensure that she did not die in obscurity." He reminded us that she was not forgotten then, and that she has not been forgotten now.

On September 9, 2008, the Boulder County Sheriff's Office reburied Jane Doe in her former grave in Columbia Cemetery. Left to right, behind the casket, are Commander Phil West, the author, and Reverend Andy Wineman. Visible on the right, with their backs to the camera, are Crist Mortuary general manager Michael Greenwood and Detective Steve Ainsworth. Between them is Columbia Cemetery Preservation project manager Mary Reilly-McNellan, and to the right are two employees of Crist Mortuary. Photo courtesy of Alan Cass.

When Reverend Wineman commented that the Lord knows the victim's identity, he sounded very much like Reverend Charles Franklin Parker, who said at Little Miss Nobody's burial in Prescott, Arizona, "There are no unknowns, no orphans in God's world." Reverend Wineman told us that at the victim's first burial, another reverend—Paul Fife, of Boulder's Sacred Heart of Jesus Church—recited a portion of Psalm 130, and that the psalm was still appropriate today.

I spoke briefly about the many people who care for Jane Doe, and I reminded this small group that they, too, are a part of her family. I also mentioned that a newspaper account after her original graveside burial spoke of "restoring the dignity that was taken from her in the last hours of her life." In thanking those assembled again at her grave, I said that through the joint efforts of so many people, this had been accomplished—and, in doing so, we had honored both her life and her death. I had planned to read the lines from "Elegy to an Unfortunate Lady," but I choked up and handed the text to Commander West, standing next to me, who read: "By foreign hands your dying eyes were closed. By foreign hands your comely limbs composed. By foreign hands your humble grave adorned. By strangers honored and by strangers mourned." The commander then reminded us that the case was still open, and that the search for Katharine Farrand Dyer's family members would continue.

Then the groundsmen from the mortuary slowly lowered her casket into the ground and refilled the grave with the dirt they had removed that morning. A member of the Boulder Parks and Recreation Department reset the original gravestone that had been stored off-site for more than four years. Future passersby may think nothing has changed, but those who have followed Jane Doe's quest know that, under the ground, the victim's tenderly cared-for remains reflect the latest advances in forensic science as well as the love of an extended family.

Before leaving the cemetery, I placed on the grave what I had held throughout the service—a spray of red gladiolus. They were the same kind and color of flowers that were sent fifty years ago by another stranger—along with the card that was simply inscribed, "To Someone's Daughter."

ACKNOWLEDGMENTS

Jane Doe touched many lives, and hundreds of people—those I call her extended family—contributed to her story. I am unable to publicly recognize them all, but I do wish to particularly acknowledge the roles of the following individuals.

First of all, revisiting the Jane Doe case could not have been possible without the cooperation of Sheriff Joe Pelle and Division Chief Phil West of the Boulder County Sheriff's Office. I have great appreciation and respect for them, personally, and for the professionalism they showed me in our interactions. I also am grateful for the input and assistance of Detective Steve Ainsworth, Deputy John Appelmann, Sergeant Dan Barber, Deputy Sue Cullen, Commander Joe Gang, retired Division Chief Dennis Hopper, Deputy Steve Kellison, Evidence Technician Debbie Trever, Sergeant Mike Wagner, sheriff's chaplain Reverend Andy Wineman, former Detective John Zamora, and the many other officers and employees who worked behind the scenes. Retired Boulder County Sheriff George Epp, former Boulder County Sheriff Brad Leach, and former Boulder County Under-Sheriff Dorse "Dock" Teegarden also took the time to discuss the case with me.

Law-enforcement personnel outside of the Boulder County Sheriff's Office were very helpful, as well. From the Boulder Police Department, I wish to thank Chief Mark Beckner and Deputy Chief David Hayes, as well as retired officers Greg Bailey and Larry Kinion. Ron Hendricks introduced me to his late father, retired Detective Roy Hendricks, who was the last surviving detective on the Jane Doe case. Naomi Cole introduced me to Ethel Hill, widow of Detective Roy Hill, while Darlieen Del Pizzo provided important historic context. I also enjoyed the lively discussions I had with former Boulder County district attorney Stan Johnson.

Also sharing insight and ideas were former senior criminalist Thomas W. Adair of the Westminster Police Department, technician Bruce Adams of the Littleton Police Department, retired FBI criminal profiler Roy Hazelwood, and cold case investigator Cheryl Moore of the Jefferson County Sheriff's Office. Sergeant John Umenhofer of the Springfield Police Department, in Oregon, provided the original Harvey Glatman case files that had been passed down to him from the Los Angeles Police Department's lead investigator, the late Pierce Brooks. Lieutenant Rex Gilliland of the Coconino County Sheriff's Office kindly contacted me in response to my request for information on Katharine Farrand Dyer.

Frederick Bornhofen was my first contact with the forensic community. As chairman of the board and case manager of the Vidocq Society, he brought in Dr. Walter Birkby, Dr. Richard Froede, and Dr. Robert Goldberg, who all worked pro bono with the Boulder County Sheriff's Office to exhume Jane Doe's remains and then stayed on as consultants. In addition, Dr. Birkby reconstructed the victim's skull from more than one hundred pieces. I am grateful, too, to additional Vidocq Society members—Frank Bender for his sculpture based on the victim's reconstructed skull and Richard Walter and Richard Walton (everyone gets their names mixed up), who offered advice and assistance along the way.

I also particularly want to thank Dr. Todd Fenton and his graduate student, Carolyn Hurst, of the Michigan State University Forensic Anthropology Laboratory for their superimpositions of Jane Doe's skull with photographs of Marion Joan McDowell, Twylia May Embrey, and Katharine Farrand Dyer. Doe Network area director Barbara Lamacki put me in contact with forensic dentist Richard M. Scanlon, DMD, who provided valuable information on Jane Doe's teeth. All of these experts' services were free and were much appreciated. In addition, Dr. Terry Melton, of Mitotyping Technologies LLC, profiled Jane Doe's mitochondrial DNA and has pledged to continue on the case.

Former Boulder County medical investigator Beth Conour (now Beth Buchholtz, community service officer in the Detective Division at the Longmont Police Department) worked tirelessly, and on her own time, to assist Dr. Walter Birkby in removing Jane Doe's remains from her grave. Dr. Freburn L. James, the pathologist on the case in 1954, graciously forwarded his original autopsy report.

In addition to law-enforcement personnel and forensic contacts, an invaluable component of the Jane Doe investigation was the core group of volunteer researchers mentioned here in the order that they first contacted me—Micki Lavigne, Cindi Eichorn, Dave Frederick, Karen Anne Nicholas, and Sandy Bausch. They will remain my lifetime friends. Throughout the years, other researchers came and left, and I thank them for the information they shared, as well. Carol Gregory worked extensively on Farrand family histories. Two men, known to me only as Paul and Jim—of the organization Random Acts of Genealogical Kindness—spent many volunteer hours on the investigation.

Many others also made important contributions. At the top of the list are Crist Mortuary general manager Michael Greenwood and his crew—who, at their own expense, both opened and closed Jane Doe's grave, with the generous cooperation of Columbia Cemetery Preservation project manager Mary Reilly-McNellan. I also wish to thank the donors in 2004—especially Carl Wright—who pitched in to make the revisiting of the case possible in the first place, and to their predecessors in 1954, who provided Jane Doe's grave with a stone. Sierra Bufe set up and maintained the Jane Doe website, and director Nancy Geyer of the Boulder History Museum administered the Jane Doe Fund. Hotel Boulderado general manager Sid Anderson provided complimentary rooms for Vidocq Society visitors, and Roxy Walker and her colleagues at Sturtz and Copeland Florists donated flowers for Jane Doe's grave.

Todd Matthews, media director of the Doe Network, was my initial inspiration, and archeologist Jack Smith was the first to suggest that DNA comparison could also be done with Jane Doe. I also appreciate my contacts with executive director Howard Morton and former treasurer Dr. Michael Radelet, of the Colorado-based organization Families of Homicide Victims and Missing Persons.

Former *Daily Camera* librarian and longtime friend Carol Taylor discovered the morgue photos, taken by retired editor Laurence Paddock. Kathryn Keller and her daughter, Eleanor Wedum (recent portrayer of Jane Doe at "Meet the Spirits"), have championed the victim's story for years. The media spread it far and wide, and I would particularly like to thank Pauline Arrillaga, P. Solomon Banda, Shaun Boyd, Drew Griffin, Fred Peabody, Christine Reid, Marilyn Robinson, Pierrette J. Shields, and Diane Wetzel, as well as Doug Looney, who relayed stories about his late reporter-father, Bob Looney.

I also valued the assistance of research librarians from the following facilities: Carnegie Branch Library for Local History (Boulder), Cline Library of Northern Arizona University, Colorado State Archives, Colorado Historical Society, Colorado Mountain Club, Denver Public Library, and the San Antonio Public Library.

Even with the contributions of so many, the Jane Doe story would not exist without the input of many additional individuals, and I would particularly like to mention the following (some last names are withheld to protect their privacy):

- The late Wayne Swanson and his brother, Denny Swanson, for telling me about the discovery of Jane Doe's body.
- Debbie, daughter of Bruce Weibel, for discussing her connection with Jane Doe.
- Jennifer Kitt and Mildred "Midge" Garner, for introducing me to the life of Twylia May Embrey. Others who helped flesh out her story include James Conner, Eula Kramer, and Virgil Valentine.
- Susan Ridpath, for sharing her family's thoughts on Marion Joan McDowell.
- The ephemera collector (who wishes to remain anonymous), for lending me a copy of *Dood*, and former editor Bob Latham, who still likes to talk about it.
- Richard Nelson, for providing Denver East High School records on Harvey Glatman, and Pat Palmieri, for corresponding with me about "lonely hearts clubs."
- Eula Jo Hand "Jody," for being a true survivor and telling me her story, as well as her grandson, James C. Oleson, who told me how to find her.
- Orvella, daughter of Norene Lauer, for meeting with me to discuss her mother's assault by Harvey Glatman.
- Relatives of Jimmie Dyer, for aiding in my search for Katharine Farrand Dyer. I am grateful to Jimmie's subsequent wives—Joan, Ann, and Maxine—as well as Jimmie's daughter, Chris, and his niece, Berta.
- Friends of Jimmie Dyer, especially Navy buddy Clayton Donton and classmate Chuck Pullen.
- Pamela Anastassiou, registrar of Northern Arizona University, for discussing Jimmie's college record with me.
- Hugh "Huck" Acton, for telling me about Jimmie and Katharine Dyer's wedding.
- Pat Crawley, for being my enthusiastic tour guide and research assistant in Flagstaff, and Billie Ruth and Jay Hubbs, as well as Shirley Ostrander, for sharing what they personally knew and remembered about Katharine.

Agents Todd Shuster and Rachel Sussman, of Zachary Shuster Harmsworth, patiently worked with me to shape the Jane Doe story into a narrative, which Taylor Trade's publisher Rick Rinehart and editors Dulcie Wilcox, Janice Braunstein, and Amanda Gibson refined to its finished product.

A special thank-you also goes to Alan Cass for his compassion, friendship, and commitment to bring justice—not just to Jane Doe, but to all murder victims. Lastly, I wish to thank my family: my daughters, Daisy and Clara, and my husband, Ed Raines—a willing sounding board and valuable critic during every aspect of the quest.

HARVEY GLATMAN TIMELINE

December 10, 1927—Harvey Glatman was born in the Bronx, New York, to Albert and Ophelia Glatman. Prior to 1930, Albert, Ophelia, and Harvey moved to Denver.

1930—The Glatman family lived briefly lived in Denver before moving back to New York. Harvey was an only child.

1937–1944—The Glatmans returned to Denver and moved in with Ophelia's sister, Rosalie Gold. Harvey Glatman attended Denver East High School, where he was in the top seventh percentile of his class and played the cornet in the high school concert band.

1944–1945—During Glatman's senior year in high school, he started binding, gagging, and molesting Denver women, while robbing them of small amounts of money.

May 4, 1945—Glatman bound, gagged, molested, and robbed Eula Jo Hand and two other women in the Capitol Hill neighborhood of Denver.

May 18, 1945—Glatman was arrested—for the first time—in Denver, for the "robbery" of Eula Jo Hand and two other women.

May 18–21, 1945—Glatman was confined in the Denver County Jail and, reportedly, did not get to graduate from high school.

May 21, 1945—Glatman's mother Ophelia bailed him out of jail, paying $2,000 in three separate checks.

July 15, 1945—While out of jail on bond, Glatman bound, gagged, molested, and robbed Norene Lauer in Boulder.

July 17, 1945—Glatman was arrested—for the second time—in Denver, for his Boulder assault of Norene Lauer. He was transported back to Boulder and confined in the Boulder County Jail.

July 23, 1945—Glatman was released from the Boulder jail after a bonds-man paid his $5,000 bail.

July 31, 1945—Glatman's bond on the Lauer case was reduced to $2,000, and he was committed to the Colorado Psychopathic Hospital, in Denver, for evaluation.

July 31–September 8, 1945—Glatman was confined in the Colorado Psychopathic Hospital.

September 27, 1945—While out of the hospital and out on bond from both the Denver and Boulder county jails, Glatman bound, gagged, molested, and robbed two women in the Park Hill neighborhood of Denver. He also molested another Denver woman, who screamed and ran out of her house.

September 30, 1945—Glatman was arrested—for the third time—in Denver, for the Park Hill neighborhood assaults.

September 30–October 8, 1945—Glatman again was confined in the Denver County Jail.

October 8, 1945—Glatman was ordered by the court to go back to the psychopathic hospital for "a period not exceeding 10 days." On the same day, the court released the $2,000 bond on the Eula Jo Hand et al. case.

November 4, 1945—Glatman's third charge—for the Park Hill assaults—was dismissed.

November 19, 1945—Glatman pled guilty, in Denver, in the case of Eula Jo Hand et al. Dr. Hilton was his only defense witness and recommended insulin shock treatments.

November 26, 1945—Glatman appeared at a hearing in Boulder on the Norene Lauer case, which was continued because of his conviction in the Eula Jo Hand et al. case.

December 1, 1945—Glatman was sentenced to one to five years at the Colorado State Penitentiary in the case of Eula Jo Hand et al.

December 5, 1945—Glatman began his first prison term—as prisoner number 23863—at the Colorado State Penitentiary.

July 27, 1946—Glatman was paroled from the Colorado State Penitentiary after less than eight months of his one- to five-year sentence.

July 27–August 25, 1946—While out on parole for the Eula Jo Hand et al. case, and still under the $2,000 bond from his assault on Norene Lauer, Glatman went with his mother to New York State. There, he committed several more robberies and assaults on women.

August 25, 1946—Glatman was arrested and confined in jail in Albany, New York.

October 10, 1946—Glatman was sentenced to one to five years for the first of his New York robberies and assaults.

October 24, 1946—Glatman entered the New York State Reception Center at Elmira.

October 28, 1946—Glatman's bail on the Boulder case of Norene Lauer was reduced from $2,000 to $500. The case was continued until his release from New York authorities.

September 8, 1948—Glatman was transferred to Sing Sing Prison at Ossining, New York.

November 27, 1950—A Boulder judge dismissed the case of Norene Lauer so that Glatman could be paroled from Sing Sing Prison.

April 16, 1951—As soon as Glatman was released, he immediately was arrested and jailed again for his outstanding charges from 1946. Two were dismissed and one was suspended.

May 2, 1951—Glatman returned to Denver, where his parole stipulated that he be under the care of Dr. Franklin G. Ebaugh, a psychiatrist.

1952—Glatman's father, Albert Glatman, died.

1953—Glatman's psychiatrist, Dr. Ebaugh, retired.

April 8, 1954—The body of Jane Doe was found west of Boulder. *If Glatman committed any crimes in Colorado between 1951 and 1957—including the murder of Jane Doe—he was not caught.*

January 1957—Glatman moved to California, although he occasionally returned to Denver to visit his mother.

August 1, 1957—Glatman murdered Judy Ann Dull in Riverside County, California.

March 9, 1958—Glatman murdered Shirley Ann Bridgeford in San Diego County, California.

July 24, 1958—Glatman murdered Ruth Mercado in San Diego County, California.

October 27, 1958—Glatman was arrested in Orange County, California, while assaulting Lorraine Vigil.

October 31, 1958—Glatman was arrested for the murders of Bridgeford and Mercado, but not for Dull.

November 4, 1958—Boulder County Sheriff Art Everson sent his Jane Doe case file to California authorities, asking them to "question Glatman again using details of the case," but there is no record that they ever did.

December 16, 1958—Glatman was sentenced to death for the murders of Bridgeford and Mercado.

December 1958–September 18, 1959—Glatman was confined on death
row at San Quentin State Prison in Marin County, California.

September 18, 1959—Glatman, age thirty-one, was executed at San
Quentin. His cremated remains were buried in the San Quentin
Cemetery.

INDEX

Connie, available to compare to, 200; Tent Girl, used to identify, 27–28; World Trade Center, used to identify victims of, 127. *See also* Combined DNA Index System; National DNA Index System

Doe Network, 44, 46, 61, 96, 118, 235, 244–245

Dolan, Deputy District Attorney Joe, *17*

Donton, Clayton, xi, 220–221, 246

Dood. See magazines

Doyle, Sir Arthur Conan, 31, 98

Dr. McAdoo, 33–35, 49, 100, 227

Dull, Judy Ann, 251

dummy-toss, 93–*95*

Dyer, Jimmie "Jim," xi, 246; Arizona State College (now NAU), student at, 179–180, 199, 209, 221–224, 226, 233, 237; Farrand, Katharine E., marriage with, 183–184, 189, 232–233, 236; Flagstaff High School, student at, 226, 235; initial research on, 177–181; residence (in 1954), *202–203. See also* Donton, Clayton; Dyer, Jimmie "Jim," wives

Dyer, Jimmie "Jim," wives: Ann, 220–222, 246; Joan, 181, 207–209, 220–223, 235, 246; Katharine. *See* Farrand, Katharine E.; Maxine, 179, 181, 220, 222, 246

Dyer, Katharine. *See* Farrand, Katharine E.

East York Police Department (Toronto), 99

Ebaugh, Dr. Franklin G., 166, 172, 251

Eichorn, Cindi, xi, 237–238, 244; *America's Most Wanted*, ruled out leads from, 197; Dyer, Katharine Farrand, corresponded on and

researched, 184, 187–188, 225, 229; Glatman, Harvey, suggested as suspect, 128, 132, 134, 173; missing women, searched for, 138, 176; unknown victims, corresponded on, 201

Eighth Judicial District of the state of Colorado, 146

Eisenhower, President Dwight David, 20, 58

Elegy to an Unfortunate Lady, 59, 241–242

Elmira. *See* New York State Reception Center at Elmira

Embrey, Twylia May (aka Theresa), xi, 244, 246; age-progression drawing of, 138; closure for family of, 207, 238; continued research on, 115, 122, 148, 159, 188, 230; discovery of hidden life of, 174–176, 178, 184, 187, 189, 192; DNA comparisons with, 124–128 (first), 138 (second), 218–219, 227; initial contact by family of, 103, 105–*106*; Nebraska, family visited by author in, 109–113; photo-superimposition of, 105, 107, 136, 224–225, 227

Epp, retired Sheriff George, 47, 243

Evans Investment Company, *202–203*

Everett, Vaughn, 115

Everson, former Sheriff Art, xi; *Dood* editor, contacted, 86; Glatman, Harvey, considered a suspect (in 1958), 129, 131–132, 139, 226; Glatman, Harvey, jailed (in 1945) in Boulder, 151; visited crime scene, 14–*17*, 55; worked and lived in Boulder County Courthouse, *21*, 150. *See also* Boulder Crime School; investigation (initial 1954)

exhumation. *See* Columbia Cemetery (Boulder), exhumation (in 2004)

Tropics nightclub, 86
truth serum, 36, 165
Twentieth Judicial District of the state
of Colorado, 43, 146, 204

Umenhofer, Sergeant John, xiii, 139,
145, 171, 216, 221, 244
unidentified flying objects, 209
United States Department of Justice,
31, 59, 75. *See also* National
Institute of Justice.
United States Supreme Court, 83
University of Arizona, 73–74, 92, 226
University of California, Berkeley,
35–36
University of Colorado, Boulder:
author attended, 18–19; cold cases,
researched by students, 45, 115;
no missing students from, 20. *See
also* Andes, James "Jim"; Cass,
Alan; Foster, Theresa; Jaquette,
Elaura; Rippon, Mary; Spore,
Roy; Swanson, Wayne; Tempest
Storm
University of Denver, 132–133, 173,
180, 201
University of Kansas, 74
University of North Texas Health
Science Center, 118
USS *Halford*, 179

Valas Motor and Radio Center, 171,
202–203
Valentine, Virgil, 112–113, 246
V-E Day, 160
Verdict of Jury, 29–30, 53, 61
ViCAP. *See* Violent Criminal
Apprehension Program
Vidocq Society, 244; *America's Most
Wanted*, contributions acknowledged
on, 196; Bornhofen, Frederick,
commented on, 216; initial contact

with, xvii, 59, 61–62; poster
session at AAFS (2007), members
participated in, 218–219; Vidocq,
Eugène François, named for, 59.
See also Bender, Frank; Birkby,
Dr. Walter; Bornhofen, Frederick;
Froede, Dr. Richard; Fleisher,
William; Goldberg, Dr. Robert;
Walter, Richard; Walton, Richard
Vigil, Lorraine, xiii, 134–135, 144, 251
Violent Criminal Apprehension
Program, xviii, 139
Vollmer, August, 36

Wagner, Sergeant Mike, 75, 243
Walker, Charles, 24
Walker, Joe Sam, 25, 149–151
Walsh, John, 192
Walter, Richard, 244
Walton, Richard, 192, 219, 237, 244
Wecht, Dr. Cyril, 219
Wedum, Eleanor, xiii, 239, 245
Weibel, Bruce, xiii, 76, 78–83, 141,
246
Weibel, Debbie, 76, 78–83, 141, 246
Weibel, Geraldine, 76, 79–80, 82–83
West, Lieutenant (then Commander,
now Division Chief) Phil, xiii, 237,
243; crime scene visits (including
dummy toss), participated in, 69,
93–95; Dyer, Katharine Farrand,
made contacts and issued press
release on, 180, 224–225, 227,
229; Embrey, Twylia May, made
contacts and issued press release on,
105, 107, 125; exhumation, planned
for and participated in, xxi–xxii,
61–63, 74, 77; facial reconstruction,
requested, 107–108; Glatman,
Harvey files, shared thoughts on,
144–145; integrity of the case,
commented on, 124; McDowell,